Eight Days in September

Eight Days in September

The Removal of Thabo Mbeki

Frank Chikane

PICADOR AFRICA

First published in 2012 by Picador Africa

This edition published in 2017 by Picador Africa
an imprint of Pan Macmillan South Africa
Private Bag x19, Northlands
Johannesburg, 2116

www.panmacmillan.co.za

ISBN 978-1-77010-562-1
ePub ISBN 978-1-77010-565-2

Editing by William Saunderson-Meyer
Proofreading by Lisa Compton
Design and typesetting by Triple M Design, Johannesburg
Front cover photograph by Georgio, Wikipedia
Cover by K4

Printed and bound by Bidvest Data, Cape Town.

CONTENTS

ABBREVIATIONS

ADB   African Development Bank
ANC   African National Congress
ANCYL   African National Congress Youth League
APF   Africa Partnership Forum
APRM   African Peer Review Mechanism
AU   African Union
AZAPO   Azanian People's Organisation
CAFRAD   Centre Africain de Formation et de Recherche
            Administratives pour le Développement
CODESA   Convention for a Democratic South Africa
COSATU   Congress of South African Trade Unions
DG   director-general
DRC   Democratic Republic of Congo
DSO   Directorate of Special Operations
ECA   Economic Commission for Africa
FOSAD   Forum of South African Directors-General
G8   Group of Canada, France, Germany, Italy, Japan,
            Russia, United Kingdom and the United States
G13   The G8 plus Brazil, China, India, Mexico
            and South Africa
G20   Group of 20 major developed and major emerging
            countries
G77   Group of 77 developing nations
GEAR   Growth, Employment and Redistribution,
            (a macroeconomic strategy of government)
GNU   Government of National Unity (South Africa)
GPA   Global Political Agreement (in Zimbabwe)

ICC	International Criminal Court
IEC	Independent Electoral Commission
IMF	International Monetary Fund
MANCO	management committee of FOSAD
MAP	Millennium African Recovery Plan
MDC	Movement for Democratic Change (Zimbabwe)
MISS	Minimum Information Security System
MK	Umkhonto we Sizwe, the ANC's military wing
NAM	Non-Aligned Movement
NCCR	National Coordinating Committee for the Return of Exiles
NCP	National Council of Provinces
NDPP	National Directorate of Public Prosecution
NEC	National Executive Committee (of the ANC)
NEPAD	New Partnership for Africa's Development
NGC	National General Council (of the ANC)
NIS	National Intelligence Service
NRLF	National Religious Leaders' Forum
NSC	National Security Council
NUM	National Union of Mineworkers
OAU	Organisation of African Unity
OECD	Organisation for Economic Co-operation and Development
PCAS	Policy Coordination and Advisory Services, Presidency
POA	Programme of Action
PRC	Presidential Review Commission
PRC (AU)	Permanent Representatives Committee (of the African Union)
RDP	Reconstruction and Development Programme
REC	Regional Economic Community
SA	South Africa

SABC	South African Broadcasting Corporation
SACC	South African Council of Churches
SACP	South African Communist Party
SADC	Southern African Development Community
SANCO	South African National Civic Organisation
SANDF	South African National Defence Force
SAPS	South African Police Services
SCA	Supreme Court of Appeal
UN	United Nations
UNAIDS	Joint United Nations Programme on HIV/AIDS
UNCHR	United Nations Commission on Human Rights
USA	United States of America
WDB	Women's Development Bank
WMD	Weapons of Mass Destruction
WTO	World Trade Organization
ZANU-PF	Zimbabwe African National Union–Patriotic Front

DRAMATIS PERSONAE

Nkosazana Dlamini-Zuma
Mbeki's minister of foreign affairs

Trevor Fowler
Chief operations officer in the presidency and accounting officer

Mojanku Gumbi
Mbeki's legal adviser

Winnie Madikizela-Mandela
Former wife of Nelson Mandela

Titus Mafolo
Mbeki's political adviser

Julius Malema
President of the ANCYL

Nelson Mandela
Former president of SA

Gwede Mantashe
Secretary-general of the ANC

Trevor Manuel
Mbeki's minister of finance

Ivy Matsepe-Cassaburi
Mbeki's minister of communications, briefly
acting president of SA

Govan Mbeki
Deceased father of Thabo Mbeki

Moeletsi Mbeki
Brother of Thabo Mbeki

Thabo Mbeki
President of ANC and of SA

Zanele Mbeki
Wife of Thabo Mbeki

Baleka Mbete
Speaker, chairperson of the ANC

George Meiring
Former head of the SANDF

Phumzile Mlambo-Ngcuka
Mbeki's deputy president after Zuma's exit

Kgalema Motlanthe
Deputy president of the ANC; president of SA

Chris Nicholson
KZN High Court judge

Essop Pahad
Mbeki's minister in the presidency

Mathews Phosa
Former premier of Mpumalanga

Cyril Ramaphosa
Former trade unionist, businessman and ANC member

Mukoni Ratshitanga
Mbeki's spokesperson

Tokyo Sexwale
Businessman and ANC member

Schabir Shaik
Former financial adviser to Jacob Zuma

Manto Tshabalala-Msimang
Mbeki's minister of health

Jacob Zuma
Deputy president of the ANC and of SA; president of the ANC
and SA

PREFACE

No one could experience the removal of President Thabo Mbeki from office in September 2008 without stopping and reflecting on those events, especially if one was caught in the middle of it as secretary of cabinet and head (director-general) of the presidency.

It would be an understatement to say that those eight days in September (from the 19th to the 26th) were momentous days in the history of post-apartheid South Africa, which tested the foundations of our newborn democratic state to the limit with a great risk of destabilisation and reversal of the democratic gains made.

The challenge with this recollection is that it is risky in many respects, as it constitutes what I have rediscovered in the last three years or so to be in the category of 'dangerous memory'. Firstly, for those who worked on the removal of Mbeki, the story is better forgotten and erased from the annals of history, unless it is told only from the perspective of those who engineered his removal.

In response to some of the articles that were published as extracts from this book, some retorted: 'Eish! Why do you raise this matter at all?' or 'Why don't you just let sleeping dogs lie?' Some expressed deep anger that I wrote about this subject at all and saw this as an expression of disloyalty to the African National Congress (ANC) or the leadership of what is now called 'the Polokwane Project'. The July 2010 statement of the National Executive Committee (NEC) of the ANC on this matter indicates the levels of anger relating to this recollection of the manner in which Mbeki was removed from office.

In my discussions with the officials of the ANC in November 2010, I made clear that this book is not about the ANC or individuals within the ANC. It is about my experiences in government, one of which was the removal of Mbeki from office. Accordingly, it could not be construed as an expression of disloyalty to the party. In any case, we also agreed that ANC members have the right to write about their experiences, as well as express opinions about matters which affect the people or the country.

For those who would want to present Mbeki as the embodiment of all the challenges the ANC faced at the time, any recollection of the positive legacy of Mbeki (even the African Renaissance vision and programme, which is regarded internationally as one of the best legacies Mbeki left for the continent and the world) has to be discounted as if it never happened, since it contradicts the storyline of him being the embodiment of all evil in the ANC and the country.

Secondly, any recollection of this momentous event is taken as support for Mbeki against the Polokwane Project. This had dire consequences, as I was either blocked from existing business interests, including opportunities for employment, or business was made to understand that I was a *persona non grata* and that they should have nothing to do with me. This also closed opportunities to serve on the boards of private companies. The consequences of defying this injunction were very clear and business ensured that they did nothing that would suggest they had any relationship with me. In Setswana one would say that they were scared of being splashed with *madi a kgofa* ('the blood of a bug') as it is bashed and killed.

Thirdly, for Mbeki's family and friends this story was just too early to recount, as the deep wounds it had inflicted were still too fresh to be opened again. They needed time to heal.

The reality, though, is that the story is so profound that the history of this country cannot be told without referring to it. Unfortunately, the story as presented by the media and the actors of the day is woefully incomplete and some aspects clearly false. Some publications I have read are more about 'the bashing of Mbeki' or attitudes or opinions against him, rather than the actual story. Many commentators seem to think that Mbeki-bashing is what audiences would want and they do this repeatedly and effectively. But this only works with those who are comforted by bashing him. The silent majority might just surprise us.

Those of us whom history destined to be caught in the storm – dangerous and risky as it became – unfortunately have a responsibility to record the story while it is fresh in our minds lest it fades and is lost to posterity, pleasing those who want these events to remain untold.

An initial commitment by the presidency to assist me with whatever I needed in writing this book was regrettably withdrawn following the publication of the first set of articles in July 2010, although it took six months before I was informed about this decision. From then I had to rely on my own devices, without the references and information that would have made my task easier.

The articles in Independent Newspapers prior to the publication of this book were surprising to some, especially those who are in the book business. Indeed, this was out of the ordinary. My view has always been that there are a negligible number of people who buy and read books. The masses, for whom this book is written, do not. It is for this reason that I agreed with Independent Newspapers to release summaries of sections of this book before publication. I accept that there are other publications which could have reached some of the grassroots better, but their overall reach was too limited.

The summaries were about a quarter of some chapters and the responses were very useful in enriching the book in a way that otherwise would never have been achieved. I wish to express my appreciation to all those who gave me feedback by writing or calling, those I met in the streets of the cities, towns, townships, villages and rural areas of this country, in airports and in the air, at public events including church, and from neighbouring countries and the wider world. *Nangonso. Le ka moso* ('I hope you do the same in future').

For now I leave the text in the hands of the readers.

Frank Chikane
November 2011

The Challenges of Telling this Story

Many people I met who have read the summary articles of sections of this book said to me that I must be 'very brave' to write about the removal of Thabo Mbeki, because of the risks it entails. In response, I have often said that it is not a matter of being brave but an unavoidable burden of responsibility. I might have fears about the implications of writing this story – the fears are real and the consequences dire – but my conscience never walks away just as it never walked away during our struggle for liberation. I wish it could, but it does not. It is always there, making the point that I have a responsibility that no one but me can now discharge.

My disposition towards taking my faith in God seriously does not help in this regard. Instead, it compelled me to do what all of us would really want to avoid – take a risk that could have an enormous impact on one's life, career and future. My conscience gave me no option but to take responsibility for this task regardless of the consequences, because this is about God's people, the people of this country, the continent and the world.

The reality is that I happen to be among the few who had the privilege to offer services to the people during the presidencies of Nelson Mandela, Thabo Mbeki, Kgalema Motlanthe and Jacob Zuma over a period of thirteen and a half years, between 1995 and 2009. With the exception of Professor Jakes Gerwel, who was the head of President Mandela's office between 1994 and 1999, I happen to be the only one who was both the head of the presidency (the president and the deputy president's offices together) and the secretary of cabinet. When the National Security Council (NSC) was established in 2000, I became its secretary and chairperson of the NSC Director-General's (DG's) committee.

I had the privilege also of seeing government through multiple windows over this period, as I was chair of the Forum of South African Directors-General (FOSAD) and the FOSAD MANCO (its management committee) where all programmes of government were discussed and strategies developed. Another responsibility was to assist the president in situations where there was tension between an executing authority (minister) and a head of department (director-general), especially where this impacted on the department's delivery of services.

Aside from my service in government, I also served as a member of the National Executive Committee (NEC) of the African National Congress (ANC) for ten of these thirteen and a half years (between 1997 and 2007), which was one of the most difficult periods (in my view) in the existence of the ANC. This gave me the opportunity and advantage of seeing the unfolding drama from the perspective of the party as well as that of government. My NEC role was less conspicuous, since the Public Service Act limited my participation and public expression.

One could say that I have seen it all from my vantage point at the apex of government and within the leadership of the ANC. I have seen the dark clouds gathering, leading to the removal of Mbeki from office during the last five years of his service as both the president of the country and of the ANC.

I was in the president's office when dubious intelligence reports accused Mathews Phosa, Cyril Ramaphosa and Tokyo Sexwale of plotting to take over the presidency. I was there when circumstances as yet unclear led to the then deputy president Zuma making a public statement that he was neither campaigning for, nor interested in becoming, president.

I was the director-general in the presidency when Mbeki and Zuma were president and deputy president of the country and of the ANC respectively, from 1999 to 2005, making them my responsibility.

I was in the presidency when the Arms Procurement Programme was developed, starting with a White Paper in parliament, followed by decisions of cabinet. The programme was executed and, as can be expected, the huge sums of money involved attracted corrupt elements internationally, nationally and within and outside government and the ruling party. I was there when some of our comrades were charged with corruption, fraud or related offences, and these were painful experiences for the family that is the ANC.

Among the most challenging of these were the charges against Schabir Shaik, which implicated the then deputy president of the country, Jacob Zuma. I was in the presidency when President Mbeki removed his close comrade and colleague of many years, Zuma, from his position as deputy president of the country at the conclusion of Shaik's trial. Shaik had been found guilty and the verdict implicated the deputy president. The pain of this surgery, the removal of Zuma, was felt to be unbearable within the ANC. It went deep into the heart of the party. All who were disgruntled for any reason sought an opportunity to express their views in support of Zuma.

I painfully watched as the drama about charges against Zuma unfolded, leading to an unprecedented and emotional campaign in his
support, taking the form of a vicious anti-Mbeki crusade. The of-
fensive deteriorated to a level where some ANC members publicly
burned ANC T-shirts with Mbeki's face on them, in the presence
of fellow leaders of the movement. Many of those involved believed
that Mbeki was either responsible for the charges against Zuma or
that he had not done what he was expected to do: to cause the
prosecution authority to withdraw the charges or stop the trial.

I witnessed the painful and rapid pace of divisions that occurred
from top to bottom within the ANC. I personally experienced the
force of the storm that rattled the unity of the NEC and spilled into
its membership.

To intensify this division and conflict, devious and unscrupulous
intelligence projects were devised to deepen the crisis within the
ANC, to break it from inside. Among these were the fake e-mails
about ANC leaders and the so-called Browse Mole document,
which was produced by some elements of the Directorate of Special
Operations (DSO) within the National Directorate of Public
Prosecution (NDPP). All these projects shared two key elements:
the collaboration of the worst of the old and the new intelligence
operatives, and the hand of foreign intelligence elements.

Surprisingly, when information about the involvement of these
elements surfaced, the people's revolutionary movement appeared
unconcerned, nor did anyone within the party express alarm. Those
troubled by this development simply went underground for fear of
victimisation or being thrown out of the party. The reality is that
these elements could corrupt our intelligence services to an extent
that foreign entities or their agents or national proxies could take
over government. If this happened, all that our people had struggled
for and made costly sacrifices for would have been in vain.

As we drove to Polokwane, those who are honest will testify that we did so knowing that there were two ANCs at war with each other heading to that city. Even during our breakfast in Polokwane on the day the conference started, we had difficult discussions amongst the leadership at the hotel where we were being accommodated. We knew that there was going to be a bitter fight to the end and that the winners would take all the spoils or entrench a spoils culture.

Indeed, Polokwane led to radical changes in government, as if a hostile opposition political party had taken over, and the purging of comrades who had made enormous sacrifices to achieve our liberation became an acceptable practice. Even innocent VIP Protection Unit members were victimised, not because they were disloyal to the state, but simply because those who returned from Polokwane seemed not to trust anyone who had served during Mbeki's time.

From that moment on, everyone knew that the ANC and the country would never be the same again. The events of the past four years or so testify to this.

I have also seen the frightening spectre of factions within the party battling to control or corrupt elements of the intelligence services to ensure that they served their party factions or individuals, rather than the security interests of the state and people of South Africa. At this point, I feared for the future of the country that many of our comrades had suffered for, were tortured for, were put in detention for, were imprisoned for, were exiled for, and even laid down their lives to free the country from the brutal forces of apartheid and racism.

It was at this stage that I thought of Albert Luthuli, Oliver Tambo, Govan Mbeki, Nelson Mandela, Joe Slovo, Chris Hani, Lillian Ngoyi, Beyers Naudé, Albertina Sisulu, Solomon Mahlangu, Neil Aggett, Ernest Dipale, and many others who made great sacrifices for the struggle and even died for it. One could not traverse this gallant history of the people's struggle and not shed tears at having to watch an unfolding rot that had the potential of destroying the organisation and the future of the country.

As I write this story, I fear for the future of the country no less than I did then. The apparently united front of the Polokwane Project is unravelling, threatening the stability of South Africa and its future. The questions we have to ask are, where are we going and where we are likely to end up?

The challenge is that these questions cannot be answered intelligently without knowledge of why we are where we are, in the first place. The story I have no choice but to tell is part of an important reflection that our people must engage in, without fear of victimisation or loss of life. My experience following the publication of the articles related to this book shows that indeed what I am writing about is what has been called 'dangerous memories' that some don't want to hear about. Dangerous memories naturally attract threatening responses that go beyond the necessary discourse we need to engage in as a people, a nation.

Another challenge is that many of the players who could contribute to make this story as balanced and complete as possible are either not yet ready to talk about it, or fear for their lives and their future. Many have said to me that this is not just risky but it is also career limiting, as the doors of opportunity could be closed to them both in the public and the private sectors. In some cases, names of people who were involved have been left out to save them from the fire that might be directed at them. I have tried my best to ensure that this book does not become a lightning conductor that could imperil some comrades.

The book is thus about my knowledge of the events as I experienced and understood them. It is my account during a momentous time in our history. Indeed, my perspective may differ from that of others who may have been involved or affected by these events, depending on our vantage points and our *a priori* views. Fortunately, in the real world, no one would expect us to agree in all respects as we are mere humans.

While I am committed to recounting the story as accurately and objectively as possible, there is a challenge in that none of the players, including myself, participated in all the events and meetings relating to the crisis. Those who were at ANC headquarters in Luthuli House were not necessarily the same people who were at the Union Buildings; those who were in Forest Town, at the residence of ANC President Jacob Zuma, were not the same as those at the presidential residence, Mahlamba Ndlopfu; and those who were at Esselen Park in Pretoria, where the ANC's NEC was meeting, were not the same people as those who were in Cape Town.

Some held their own meetings: some secret, others open; some legitimate, others downright factional but dignified as 'lobbies'. Lobbies do indeed lobby for particular positions, to serve specific interests. At one stage there was even talk about a powerful 'extra-organisational' cabal that made decisions that were imposed on the organisation. Many resented this development but could not do much about it given the climate of the time and the heavyweights involved. In a crisis of such magnitude, cabals and secret groups thrive and assume a semi-official status. And, because they are not fully official, their funding also becomes cabal-like, with the risk that those with more resources could assume control of the cabal and thence the party. The result was that when someone spoke to you, you had to work out whether or not he or she represented the official position of the organisation or that of a faction or cabal.

In short, under such complex circumstances, no one can claim to know everything that happened. Only God, who is omnipresent and omniscient, can know. My faith is helpful in this regard as I believe that God indeed does know what happened and who was involved, however clandestine the circumstances.

It would be helpful if everyone remembered and took heed

of the scriptural saying that 'there is nothing hidden that will not be disclosed, and nothing concealed that will not be known or brought out into the open'. The passage ends with the advice that 'those who have ears to hear let them hear'. Another lesson to be learnt from the last year or so is 'do not do anything that you would not want anyone to remember' as it may be made public.

Unfortunately, we humans (*Homo sapiens*), who are supposed to be sensible or have some level of wisdom (*sapire*, 'be wise or sensible'), are able only to know about those events we were involved in. For the rest we depend on reports, which are often inaccurate or merely an interpretation of what happened.

So it was, during those September days, that false information was fed deliberately into the discourse to mislead or produce a particular outcome and many relied on rumours and distorted information obtained through the grapevine. Until all that is hidden is revealed, including conspiracies hatched in secret places during secret meetings, we must live with our incomplete knowledge.

Despite this challenge, I am determined to present these events as accurately as possible. Although my vantage point is bound to colour some of my perspectives, I will present the facts as accurately as I can, while also analysing and interpreting them in order to make sense of them.

In doing so, I unfortunately cannot make use of classified information, as it is governed by laws for which I have total respect. Public servants are required in terms of the Minimum Information Security System (MISS) document and other relevant secrecy laws to protect the integrity of all classified information, from 'restricted' to 'confidential', to 'secret' and 'top secret', until it is declassified. There is a further requirement, in terms of tradition within the presidency, to treat all discussions with the president as privileged, disclosing nothing without the president's consent.

In my case, as secretary of the cabinet, chairperson of the NSC committee of security-related officials, and secretary of the execu-tive level of the NSC, the bar was raised even higher. In these fora one operates strictly at a 'top secret' level – what, in Afrikaans, is called *streng geheim*. At this level, some of the information will never be declassified during our lifetime. In most instances, this has to do with the security of the state or with a risk to people's lives, espe-cially those of informants or agents.

This obviously limits the public's understanding of those events, specifically the degree to which this country's peace was threatened. Some things will have to remain unknown and in certain cases a mystery to many. We have to live with the reality that there are aspects of what happened that will never be properly understood.

Although a handful of people know about one aspect or another of this classified world of information, none of them can know every aspect of it. Even classified intelligence information fed into the system and analysed can be falsified to produce a particular outcome, or to support a specific cause or interest.

Some may not believe that even after leaving government I am still bound by the laws and regulations that protect classified and confidential information. In fact, there are some things I will be un-able to discuss unless I live to the age of 90, by which time they may well be declassified. As a result, some things may never be said at all.

I believe it is important to deal with this limiting regulatory framework to give the public a better perspective of the scope of what can and cannot be said and why.

It is in the nature of the state that those who lead it know more than ordinary citizens do. Governments are custodians of the per-sonal details of individuals, as well as of information about gov-ernment structures, institutions, programmes, projects, budgets, and so on. With this information at their disposal and given their ac-cess to intelligence information, states naturally know more both at national and international levels. Some of this information is available to the public and some of it is used for public or private purposes. Some is confidential and cannot be disclosed to third parties who have no right of access to it. In such cases, confidentiality builds trust and opens the doors to the sharing of more confidential information.

Each state or government possesses information that is classified and to maintain the integrity of this system public servants who deal with such sensitive information are vetted for particular levels of secrecy. Your classification determines the level of sensitive information to which you can have access.

In South Africa, a MISS document regulates the way in which sensitive information is managed by public servants. In terms of this document, the director-general or head of a department or entity of government is responsible for the effective management of security of information. A head of department is required to report any violation of the rules and regulations contained in the MISS document, as well as to take the necessary steps to remedy the situation.

Public office bearers take an oath of office and are bound by it. Sections 1–3 and 5 of Schedule 2 of the Constitution of the Republic of South Africa provide for 'oaths and solemn affirmations' for members of the executive at both national and provincial levels, which includes the matter of the management and handling of secret information. When they assume office, members of the executive at national and provincial levels take an oath 'to respect and uphold the Constitution and all other law of the Republic'. They also undertake 'to hold' their office 'with honour and dignity' and *'not to divulge directly or indirectly any secret matter entrusted'* to them (my emphasis).

All these rules and regulations are necessary for the proper functioning of the state and for the security of the country. They ensure that officials at both political and public service levels maintain the integrity of information that is in the possession of the state. As I have indicated, in my case the bar was raised even higher as I was both secretary of cabinet and secretary of the NSC and was thus one of the key custodians of such information and documents. As a result, I had to be responsible about what I said or communicated publicly.

Unfortunately, notwithstanding all these strictures, there have been gross violations at high levels that have seriously threatened national security. As the story of the removal of Mbeki unfolds, the degree of regulatory violations will become apparent, though not much detail can be given, since these are in the realm of classified information. The consequences of some of these violations have implications for the future and may yet come back to haunt us and impact negatively on the country.

There is a further security requirement for which there is no legislation. As I have already mentioned, any discussion with the president is considered privileged and all information acquired during such a discussion is treated as confidential unless otherwise stated. No one – not even presidential envoys – may disclose such information without the president's approval.

There is also an international element to information security. 'Friendly states' from time to time share sensitive information relating to matters of mutual interest or security, sometimes in relation to combating crime at an international level and sometimes in dealing with matters such as terrorism. States that share sensitive information to assist an ally to deal with its own national security matters, or with partners involved in combating a common challenge such as crime or terrorism, need the assurance that the integrity of the information will be maintained.

An environment of fear can also inhibit the free flow of information, dialogue or truth telling. Some things will never be said because of risks to the person who divulges the information. The political climate can at times determine which truths can be told and which cannot. Power dynamics, fear and risk can distort facts and colour the story. In short, those who are in power can rewrite history, just as the colonialists did. One thing I can say is that my deployment as a public servant frustrated me greatly at critical moments as the crisis within the ANC intensified. My efforts to help within the party as a responsible and disciplined cadre of the movement were at times ignored or simply put aside. In these cases, I could not resort to the public arena as this was not open to me. If the issues involved became subjects of a public debate, neither could I enter the debate. In a sense I was forced to *lala ngenceba* (literally, 'sleep on one's wound').

Even today, there are things that cannot be said because they may widen the divisions within the party. As regards these, I may have to continue sleeping on my wounds, specifically those that were inflicted by the politics of the past five years or so.

There is another challenge that is usually underplayed. In many instances, the truth cannot be told if you do not have sufficient evidence to stand up in court if sued. There are many cases where the community knows about the criminal activities of someone and cannot understand why that person is not arrested. The challenge is to obtain evidence that goes beyond intelligence information and hearsay. In other words, intelligence must be translated into evidence to stand the test of our courts.

So, in writing this book, I undertake a risky endeavour – saying things that skirt the bounds of the law on the one hand, and avoiding being sued on the other.

This account is also not a product of interviews with all the players involved or affected. It is based purely on my recollection of the events, documents, notes and other sources regarding those fateful eight days in September 2008, as well as the events preceding and the aftermath. Many aspects that were not part of my experience are not included in this account. There are also characters missing who

I did not want to expose without their consent, especially because the writing project had become risky and career limiting. When it is safer to engage these players and include them in the record, the story will be more complete than it is now. Unfortunately, this remains a project for the future.

One thing is certain. Having been in the presidency from the time of Mandela to that of Zuma, I am one of the privileged few who has seen it all, rather than hearing it via the grapevine. The challenge is to say 'the things I could not say' in a responsible way that helps the country to move forward rather than backwards.

I must state from the outset that my intention in this book is not to attack individuals or organisations or parties. If there is a reference to anyone or any party, it will be because it is unavoidable in order to tell the story. My task is not to deal with individuals but with issues of strategic nature and importance.

My overall objective is to assist the nation to avoid the pitfalls of the past and move forward to build a better South Africa, of which we can all be proud.

PART ONE

The Removal of Mbeki
and its Aftermath

CHAPTER 1

After Midnight

The Removal of Mbeki

It was after midnight of Friday, 19 September 2008 – to be precise, just before 1.00 a.m. on Saturday – when the first text messages began to come through: 'the NEC has decided to recall Mbeki as president of the country'. Another said that ANC officials had been appointed to visit Mbeki immediately, that night, to inform him of the NEC decision.

Other text messages kept coming from NEC members in Esselen Park celebrating that they had won and that Mbeki was to be removed or else expressing concern over the consequences of the NEC decision. Some text messages came from journalists who wanted more information and responses. Yet others came from concerned ANC members who were not at Esselen Park and some came from concerned South Africans.

If you monitored cyberspace during those early hours of that fateful day you could have written a prize-winning drama. This cyberspace record would have given us the totality of what happened and the feelings of those involved.

Earlier on that critical Friday, reports emanated from the meeting telling of tough debates, lasting into the early hours of Saturday morning. The voices of reason which pleaded that Mbeki be allowed to complete his term, perhaps bringing the election date forward, were drowned out by the angry voices of the night.

Even the proposal that he should be allowed a month or so to complete some of his critical commitments of state was shot down. Among these commitments was a United Nations (UN) meeting the following week to consider the Millennium Development Goals. Another was the African Diaspora Conference, scheduled for 7–10 October 2008, which would bring together African leaders on the continent and those in the Diaspora, in line with an African Union (AU) resolution. The Permanent Representatives Committee (PRC) of the AU meeting scheduled for 24 September 2008 to prepare for the Africa Diaspora Conference was also postponed.

In the end, the *ngoko* ('now!') chorus won the day.

Calls also began to come through from Mbeki's advisers asking what they should do. Advocate Mojanku Gumbi, the president's legal adviser, was among the first to call and we discussed what the presidency needed to do. Her second call concerned a message from the staff at Mahlamba Ndlopfu, saying that they had been asked to wake the president as a delegation from the ANC was coming to inform him about the NEC decision.

Presumably the thinking was – as a matter of courtesy – that he should learn about the decision from the party, not from the media or third parties, but we believed he should not be woken. Advocate Gumbi and I would be at Mahlamba Ndlopfu early in the morning to inform him about the impending visit. We instructed the staff accordingly and made arrangements with the ANC to send their delegation at about 9.00 a.m., by which time we thought the president would be ready to start his day.

Advocate Gumbi and I agreed that she (together with the legal unit in the presidency) would review all the legal issues related to the decision and advise how the government would handle the matter – a procedure dependent on the nature of the decision, which we would only hear officially from the delegation later that morning.

At the forefront of our thinking was how to preserve Mbeki's legacy, particularly his African Renaissance vision and programme, his extensive attempts to end conflicts on the African continent and create the peace necessary for its development, and his leadership in the development of the New Partnership for Africa's Development (NEPAD) and the African Peer Review Mechanism (APRM). There was also the AU project of bringing together African leaders on the continent and those in the diaspora, a project close to Mbeki's heart. Nothing should be done to affect negatively this legacy, which no one could take away from Mbeki.

The next conversation, covering much the same ground, was with Trevor Fowler, the chief operations officer and accounting officer in the presidency, who was my second-in-command. Fowler, who had been a member of parliament and a speaker of the Gauteng Provincial Legislature for a number of years, focused on what needed to be done in relation to the executive and parliament. We agreed on several possible ways of handling the situation, which we would discuss with the president when we met him.

At about 3.30 a.m. we completed our preparations for the events that would unfold later in the day. I was due to conduct a wedding at 10.00 a.m. at my church in Naledi, Soweto, and had planned to leave Soweto at 6.00 a.m. in order to reach Mahlamba Ndlopfu at 7.00 a.m. I estimated that the mission to Pretoria would cost me four hours, which I had to make up for. Instead of retiring to bed, I went to the study to prepare for the wedding.

It was difficult to close the window on the crisis and open a new window on the wedding, but this was not the first time I had faced such a challenge in the presidency.

Emergencies arise at times when one needs to focus on a sermon or service, but as I could not be released from my calling as a pastor, I continued to serve the church irrespective of the challenges. At such times the spiritual adrenalin takes over with a special inspiration to be an even greater blessing to the church than I would have been in normal circumstances. Fortunately, I had prepared the sermon in advance and only had to clean it up. I then focused on the liturgy and order of proceedings. I also ensured that all the participants were aware of the new pressures I was subjected to. Fortunately, again, the congregation had handled emergencies like this before and simply engaged their emergency gear.

I left home at 6.00 a.m. and the first sign that something had happened during the night was newspaper headlines on the streets of Johannesburg and Pretoria: 'Mbeki recalled' ... 'Mbeki removed' ... 'Shocking decision by the ANC' ... and so on. This reopened the Mbeki file in my head. The questions in my mind were: 'How is the president likely to respond? How do we assist him as his support staff and advisers to manage this crisis? How did we come to this point? How did the ANC, as the ruling party, find itself in this situation? What were the mistakes made within the ANC? What mistakes could Mbeki have made both as president of the ANC and as president of the country? Could the situation have been managed differently?'

It was obvious that I could not answer all these questions at that moment and alone. We would require an extensive evaluation workshop to reflect on this period. Unfortunately, events of this nature do not allow for the luxury of time for reflection, as this could be construed as conspiratorial.

As I was driven along the M1 North towards Pretoria I could not stop thinking about the implications of the decision. The reality is that every event in the life of a nation or country defines what that country or its people become. Post-colonial countries where coups are part of the culture have learned that once such events are set in motion they are difficult to stop. Fortunately, no such culture has developed in either the old or the new South Africa.

But a new, worrying culture has been introduced that might come to haunt us – the culture of ruling parties recalling or removing their own presidents, purely because of intra-party dynamics rather than their performance in government. As a member of the ANC, I wondered whether this was the precedent my organisation wanted to establish. But it did and indeed it will haunt us into the future unless there is a radical change in the way the organisation conducts itself.

With regard to Mbeki, his history and the fact that he had lived his whole life for the ANC and had no life outside the party, this action felt like 'feeding on your own' or ending his life. What would he be without or outside the ANC? What would become of his life outside the ANC? What would South Africa be like after his removal? What would happen to the ANC? As my brain went into overdrive on these matters, I could not but conclude that South Africa would never be the same again … and neither would the ANC.

We arrived at the gates of Mahlamba Ndlopfu at exactly 7.00 a.m. thanks to the efforts of the VIP Protection Unit, which had moved me physically from Soweto to Pretoria while my brain remained in another world.

The household staff received us at the house, where, as one would expect, the mood was sombre. Concern and uncertainty were written on the faces of all those who met us but they were unable to express their fears, trained as they were to serve the president irrespective of who it was rather than engage in the political processes which affect the party or government. They were civil servants and served the president or government of the day.

Advocate Gumbi, with whom I had been in contact en route to Pretoria, followed hot on my heels. The last to arrive was Trevor Fowler. Told that the president was still resting, we suggested he be left for a while. We were ushered into the historical lounge where we had spent many hours with the president over the years, discussing government and developing strategies to manage it as effectively as we could, as well as strategising about the continent and the world. As we sat there, we knew that this meeting with Mbeki might be our last with him as the country's president.

We used the opportunity to exchange notes and reflect on how we would handle the situation. As usual, Advocate Gumbi was ready with the legal complexities. As a good lawyer she always made our lives more difficult. Nothing is obvious and few things are the way they look like and the way we might want them to be. She mapped out the challenges, uncertainties and dangers of the legal route to dealing with the crisis. The risk of the country sliding from a constitutional state to one with no respect for its own Constitution and laws was staring at us.

Our deliberations were interrupted constantly by our cellphones, as one person after another voiced their shock at the decision. Some wept, some were disgusted and others wondered what had happened to their ANC. Still others were concerned about the effect of it all on Mbeki, the person. 'Remember that he is a human being as well and must feel the pain of what had happened,' said one caller. But we had passed that stage during the night and were more concerned now about managing the crisis in a way that would not cause pain to the people of South Africa, accepting that we could not at that stage do much about the decision of the ANC and the pain Mbeki was going to go through, except for the limited support we could give him.

The first person to make an appearance, at about 8.00 a.m., was the president's wife, Zanele Mbeki, who was surprised that we were already in the house so early and surmised that we were there to talk about *ntho tsa masiu* ('the night's events'). We informed her that an ANC delegation was scheduled to arrive at 9.00 a.m. She was not surprised, just stared at us, shook her head and proceeded to go where she was going within the house.

Mbeki followed later. As usual he was cool and collected but was walking more slowly than usual. He took his normal seat and listened to us as we told him that 'it had happened'. It was almost like saying *sekunjalo* ('now is the time') or *sekwenzekile* ('it has happened'). As usual, one could not read his body language as he listened without emotion to the story of *ntho tsa bosiu*. The closest to an expression of emotions was when he repeated his belief that no true cadre of the movement (the ANC) could make a decision of that nature given the circumstances and issues involved. Not on the basis of such an obviously faulty judgement of Judge Chris Nicholson (discussed in detail in Chapter 7). For him this meant that something had gone radically wrong in the ANC and it was a cause for great concern. It was out of character and a manifestation of the first fruit of the Polokwane Project.

Mbeki repeated his view, expressed earlier in the week, that if his organisation asked him to leave office he would comply, since he saw his role as that of 'service to the people' rather than 'a position' that he needed 'to fight for'. He had not fought for positions in the ANC before and he was not about to do so now. He re-emphasised his commitment to ensuring that the country was not destabilised by his problems with the ANC. No one should pay a price for the negative politics of the party. He was ready to meet the ANC delegation at any time. At this stage he looked like a soldier who was ready to die, if he had to, for the sake of the country; a lamb to be slaughtered for a cause.

In the hour that remained before the arrival of the delegation, the four of us passed the time discussing the changes in the movement to which Mbeki had devoted his life. He could not accept, just as he had been unable to accept at Polokwane, that there had been enormous changes in the ANC since it had assumed power as a ruling party. He still believed no genuine cadre could behave as the delegates at Polokwane had behaved or could take a decision like the one that had been taken in the early hours of that day. He believed such behaviour disqualified those responsible from remaining cadres of the ANC.

At about the time the ANC delegation was due to arrive, I had to return to Soweto to be on time for the wedding ceremony. In any case, I was not needed for that meeting as the director-general and secretary of the cabinet as this was a purely party matter. Once more the VIP Protection Unit swept me off to my destination while I ran through my sermon. The wedding went well and as usual the Lord took over and it was a great blessing to many. As a disciplined pastor I kept the politics of *ntho tsa bosiu* outside the wedding, although one could not miss the bewilderment of many in the audience. Some of the leaders expressed concern, when they got a chance after the service, but there was no time to discuss this matter and as a result they just prayed and left this with the Lord.

After it was over, I returned to Mahlamba Ndlopfu, informed en route that the president had met the ANC delegation consisting of comrades Kgalema Motlanthe (deputy president of the ANC) and Gwede Mantashe (the ANC secretary-general). They informed him that the party had decided to 'recall' him as president, and in response the president told them that he would leave as soon as his party wished him to.

It was interesting for me that the party used the concept of a 'recall'. There were problems, though, about this concept in relation to a sitting president, since the president is elected by parliament and not the party. The concept of a 'recall' makes sense within the context of the 'deployment' policy of the ANC but could not be applied directly to a president who is elected by parliament. The language of 'recall' is usually used by presidents to 'recall' an ambassador who is appointed by the president, but could not legally be used to remove the president from office. Only parliament could remove the president, in terms of s 89 and s 102 of the Constitution. Though the concept of a 'recall' was an innovative one to try to remain within the law, it did not pass the test, and it left many questions in the minds of many South Africans.

Constitutionally, the president could have ignored the 'recall', to force the party to use the constitutional mechanisms to remove him from office, if they could achieve the voting threshold required, which was unlikely at the time. All other options would have been illegal or unconstitutional and would not only have risked destabilising the country but would have led to destabilisation. To avoid this risk, he chose to leave voluntarily. He did not want to give anyone an opportunity or be the reason for anyone to act unconstitutionally.

The president had, though, asked the ANC delegation two questions. The first concerned a constitutional way of leaving office without leaving a vacuum, as the Constitution did not provide for the resignation of the president in the way it was contemplated. The second concerned the immediate responsibilities of the president, which had to be carried out while they were mulling over these matters. The delegation promised to come back to him later that day.

On my return I found the president's official residence full of comrades and some family members who had come either to express their support for Mbeki or just to sympathise with him. Some wept in disbelief at what had happened and others pondered why he could not be allowed to finish his term of office, as he was left with only seven months. Greeting them was as much of a challenge as doing so in a bereaved family.

Gumbi, Fowler and I retreated to the lounge again to continue with our strategic discussions and planning, joined by the president's political adviser, Titus Mafolo, and his spokesperson, Mukoni Ratshitanga, both of whom had arrived while I was away. We returned to the subject of preparations for the announcement, meticulously putting into place procedures for dealing with the crisis. We had to banish our emotions and engage our rational sense to execute our responsibilities in a highly charged and emotive environment.

The plan unfolded as follows: firstly, once the delegation of the ANC had answered the two questions, details of how we would manage the process of the departure of the president would be formalised. Secondly, and whatever the responses of the party to the questions the president had asked, the president would meet his cabinet to inform them of his decision to resign in response to the 'recall' decision by the ANC. The cabinet secretariat was commanded to set the meeting up for 4 p.m. the following day, the Sunday afternoon, when it was expected that the NEC would have concluded its meeting, given that most members of the cabinet were also members of the NEC.

Thirdly, the president would inform the country about his decision. We agreed that this should be done on the Sunday evening, after the cabinet briefing. The timing for the announcement was precipitated by the demand expressed later from Esselen Park, where the NEC of the ANC was meeting, that Mbeki deliver his letter of resignation before 7.00 p.m. on Sunday. In this regard, Ratshitanga was mandated to interact with the South African Broadcasting Corporation (SABC) to make the necessary arrangements. The preferred time was 7.00 p.m.

Fourthly, to ensure stability in the country, Mbeki would meet the command structures of the security forces (the South African National Defence Force [SANDF], the South African Police Services [SAPS] and the intelligence service), brief them about his decision to resign and impress upon them their professional responsibility and the imperative to ensure that there was stability, safety and security in the country. Not only did the president need to do this, he must also be seen by the nation to have done so, in order to assure the people that everything was under control and that there was no risk of instability.

The secretariat of the National Security Council (NSC) was instructed to arrange these meetings one after another on the Monday morning. This was the responsibility of Loyiso Jafta, head of the NSC secretariat, who had also joined the meeting at that time. He began to do so accordingly. An announcement would be made once the meetings were arranged, to ensure that there was no anxiety amongst the command structures of the security forces. Ratshitanga would take care of the media side in this regard.

Finally it was agreed that the presidency would interact with parliament to determine the best way to handle the resignation, including the way in which he would bid farewell to parliament. This discussion, which would have to take place with the speaker of the National Assembly and the chairperson of the National Council of Provinces (NCP), could only take place on the Monday. Trevor Fowler was delegated to organise and manage it.

On the international front, the minister of foreign affairs, Nkosazana Dlamini-Zuma, was already in New York to participate in UN annual meetings, including preparations for the president, who was due to follow. She had to deal with the immediate programmes of the president that were likely to be affected by the decision on recall, starting with the UN meetings scheduled for Monday morning.

In the midst of these discussions, a message came from the ANC NEC meeting in Esselen Park to say that the president could not continue with any of his responsibilities, particularly his international commitments. This was disturbing, to say the least, in view of the fact that he was due to be the keynote speaker at the UN

Summit on Africa on the following Monday. The party determining what the president could do and not do while he was in office was a clear violation of the Constitution, including the oath of office of the president. This decision turned a party 'recall' of the president of the country, which in itself was problematic and a challenge constitutionally, to an act of stopping the president from executing his responsibilities.

This act brought us close to the definition of a *coup d'état*. The act of stopping the president from exercising his constitutional responsibilities and mandate was tantamount to 'an illegal change of government' – in this case, the president. As long as a president is in office, no one can stop him or her from executing his constitutional responsibilities and duties. Interestingly, there was no response (as far as I can recall) to the second question the president had put to the ANC delegation that the ANC advise about a constitutional way in which his 'recall' could be effected. For those of us who were outside the decision-making machinery at Esselen Park, it would seem that issues of constitutionality did not matter. What was urgent was the 'removal' of Mbeki *ngoko,* which meant that he had to be stopped immediately from continuing to act as president even before he resigned.

The president could have ignored this directive as well. But he didn't. He took this instruction, too, in his stride, saying he would do nothing that might suggest that he wanted to remain in office against the wishes of his party. However, he had a responsibility to ensure that the transition was as smooth as possible and on this matter he was not going to relent. Stability, stability, stability – this was the priority for all who were involved in the decision-making process within government in relation to the 'recall' of the president.

Fortunately, and in the midst of all the madness, the ANC leadership also took the same view. In its statement, released on that Saturday, the NEC said:

our most important task as a revolutionary movement is the *stability of our country* ... We will follow *with precision all the constitutional requirements* to ensure that interim arrangements are in place to ensure the smooth running of the government ... we share the *desire* (together with the citizens of South Africa) *for stability* and for a peaceful and prosperous South Africa [my emphasis].

This statement by the ANC was reassuring indeed and made our efforts to manage the transition much easier. There would be no differences within the ANC on this matter irrespective of the mood of some, which was described as 'foul' and bordering on irrationality.

Notwithstanding this statement, and the particularly reassuring part which stated clearly that the ANC 'will follow *with precision* all the constitutional requirements', the leadership still made the decision to stop Mbeki from carrying out some of his immediate responsibilities. This was disturbing indeed. It contradicted what Mantashe had said on behalf of the NEC. Until Mbeki's resignation took effect, he remained constitutionally bound to execute his duties. The president, however, dealt with this matter in a pragmatic way.

The decision meant that the UN had to be informed that he would not be attending the summit and a special apology conveyed to those African leaders who had already arrived in New York. This task was left to Dlamini-Zuma, who was in New York, along with other ministers, including Trevor Manuel, then minister of finance.

Another problem we faced was uncertainty about the implications for ministers and deputy ministers of the president's resignation, for he had appointed them. Manuel had, in fact, left a letter of resignation with the presidency before travelling to the UN, in case all the ministers had to resign. Dlamini-Zuma inquired whether she was required to return but was advised to continue with her responsibilities until there was clarity about how parliament would respond to the resignation. Delegates to the UN summit and the president's advance team thus continued with their responsibilities.

Mbeki's absence was certainly felt in New York. As investigative journalist Joe Lauria put it in a report published in *The Star* on 23 September:

> the shadow of Thabo Mbeki followed foreign minister Nkosazana Dlamini-Zuma ... as she sought to replace the experience and clout of a man who knew his way around world leaders at the annual UN General Assembly summit. There were reminders of Mbeki wherever she went on Monday.

At the round-table discussion on African development issues the Ghanaian President John Kufuor told the gathering (which included several heads of state) that

> I take the chair at the invitation of the UN Secretary-General in the place of my colleague and friend, Thabo Mbeki of South Africa, who should have been here but for matters of state. We all know the role President Mbeki has been playing on the continent of Africa, and indeed on the international scene, during the past decade. He is one of the main architects of the African Union and a key initiator of ... the New Partnership for African Development.

Kufuor's statement was a powerful testament to Mbeki's role on the continent and the international scene as he was removed from office by his own party. In line with Mbeki's foreign policy perspectives, which were based on ANC policies, the missed opportunities occasioned by his absence were seen in terms of his work on the continent rather than only about South Africa as is clear from

Lauria's report. He continues to say, 'Mbeki's absence ... was felt everywhere', and his

> missed meetings could spell missed opportunities for South
> Africa to achieve its two main goals at this General Assembly:
> getting aid and international support for post-agreement
> Zimbabwe, and blocking the Security Council's endorsement
> of the International Criminal Court's indictment of Sudan's
> President Omar Bashir.

Messages came from Dlamini-Zuma to say that this was one of the most painful assignments she had had to undertake, especially having to explain the situation to African leaders who were terribly shocked by the news, feeling it was not possible that the ANC they had known and respected had taken such a decision. They could also not understand why the decision could not have been postponed until after the summit, since Mbeki was a critical part of the African project and the decision had severely disrupted the programme.

Some leaders felt the ANC should have taken them into its confidence and alerted them about the decision. They also felt strongly that the ANC should have understood that any decision about Mbeki's attendance at the UN would affect them directly. There was a sense that, for some of these leaders, the ANC was their liberation movement as well. After all, in the years of the Frontline States, the Liberation Committee for Southern Africa, and the support the region gave to the liberation movements in the southern African region, the ANC could not take any major decisions without taking them into its confidence.

Clearly, this was not in the minds of those who were making decisions at Esselen Park. What preoccupied them was how to remove Mbeki from office rather than the international implications thereof. We learned that some comrades tried to bring this perspective into the debate but it was drowned out by the *ngoko* chorus.

Back at home, the atmosphere at Mahlamba Ndlopfu was like that of an African home where death has struck, with people coming and going, people wandering about, people weeping. The household staff, battling with their own emotions, had their hands full offering refreshments and food to large numbers of unexpected guests. Every sitting room or space was full of guests, with an overflow into the garden. Staff reinforcements had to be brought in from other official households to assist.

It was impossible for the president to attend to everyone who had come to express their solidarity, sympathy or frustration. He also could not take all the calls that were clogging the telephone lines, nor was he able to cope up with all the personal e-mails from friends and leaders who also expressed their sympathies and solidarity. The crisis went on into the depths of the Saturday night, turning the activity in the house into something like a night vigil.

As we went deep into the night I was becoming restless, as I had a sermon to deliver the following day, the Sunday. By then everything had been taken care of except for the president's letter of resignation, which had to be drafted carefully in the light of the constitutional challenges involved. Advocate Gumbi agreed to think about the formulation of the letter from a legal perspective and discuss it with the president. The second consideration was the president's speech to the nation scheduled for the Sunday evening. Titus Mafolo, who normally drafted or facilitated the drafting of Mbeki's speeches, felt that this had to be done by the president himself as it was critical. This, of course, was agreed with by Mbeki, as such important texts he produced personally.

When I left Mahlamba Ndlopfu that night, we agreed that I would return after the Sunday morning service to look at the resignation letter together with Mojanku Gumbi and Trevor Fowler, and at the draft speech with Mafolo, Gumbi, Fowler and Ratshitanga.

The night trip from Mahlamba Ndlopfu to Soweto, the second in a day, was a time of reflection about the extraordinary events of the past 24 hours or so. I wanted to focus on the sermon but my mind kept on drifting from one event to another, from one issue to another, and the implications of it all. I had to do a forced shutdown to open the window on the sermon and service for the next day.

Sunday, 21 September 2008

During the Sunday service the national crisis was only referred to when the time came for prayers and intercession. Over the years my congregation has been extremely careful not to use the church for party political matters, conscious as we are that members probably belong to many different parties. Although the congregation was aware that I was not just a member of the ANC but that I had been a member of the NEC for ten years, at no stage did I use the church to promote sectarian party politics or factional interests within the party.

It is for this reason that I have problems with comrades who use funerals to promote not only a particular party, but a faction or individual within a party. People forget that at a funeral the mourners, particularly family members, do not all belong to the same party. One can speak about the party the deceased belonged to but cannot use a funeral to promote one party against another or one individual leader against another within the same party. It is worse when leaders use a funeral to attack other leaders or parties. An extraordinary level of sensitivity is required in this regard.

In my sermons I have always distinguished between party politics and the cause of justice. My involvement in the liberation struggle

33

was about the struggle for justice and not about a particular political party. The liberation movement (the party) was the means to an end rather than an end in itself. I was involved in the struggle to save our people from the brutal violence of the apartheid system and its crude racial policies, which treated black people as less than human. This to me was a negation of the image of God in us. Justice and righteousness were the operative words. It is for this reason that I stated in the early 1990s that if blacks took over government and oppressed whites, I would go to prison again.

For many of us in the struggle it was not about the colour of the people, the party, a group or a faction. It was also not about narrow personal interests. The brutality of the system took away any narrow personal interests, since it dealt with us as a group and not as individuals. In any case, during those days, there was no patronage, tenders or deals as there is today. In all ways blacks were excluded from the system. The struggle was about the people – the people of God who were oppressed and exploited by an evil and brutal system.

Although concern was expressed for me and for the president on this particular Sunday, the congregation stuck to the tradition of focusing on the bigger picture of peace and stability for the country, and that is what they prayed for. They also prayed that God should give me, the president and the leadership of the ANC the wisdom to avoid actions that might destabilise the country and again cause pain to the people.

In their prayers of intercession one could not miss their deep concern that the people of South Africa had suffered enough under apartheid and during the war with the regime's security forces. As a congregation they had witnessed and experienced the pain and suffering brought about by the apartheid regime and the struggle to remove it. At the backs of their minds were the experiences of their own pastor, as well as those of other congregants and their families.

34

No doubt many were recalling the experiences of members of the congregation such as Abbey and Kgotso Chikane, France and Prince Ranoto, David Matsose, Tulamo and Ramodikoe Thipe, all of whom had been harassed by the security forces until they were forced into exile, some because they had been involved in combat action as part of Umkhonto we Sizwe (MK). Prince Ranoto died in exile and Tulamo Thipe lost some of his fingers in combat. An older member of the congregation, Phineas Ranoto, was detained and subjected to extreme forms of torture, while his daughter, Rebecca, was subjected to electric shocks in the bushes next to Merafe Station in Soweto to force her to give information about her brothers. The younger brother, Abbey Ranoto, also later went into exile. On one day in early 1977 the homes of almost all the young people in the church were raided and they were questioned. Some were taken away while others were beaten up to try to force them to give information about their peers suspected of being involved in the armed struggle.

There are those who continued with the struggle at home, such as Mzwakhe Mbuli, Oupa Radebe, Gen Nhlapho, and many others. There are also the unsung heroes and heroines – families who were harassed and traumatised because of their children or because they were suspected of giving refuge to children the security forces were looking for. The list is endless. And this is just from one congregation in Soweto.

After making this journey into the past, the congregation returned to the present and their prayers of intercession expressed that the nation was not ready for more pain. They sang '*Nkosi sikelel' iAfrika*' and '*Morena boloka sechaba sa rona*' with a prayerful spirit and prayed for God to intervene and grant them peace. Some cried to the Lord to have mercy on the people and the nation. As this is a classical Pentecostal congregation their cries were loud and reached the highest of heavens.

At this point I was reminded of one of our theological activists who visited Nicaragua during the reversals of the gains in the struggle there. He was deeply distressed and depressed, as he felt that the experience of the people of Nicaragua was like crucifying Jesus for the second time. I felt that people had died to liberate this country and we could not afford to die again because of the party's internal conflicts.

In their prayers the congregation committed all the leaders involved to the Lord to help them to avoid disaster for the people. At the end of the service they released me and wished me God's blessings, wisdom and guidance as I returned to the 'operational area' in Mahlamba Ndlopfu. Some of them could not hold back their tears as they bade me farewell.

On our way back to Mahlamba Ndlopfu I received a call conveying another disturbing message: 'The ANC say that they want the president's resignation letter today, not tomorrow!' as we had agreed with the president. Our view had been that we needed to interact with parliament before we finalised the letter, to ensure that there was a smooth transition.

The *ngoko* ('now') message made me lose my cool and I said that this could not be. The party may have the right to 'recall' its member from government but cannot determine when the president should submit a letter of resignation. I felt that *ba leka presidente joale* ('they were testing the president's patience to the limit') and that *ba batla ho ribitella bohloko bo a leng ho bona* ('they were poking their fingers into the gaping wound'). The president had agreed to resign and there was no need to set an unreasonable deadline for the letter of resignation or indeed set a deadline at all. Once they started dictating when the letter should be delivered, we began to slide into sinking sand, as this would change the status of the recall of the president to that of a *coup d'état*. The first could be considered a legitimate move for a party; the latter is a clear breach of our Constitution!

This bordered on forcing the president to resign, as if at gunpoint. Our sister country, Madagascar, had recently had just such an experience, leading to great instability. However, we were told that the mood at Esselen Park was 'foul' and it would be helpful if the letter was delivered before participants left the meeting. This argument did not help the situation as it suggested that people would not go until the letter was delivered. This sounded like an ultimatum. A 'foul mood' cannot be the reason for anyone to violate the Constitution.

My view was that the president had to be given time to think carefully through the constitutional issues involved before he wrote the letter and that the contents of the letter had to be tested against the law and the Constitution. As long as he was still president of the country he had to honour his oath by upholding, defending and respecting the Constitution as the supreme law of the Republic. I was of the view that nothing would go awry between Sunday and Monday, given the willingness of the president to resign voluntarily.

My advice was: 'Do not do it. Take your time, allow for proper consultations with lawyers and parliament and then finalise the letter.' I asked the official to communicate my view to the president.

En route to Mahlamba Ndlopfu, thinking hard about these matters, I received a call informing me that the president wished us to comply with the deadline. He repeated that he did not want it to be thought that he wished to remain in his position for a day longer than his party wanted him to. If it was *ngoko* we must do it *ngoko*! He was determined not to give anyone the opportunity to destabilise the country, as some were bent on doing.

To meet this deadline we had to work hard to ensure that the letter was delivered before 7.00 p.m. to the speaker of parliament, Baleka Mbete, who was also the chairperson of the ANC, and was at Esselen Park together with the president of the ANC, Jacob Zuma.

Many people do not understand why the president gave in so

easily and volunteered to resign. Some feel that, in doing so, he let them down. Others felt strongly that the president had not given the country an opportunity to test the constitutionality of a party 'recall' of the president of the country, who was elected by parliament. Yet many others were ready to resist or campaign against his removal but were disarmed by the president's decision to comply with the decision of the party.

In fact, in the interests of peace in the country the president had very few options that had no possibility of undesirable or unpredictable outcomes. If he had chosen not to resign, the country would have been plunged into a crisis of enormous proportions, as there was no constitutional provision for the party to do what it wanted to do except through parliament. Other options were equally risky and could not be considered. One was the 'orange revolution' method used to unseat governments in some Eastern European countries, an option that would have required the mobilisation of the masses and would have entailed considerable risk, as the people would have been deeply divided.

In addition, we had classified information that suggested refusal might have resulted in some resorting to foolish and desperate methods which, too, could have threatened the stability of the country. At this point there were a considerable number of comrades, both within and outside government, who were engaged in activities that could have easily sent them to jail, but the decision was that this was not the route we should go, as it would have deepened the crisis.

As I thought over all these matters, I was reminded of the words of an elderly member of my congregation who, angry at the events that had taken place at Polokwane, came to me during the 'peace be with you' liturgical moment and shook me, asking, 'Mfundisi, what have you done with our organisation? How could you allow this to happen?' She is tall and heavy and could have just pushed me over, as I had not expected her to go beyond the liturgical handshake to actually shaking me up. Some members of the church who witnessed this act were surprised but continued with the liturgy activity of sharing 'peace' with others.

Because it was in the middle of the service I could not answer her or respond. I just said, 'Let's find time to talk.' When we did find time she expressed her shock and disgust about what had happened in Polokwane in the presence of the leadership – the unbecoming behaviour of the delegates, the rudeness, the vulgarity, and so on – which she said was totally uncharacteristic of the ANC she has known and been a part of for many years. A few weeks later she came back to me and said that perhaps the Polokwane decision had to happen after all; that perhaps the Lord had allowed it to save us from people who might have resorted to violence, which could have destabilised the country. I was struck by the fact that this *gogo* ('granny'), relying purely on her spirituality and politics rather than intelligence information, understood so well the implications of what could have happened if a different option had been pursued.

Interestingly, the media did not examine the options that were open to the president and what their possible consequences were. There was no serious analytical work, as the focus was on his removal from the office, statements justifying his removal, his response, the resignation of his ministers, and about his successor. It was almost as if the media was happy over the outcome of the NEC deliberations. It was what they also wanted.

The one thing many commentators and analysts missed was the dangerous blurring of lines between party and state. The party made a decision to recall the president and the president responded as a disciplined cadre of the ANC who would not defy his party. The challenges of the use of the concept of a recall have already been dealt with but are worth reiterating. A party can recall a member who is deployed but no one can recall a president, as he or she is elected by parliament. If there was an agreement between the president and his party, then the president had to translate the agreement into reality in a constitutional way.

This could only be done through parliament, which was why Mbeki and we believed this should be dealt with on the Monday, when the parliamentary leadership would be in office. Both the executive and parliament needed their lawyers to put their heads together to map out the best legal and constitutional route to effect the process. Given that this was not a *coup d'état*, this should not have been a problem.

The question we had to deal with was: does the president have to prepare two letters, one to the party and one to parliament? The answer was no, he was only obliged to tender his resignation to parliament. The fact that a party had decided to recall its member could not be a basis for the speaker to act until there was an official communication either from the party or from the president, and any such communication would require the speaker to consult with parliament and secure its decision. This is where the lines became blurred. Even though the speaker (who was Baleka Mbete), in her capacity as national chairperson of the party, had chaired the meeting at which the decision was made, she could not demand the letter of resignation in her capacity as speaker. Nor could she set deadlines for the president. In the circumstances the president could have ignored the demand and a crisis might have ensued.

Thank God that Mbeki, in his magnanimity, ignored these technicalities and had the letter delivered on time to the speaker at Esselen Park. The downside of this approach is that the country was denied the possibility and opportunity of testing the 'recall' approach and its constitutionality through public debates, parliamentary processes and even the courts. It left a precedent the country may not want to have. But Mbeki would argue that it was the best way to save the country then, and he also did not want be the subject of such a debate.

During the afternoon President Mbeki had held an emergency cabinet meeting at the Union Buildings, for which the NEC, which had not completed its agenda, had to adjourn to give NEC members, who were also members of the national executive of the country, an opportunity to attend. The mood was sombre, with some cabinet members fighting back tears. Some were angry, some numb, others expressionless, and a few managed to present awkward jolly faces. Deputy President Phumzile Mlambo-Ngcuka decided that if the president resigned she would also resign. A number of ministers and deputy ministers also decided to resign, some of them as a matter of principle and for others on procedural grounds, because it was the president who had appointed them.

After the meeting President Mbeki returned to Mahlamba Ndlopfu to finalise his letter of resignation, addressed not to the ANC but to the parliament that had elected him. The letter served to inform parliament that he had decided to 'resign' his position 'as president of the country, *effective upon receiving your advice that parliament has finalised this matter*' (my emphasis). He left it to parliament to decide on the date on which his resignation would become effective. The intention was to give parliament and the executive time to consult and agree on the procedures to be followed, as was the tradition in terms of the cooperative relationship between the two arms of government.

Once the couriers had left for Esselen Park with the letter, we turned our attention to the draft of the president's speech to the nation, scheduled for 7.00 p.m. As was his habit, he drafted the speech and asked us to read it, proofread it and respond to it. On this occasion we made few suggestions – it was his speech.

By this stage the special lounge at Mahlamba Ndlopfu had become a command centre from which we monitored the progress of the couriers and helped with the preparations for the president's address while the communications, protocol and security teams worked on the logistics with the SABC studio in Pretoria, Tshwane, for the live address. As the letter was delivered, the president addressed the nation and the world:

> Fellow South Africans, I have no doubt that you are aware of the announcement made yesterday by the National Executive Committee of the ANC with regard to the position of the President of the Republic.
>
> Accordingly, I would like to take this opportunity to inform the nation that today I handed a letter to the Speaker of the National Assembly, the Honourable Baleka Mbete, to tender my resignation from the high position of President of the Republic of South Africa, *effective from the day that will be determined by the National Assembly* [my emphasis].
>
> I have been a loyal member of the African National Congress for 52 years. I remain a member of the ANC and therefore respect its decisions. It is for this reason that I have taken the decision to resign as President of the Republic, following the decision of the National Executive Committee of the ANC.

The rest of the speech was in the form of a last report to the nation, covering the vision, principles and values that had guided the ANC during the struggle and that were, among others, the 'life-long lessons' cadres of the movement learned. Mbeki informed them that

> ... wherever we are and whatever we do we should ensure that our actions contribute to the attainment of a free and just society, the upliftment of all our people, and the development of a South Africa that belongs to all who live in it.

He went on to say:

> Indeed, the work we have done in pursuit of the vision and principles of our liberation movement has at all times been based on the age-old values of Ubuntu, of selflessness, sacrifice and service in a manner that ensures that the interests of the people take precedence over our desires as individuals.
>
> I truly believe that the governments in which I have been privileged to serve have acted and worked in the true spirit of these important values.

In the speech he also alluded to Judge Nicholson's judgment, which had precipitated the decision to remove him from office, stating that 'since the attainment of our freedom' the government had 'acted consistently to respect and defend the independence of the judiciary' rather than 'act in a manner that would have had a negative impact on its work'. Even when government had to publicly express 'views contrary to that of the judiciary', it had done so 'mindful of the need to protect its integrity'.

> Consistent with this practice, I would like to restate the position of Cabinet on the inferences made by the Honourable Judge Chris Nicholson that the President and Cabinet have interfered in the work of the National Prosecuting Authority (NPA).
>
> Again I would like to state this categorically that we have never done this, and therefore never compromised the right of the National Prosecuting Authority to decide whom it wished to prosecute or not to prosecute.
>
> This applies equally to the painful matter relating to the court proceedings against the President of the ANC, Comrade Jacob Zuma. More generally, I would like to assure the nation

that our successive governments since 1994 have never acted in any manner intended wilfully to violate the Constitution and the law.

We have always sought to respect the solemn Oath of Office each one of us made in front of the Chief Justice and other judges, and have always been conscious of the fact that the legal order that governs our country was achieved through the sacrifices made by countless numbers of our people, which include death. In this context it is most unfortunate that gratuitous suggestions have been made seeking to impugn the integrity of those of us who have been privileged to serve in our country's National Executive.

Although I was a member of the team that had worked on the speech, as I listened to him speaking it struck me that the ANC seemed to have made no attempt to hear the president's side of the story; no attempt to apply the *audi alteram partem* (hear the other side) principle or the basic rules of justice. This left the president to defend himself in the public sphere rather than in a proper forum of the organisation. While Judge Nicholson's inferences would be dismissed by the Supreme Court of Appeal (SCA), the ANC's dismissal of the president was never reversed nor was there any intention to reverse it. In any case, the Nicholson judgement was simply an excuse for other interests.

The president returned to Mahlamba Ndlopfu and found us together with some of his close members of cabinet and some ANC leaders in the famous lounge, reminiscing about the unbelievable events of the past 24 or so hours and comparing them with Mbeki's illustrious career as deputy president and president of the country over a period of about fifteen years. Although there were challenges and controversial issues such as the HIV and AIDS debate which, some believe, marred his presidency, the unprecedented 24 hours

44

had nothing to do with that. Instead, they were a culmination of a vicious and debilitating internal strife within the ANC, centred on the removal of Zuma from his position as deputy president of the country and the charges of corruption preferred against him.

Mbeki's illustrious service to the people of South Africa, the African continent and the rest of the world did not matter. Of all the commendable things Mbeki did during his presidency, what loomed highest was his African Renaissance vision, which had already taken root with programmes such as NEPAD and the APRM. No one – not even his worst enemies – would be able to take this away from him.

The public statement of the president brought his presidency to an unexpected and dramatic end. It felt like the light had just been switched off, bringing to an end a fast-paced exciting movie which had ended in a tragedy. It left one feeling empty and depressed, continually asking the question of how this could have happened.

With hindsight those who sat in that lounge reminiscing about the past 24 hours were like the disciples of Jesus Christ after his crucifixion. 'He was a prophet,' they said, 'powerful in word and deed before God and all the people ... they crucified him; but we had hoped that he was the one who was going to redeem' us. Of course, Mbeki is not Jesus Christ, but that gathering in that famous lounge just after the president announced his resignation brought these thoughts about his disciples to me. I was able to understand better what they went through.

Mbeki entered the room and we all stood up in respect, congratulated him for the address to the nation and then took our seats again. We talked into the night and I then made my fourth trip back to Soweto in a period of only 48 hours.

CHAPTER 2

The Aftermath

Managing Mbeki's Resignation

Monday, 22 September 2008

On the Monday morning I had an appointment I could not change. I was scheduled to speak at a workshop on Zimbabwe, organised by the Lutheran World Federation at a conference centre in Benoni. It involved representatives of churches in South Africa and Zimbabwe and members of civil society from both countries. The focus was on what the churches could do to assist Zimbabwe, following the signing of the Global Political Agreement (GPA) more than a week earlier.

For the conference organisers life had to go on irrespective of the unfolding events in South Africa – they were determined that, in the interests of the people of Zimbabwe, nothing should be allowed to overshadow the progress being made. Others who held a contrary view on the developments still felt that the meeting was important to maintain the momentum for the resolution of the crisis. Whatever the differences in perspectives, both groups agreed on one thing: the worrying developments in South Africa should not derail them from the course of finding peace in Zimbabwe.

For me it was more awkward to honour this invitation, in the light of the unfolding events which affected me directly and required my urgent attention, especially because of the meetings with the security entities given that I was the secretary of the National Security Council. On the other hand, it was a godsend, giving me an opportunity to critically reflect on and contrast the situation in Zimbabwe with that in South Africa. I shared with the workshop participants the challenges we were facing, the risks attendant on them and how easy it was for a very stable and promising country to be destabilised to a state where everyone loses control of events. Zimbabwe, the subject of that meeting, was a living example of this tragedy.

Although conditions in Zimbabwe were different, the two countries had much to learn from each other. What was incredible, though, was the fact that a president had just been forced to resign but the participants were able to continue with their workshop without any hindrance. This gave them a sense of comfort that it is possible, even in the face of the worst crisis, to maintain stability and peace while seeking solutions.

One of the lessons we learned from the historical experiences of the two countries was that in a country which has come through war or political conflict, no negotiated settlement will ever be perfect and equally satisfactory to all the contending or interested parties. One need only look at the 1980 and 1994 settlement agreements in Zimbabwe and South Africa respectively. Secondly, where leaders focus more on their personal political interests or ambitions, narrow party interests or external interests (such as those of the major superpowers) instead of the interests of the people (the common good across party lines), the conflict is bound to worsen rather than abate.

The lesson from the unfolding events in South Africa was that leaders who care about their people are always ready to be sacrificed if that will save the country. Here national interest takes precedence over personal interests. Unfortunately, this is not the trend internationally and that is why we have intractable wars and conflicts.

I then presented the GPA, its logic and the compromises made to reach the agreement. I also had to deal with public and media perceptions and perspectives which had no bearing on the reality and content of the agreement, and the need for wise and strategic leadership to make the agreement a success. There were radical differences during the question and answer session, but at the end most of the participants agreed that there was no other agreement (without compromises) that could be used to help normalise the situation in Zimbabwe other than the GPA.

While I was at the workshop, at the Union Buildings the president was meeting, as planned, with the command structures of the security establishment – the defence force, the police and the intelligence services – to brief them about his decision to resign and his expectation of them to act professionally, as well as ensure that there was stability and security for all South Africans. The media was invited for photo opportunities to ensure that the public knew about these developments. Pictures of the president and the command structures of the security forces bidding farewell sent a very positive signal in terms of the security of the state and the stability of the country. It assured the public that the transition from Mbeki to the next president would be managed in a peaceful manner.

In my address to the workshop I used the developments at the Union Buildings to illustrate the commitment of the leadership to a stable transition. After my session at the workshop I hastily returned to the Union Buildings to manage the transitional processes.

Earlier in the day our staff made contact with the staff in

parliament to work on the constitutional and legal issues arising out of the intention of the president to resign, the timing of the resignation and procedures to be followed. While we were doing this, the president received a letter from the speaker informing him of parliament's decision that his resignation would be 'effective from Thursday the 25 September 2008' and that the new president would be elected at 11.00 a.m. the same day. The speaker did not consult the president about this matter and he had no advance warning of the letter or the contents thereof as we would have expected. (Unfortunately, despite repeated attempts to acquire a copy of the letter in question, I was unable to secure the document.)

Later we learned that the speaker had issued a note on the 'parliamentary process to deal with the resignation, of the president of the Republic of South Africa and related matters'. The speaker announced the resignation of the president in the National Assembly by reading the president's letter of resignation, and the chief whip of the majority party thereupon moved a motion without notice to the effect 'that the President's resignation will take effect on Thursday, 25 September 2008'. As there was an objection to the motion being moved without notice, the chief whip gave notice with the view to moving the motion the following day.

With hindsight, it is interesting that except for the Azanian People's Organisation (AZAPO), no other party in parliament raised constitutional issues related to this resignation. AZAPO believed that the ANC's decision undermined the office of the president and the legitimacy of the president having been elected by parliament. Moeletsi Mbeki, the brother of the president who often differed from him politically, was more vocal about this matter as an analyst. His view was that the ANC did not follow the Constitution in dealing with the matter of removal of the president from office. He thought the ANC should have lodged a complaint against the president in parliament, based on the Nicholson judgment. Parliament would have investigated the matter and a decision would have been taken in terms of the Constitution. He expressed a serious concern that 'if they [the ANC] ... continue to follow the path of not following the constitution then they are going to lead this country to a civil war'.

Whatever the case, parliament chose to deal with the matter as just a matter of moving a motion to determine the date when the resignation would take effect, followed by a letter to the president informing him about the date. Again, like the media, the political parties in parliament (except AZAPO) seemed to be ready to close their eyes to the constitutional issues, as they were happy to see Mbeki leaving as president. Self-interest weighed heavily against the interests of preserving our constitutional democracy. Their definition of 'truth' and 'justice' depends on whether or not an issue favours their position or interest rather than in itself.

There were complications occasioned by the formulation of the letter from the speaker of the National Assembly. 'Effective from Thursday' would mean that he ceased to be president at midnight on the Wednesday, creating a vacuum for the eleven hours until the new president was sworn in. An attempt to interact with parliament in this regard was met with a clear message from the speaker's office: 'The contents of the letter are final and will not be changed or amended' to address the concerns that had been raised. This was strange, as there was no legal or constitutional basis for the speaker's office or even parliament to dictate the date, time and terms of the voluntary resignation of the president. On this matter they had no authority. To be precise, the response of parliament also bordered on violating the Constitution, since the speaker and her office were acting on behalf of parliament.

At this point, given the atmosphere generated by the decision of the NEC of the ANC, I realised that cooperation between parliament and the executive had been thrown out of the window because the same players at party level were in the leadership of parliament. The lines between parliament and party were again blurred and parliament was used as if it were a representative of the ruling party rather than elected representatives of the people. Indeed, the party 'foul mood' in Esselen Park, in Gauteng, was transferred into parliament in Cape Town, in the Western Cape.

This stance put the executive in a difficult position: to find its way without the involvement of parliament. This was extraordinary and could not be done in our democracy or any normal democracy. The team from the presidency used its normal contacts within parliament, developed over many years, to continue working together below the radar of the politics of the day as we had to prepare for the swearing in of the president.

The letter from parliament generated further activity in the presidency – it gave the president very little time in which to take his leave of those who had served with him and worked for him. The president asked me, as secretary to the cabinet, to convene the last cabinet meeting in the late afternoon on the Wednesday, so he could bid farewell to his colleagues. The president also wanted to bid farewell to parliament but this was not to be, given the attitude displayed by the office of the speaker of the National Assembly – yet another instance of party issues being confused with parliamentary matters. The finality of the letter from the speaker seemed to be intended to close any possibility of the president addressing parliament to bid its members farewell.

The fact is that it was not parliament which decided on Mbeki's resignation nor were there any constitutional or legal impediments which could be used to bar the president from addressing parliament about his decision to resign. In terms of s 84(d) of the Constitution, which gives him the power to summon parliament to an extraordinary sitting, the president could have asked the presiding officers in parliament – that is, the speaker of the National Assembly and the chairperson of the National Council of Provinces (NCP) – to convene a joint sitting of the two houses to announce his resignation in parliament, rather than hand over a letter of resignation to the speaker.

His address to the nation about his resignation, which he delivered on Sunday evening, could have been presented in parliament at a time of his choosing and this could have given him the opportunity to bid farewell in a more appropriate manner. The pressure for him to deliver the letter on Sunday evening could have been intended to close off this possibility. Once he delivered his letter to the speaker, he put himself at the mercy of the speaker and the door to a parliamentary farewell was closed.

Mbeki's view would be that if he had exercised his right in the way in which the Constitution allowed, he could have created a further crisis which could have led to instability in the country. Once more he opted to avoid such a crisis, and the presidency decided not to raise any further questions about this matter. History will have it that Mbeki was denied the opportunity to say farewell to parliament based on matters that had nothing to do with parliament, governance or national interest.

Another problem was that we needed to organise a farewell function for the staff and associated institutions in the presidency, but there was no possibility of doing this before the president's resignation took effect on the Thursday morning, as too many complex issues had yet to be dealt with. The function would have to be held on the Friday, when his presidency would have been terminated, and this would require consultation with the new president. As the ANC had already announced that they had nominated the then minister in the presidency, Kgalema Motlanthe, for the post of the president, I consulted him about our dilemma. He graciously said he did not foresee any problems and plans went ahead for the function.

I also had to deploy the relevant staff in Cape Town to prepare for the swearing in of the new president following his election on the Thursday morning. The swearing in ceremony was fixed for 2.00 p.m. Since the deputy president and some ministers had resigned in response to the decision to remove Mbeki, we also had to arrange for the swearing in of a new deputy president and new ministers and deputy ministers, and Friday afternoon was chosen for this purpose.

The resignations were controversial. Some resigned as a matter of principle as they felt that the removal of the president was both unjust and unacceptable and they wished to express their solidarity with him. Others resigned because they believed they were serving at the pleasure of the president and could not remain in office if the president who appointed them was removed. Section 102(2) of the Constitution provides that where a vote of no confidence in the president is passed, both he or she and the members of the cabinet and any deputy ministers 'must resign'. This was clearly not the situation here. There was no 'vote of no confidence' in the president, and the ministers and deputy ministers could stay in office and continue with their work.

Another situation, dealt with by s 94 of the Constitution, relates to the 'continuation of cabinet' after elections, which obliges ministers to leave office once a new president is sworn in. This, too, had no bearing on the situation we were facing, which was unique and not anticipated by the constitution-makers. The section of the Constitution we relied on was the one dealing with an acting president in the case of a vacancy (s 90[1]), which leaves cabinet in place.

The ANC was concerned about the resignations and called on the ministers and deputy ministers not to resign, to ensure stability in government, and meetings were arranged to persuade them to stay in office. A few changed their minds but the rest, who had already submitted their resignations, remained adamant. Some of those who resigned felt it would be better for the new president to reappoint them rather than to inherit them from his predecessor. Not unexpectedly, the controversy escalated, with some within the ANC accusing Mbeki of encouraging resignations *en masse* in solidarity with him, an accusation denied by Mbeki and all those involved or affected.

An unprecedented situation

Although Kgalema Motlanthe was already in the presidency, he could not assume the responsibilities of president until he was sworn in; and since Deputy President Phumzile Mlambo-Ngcuka had resigned, she could not help us as her resignation took effect on the day Mbeki ceased to be president. Thus we found ourselves in a situation where we had a president whose task was all but impossible because he had been informed that he could not continue with some of his presidential responsibilities – a violation of our Constitution. On the other hand, we had a nominated president who was also not in a position to perform any presidential tasks until he was duly elected and sworn-in in terms of the Constitution.

This created an unprecedented situation where, as the most senior professional public servant, I had to assume completely unexpected responsibilities. Most importantly, I had to manage the exit of President Mbeki at the same time as I managed the entry of President Motlanthe, an extraordinary and emotionally taxing task. I had to help the man I believed had done so well for the country and for the African continent to leave office in circumstances I believed to be totally unjustifiable. But as the head of the presidency (a civil servant) and secretary of the cabinet, I had to manage this change as professionally as I could, which required me to be neutral

54

and objective.

As the most senior professional public servant I had to take responsibility once the political principals, the office bearers, were unable to execute their responsibilities, or if there was political paralysis of some kind. I also had to plan the procedures relating to the swearing in of the new president and to serve him loyally, whatever my personal views. Fortunately I had no problems with Comrade Kgalema Motlanthe. In fact, I personally believed he was the best person available at the time and, as deputy president of the ANC, was the natural choice.

All this notwithstanding, it was still emotionally very taxing to manage the transition. During the week I relied heavily on my faith, on my commitment to peace in the country and on my professional understanding of the nature of the state and the role of the secretary of the cabinet. It was also a week in which I appreciated my adrenalin glands, which kept me going as I managed this difficult situation.

Managing the interregnum

Fowler impressed on me the need to address the hiatus on the Thursday morning occasioned by the letter from parliament. This did not surprise me as Fowler had worked in parliament before and was sensitive to parliamentary issues.

Those of us who spent more time working in the presidency tended to focus more on what the president and or the executive of government was doing or should do. Fowler argued strongly that the hiatus in which we found ourselves required the cabinet secretary to take responsibility for the transitional processes. Initially I brushed off his argument, feeling that he was exaggerating my role.

My modesty in this case did not help. It later became clear to me that I had no choice but to take that responsibility.

Tuesday, 23 September 2008

'Black man you are on your own', Steve Biko famously said, and by Tuesday morning it had become clear to me that apart from the dedicated team that worked with me within the presidency I was indeed, like Biko's black man, very much on my own! Although the president had the constitutional right to exercise his powers up to and including the last second of his presidency, he chose to be cautious and was hesitant about making decisions on matters that affected him directly during his last days in office. He was also hesitant about making decisions or expressing opinions on matters which went beyond the currency of his office, except where it was absolutely necessary. Besides the party having put limitations on what he could do, this was a matter of integrity.

Motlanthe, on the other hand, had no constitutional powers at all until he was sworn in. Some among us (especially within the party) believed that Jacob Zuma, as president of the ruling party, should take responsibility for government. But this, too, would be unconstitutional and another challenge invoked by mixing government with party. Those who believed that the president of the ANC had the authority to take over presidential powers and lead the country had no respect for the Constitution.

There were moments during this waiting period when I felt that there was a cabinet outside the actual cabinet; that decisions were being made elsewhere and it was being expected that the secretary of the cabinet would execute them. But this I could not do. Actions which required a cabinet decision had to be made either by the president or by cabinet and I could act only once the real cabinet had made its decision.

Every decision I had to make suddenly had implications way beyond the presidency and government. The risks were huge. But the decisions had to be made for the sake of the country and the integrity of the state.

In an effort to address Fowler's concern about the possible hiatus on Thursday, we looked at various options the Constitution gave us. Section 90 of the Constitution states:

> ... during a vacancy in the office of President, an office-bearer in the order below acts as President:
> (a) The Deputy President.
> (b) A Minister designated by the President.
> (c) A Minister designated by the other members of the Cabinet.
> (d) The Speaker, until the National Assembly designates one of its other members.

The first option was not applicable, since the deputy president had resigned or submitted her letter of resignation. With regard to s 90(b) we agreed that it might be questionable for the president to designate one of his ministers to act as president beyond the currency of his office, although some felt that this could be done because removal from office does not reverse decisions made during the presidential term. We felt s 90(c) was a safer option. Accordingly, arrangements were made for the ministers to be enabled to act in terms of this section to designate one of their own to act as president from midnight on the Wednesday when Mbeki's resignation would take effect. The minister of communications, Ivy Matsepe-Cassaburi, was designated acting president at a meeting chaired by the outgoing president.

Interestingly, this was the responsibility of the executive rather than that of parliament, which is why it did not make sense for parliament to determine the time at which the resignation of the president should take effect, without consulting the executive. Unfortunately, given the politics of the day, this was done without thought to the consequences beyond mere parliamentary considerations. One should say, though, that the note of the speaker, dated 22 September 2008, did not see any crisis, as it clearly states that 'there will be no need to have a person acting as President pending the election'. In my view this statement was incorrect. One could not have a vacuum for eleven hours before a new president was elected and sworn in.

The next problem was the swearing in of the new president, which was the responsibility of the executive and the judiciary and had to be arranged through consultation between these two arms of the state.

Once the president is sworn in he or she becomes the responsibility of the executive, in particular the secretary of the cabinet and director-general in the presidency. Consequently, the presidency and other affected departments had to work together to manage the transitional processes relating to security, accommodation, support staff, and many other issues.

Packing up

It was reported that the suggestion that Mbeki be given two weeks to a month to complete his work and prepare for his departure was shot down at Esselen Park. His departure had to be *ngoko*! As a result, he had no chance to go to Cape Town and clear his office or the official residence at Genadendal. Given the uncertainty about what would happen after midnight on the Wednesday, staff at Genadendal were instructed to pack his and Mrs Mbeki's personal belongings and arrange for their transportation to Gauteng.

For the staff who had to carry out this instruction it felt like there had been a *coup d'état*, especially because they were not taken into confidence about the details of what was happening. Was the president packing hastily and running away? Was he forced to leave? Was he safe where he was? What was going to happen next, including to the staff at the relevant official households?

Once his term of office ended Mbeki could not be flown by the air force without the permission of his successor, so one of the first issues I had to deal with when I met President Motlanthe after he had been sworn in was to get permission from him for the air force to fly the former president to Cape Town to deal with his personal belongs. Again, President Motlanthe was very gracious, saying he had not known the former president needed his permission.

By the time permission was obtained Mrs Mbeki had done everything possible to move out of Genadendal and, in the end, Mbeki never returned either to Genadendal or to his offices at Tuynhuys, feeling it inappropriate to do so once the new president was in office.

CHAPTER 3

An Emotional Farewell

Wednesday, 24 September 2008

The cabinet meeting held in the late afternoon on Wednesday was even more emotional than the one that had taken place on the Sunday. Unfortunately, since cabinet business is classified, I cannot tell the story but I can mention three things which are public knowledge. Mbeki bade farewell to his cabinet and his deputy ministers, typically doing so in a carefully crafted letter directed to every member of cabinet, including deputy ministers, in which he expressed his views and feelings. The text was released after the cabinet meeting, making it a public document.

Because of its historical importance I quote it in its entirety here (and in Appendix 4):

24 September 2008

Dear Colleagues,

To all Members of the National Executive.

As you know, tomorrow, September 25, the National Assembly will elect the next President of the Republic of South Africa, who will also swear his or her oath of office on the same day.

By law, I will therefore cease to be President of the Republic with effect from midnight today.

I thought I should send you this letter as one of my last communications to you as Head of our country's National Executive.

First of all I would like to thank you for having agreed to serve in the National Executive when you were requested to do so.

This demonstrated your selfless commitment to serve the people of South Africa, which told me that I was indeed very privileged to have the possibility to work as part of such a collective of South African patriots.

All of us, together, have always understood that as members of the National Executive, we carry the heavy responsibility to stand in the front ranks of the national forces charged with the historic task to achieve the goals of the national democratic revolution.

All of us know that, by definition, all revolutions are not, to quote Nelson Mandela, an 'easy walk to freedom'. Accordingly, our own continuing revolution has also not been, is not, and will not be an easy walk to freedom.

It will constantly test and pose a challenge to everybody, including ourselves, to prove through our deeds, rather than our words, that we are true revolutionaries.

This will demand that we demonstrate that we are able and willing to walk the long and hard road to freedom, always conscious of our obligation to serve the people, rather than promote our personal interests.

As tried and tested combatants for the victory and consolidation of our democratic revolution, you have had no need for an instructor to educate you about the challenges we would face and face, to achieve the objectives of the revolution.

Your decision to serve in the National Executive has therefore meant that you are willing to walk a hard road that would necessarily demand personal sacrifices.

It is for this reason that I have thanked you for your conscious and voluntary agreement to join the National Executive.

In this regard I must emphasise the fact that the charge given to the National Executive during the years of our freedom, since 1994, mandated by the people through democratic elections, has been to pursue the goal of the revolutionary transformation of our country.

I make this observation in part to pay tribute to you for the loyal and principled manner in which you have consistently and consciously approached your responsibilities as revolutionary democrats.

I also make it to thank you for the contribution you have made towards the achievement of the revolutionary goals of the democratic revolution.

Fifteen years ago now, on the eve of the victory of the democratic revolution, the movement to which I belong took various decisions about the immediate tasks of this revolution. These were encapsulated in two important documents, these being:

- 'Ready to Govern'
- 'Reconstruction and Development Programme'.

Repeatedly, over the years, we have summarised the strategic focus of these documents, and therefore the democratic revolution, as:

- the creation of a non-racial society
- the creation of a non-sexist society
- the entrenchment and defence of the democratic order, as reflected in our national Constitution
- the restructuring, modernisation and development of our economy to create a prosperous society, characterised by the eradication of poverty and underdevelopment, and a shared prosperity
- the implementation of social policies consistent with the preceding goals
- the transformation of the state machinery to ensure that we build a developmental state
- the Renaissance of Africa and the building of a better world, focused on the challenge to defeat global poverty, underdevelopment and inequality.

Over the years, since 1994, the objectives of the movement to which most of us belong have served as the centrepiece of the election manifestoes on whose basis the people of our country mandated the ANC to assume the honoured position of the ruling party of South Africa.

With immense pride, I would like to convey to you my firm conviction, empirically demonstrated by life itself, that you have indeed honoured your responsibilities to our country and nation, as mandated by the people in the 1994, 1999 and 2004 general elections.

If need be, it would not be difficult to detail the factual accuracy of this statement. Neither would it be difficult to demonstrate the appreciation of the overwhelming majority of the masses of our people for what has been done to improve the quality of their lives.

Apart from the ever-increasing levels of approval stated by the people in all the general and municipal elections after 1994, I have experienced these popular sentiments personally in the many community Izimbizo we have convened in all parts of our country, both urban and rural.

The fundamental message I would like to communicate to you in this regard is that you have indeed discharged your revolutionary obligation further to advance the goals of the national democratic revolution.

At the same time, I am certain that during the years we have served as members of the National Executive we have made mistakes. I am equally convinced that the only way we could have avoided these mistakes would have been if we had done nothing to strive to achieve the fundamental social transformation of our country.

In this context, as revolutionaries, we must at all times remain open to criticism and self-criticism, precisely to ensure that we identify whatever mistakes might have occurred and correct these.

At the same time, I am aware of the reality that there are some in our country who are convinced that such mistakes as we might have made, as well as the reality that in fifteen years we have not eradicated a 350-year legacy of colonialism, as we could not, derive from our strategic commitment to a reactionary, neo-liberal perspective and programme.

In addition, it is also clear that there are different views in our country with regard to the assessment of the objective national and international circumstances within which we have sought to achieve the goals of the democratic revolution.

Some claim that we have deliberately overestimated the constraints posed by this objective reality, precisely to justify our failure to undertake what they consider to be an imperative obligation to implement what they regard as a more revolutionary and appropriate programme for the fundamental social transformation of our country.

Further to complicate the challenges with which we have had to contend, the matters that have been raised by some of our opponents have required that we engage a discourse that relates to intellectual paradigms relating to philosophy, ideology and politics.

All this, including the practical politics to which we necessarily had to respond, has imposed on the National Executive the obligation to consider and respond correctly to the dialectical relationship between the two phenomena of human existence, the objective and the subjective.

Confronted by the reality that as government we must govern, and therefore take decisions that have a national, structural and long-term impact, we have consequently had the task to relate the subjective to the objective, to find the necessary relationship between theory and practice.

During our years as members of the National Executive we have discussed all these matters, which relate to the fundamental and critically important issue of the strategy and tactics of the democratic revolution.

I remain convinced that on all occasions we have addressed these matters in an open, honest and objective manner, always informed by our fundamental understanding of the nature and goals of our national democratic revolution.

Among other things, in the end, this has found expression in various documents we have adopted, which have, without let or hindrance, sought honestly to review the performance of the government in which all of us have been honoured to serve, centred on the impact its policies and programmes have had on our society.

By decision of the ruling party, the ANC, acting within its rights, the current government I have been privileged to lead has been obliged to end its tenure a few months ahead of its popularly mandated term.

In the interest of the masses of our people and country, personally I accepted this eventuality without resistance or rancour, and acted upon it accordingly. I trust that all of us, members of the National Executive, will respond in similar fashion.

At the same time, as we bid farewell to one another as members of the elected 2004 to 2009 National Executive, we must do so with our heads held high.

- We must adopt this posture not out of any sense of arrogance or self satisfaction.
- We must do so, as I suggest, because we can honestly say that we did the utmost, to the best of our ability, as a united collective to:
  - advance the goals of the democratic revolution
  - accelerate the advance towards the achievement of the goal of a better life for our people
  - pursue the objective of the fundamental reconstruction and development of our country
  - honour the mandate, and respect the expectations of the masses of our people
  - meet our obligations to the people of Africa and the rest of the world.

I am proud without reservation of what you have done to achieve these historic achievements. I am proud of the manner in which you have functioned, in the context of the intricacies of our democratic and constitutional governance system, to do the detailed work which constitutes the daily fare of our ministries and departments.

As you lead your lives in the aftermath of the early termination of the term of the life of the 2004 to 2009 National Executive, and with all due humility, I plead that in addition to what I have already said in this letter, you should do everything you can, constantly to:

- affirm your personal integrity, refusing to succumb to the expedient
- assert your commitment to principle, rejecting opportunism and cowardice
- reaffirm your commitment selflessly to serve the people, determined to spurn all temptations to self-enrichment, self-promotion and protection of material personal benefit, at the expense of the people
- remain loyal to the values of truthfulness and honesty
- respect the views and esteem of the masses of our people.

I make these comments, at this particular moment, to reemphasise the value system that has informed all of us as we served in the National Executive, concerning our quality as individuals charged with the responsibility to play a leading role as revolutionary activists of the democratic revolution.

In this regard and in the end, the ultimate motive power that would inform and has informed our behaviour as individuals are our conscience and self-respect, individually.

I am absolutely certain that at this particular moment in the

history of our country, the masses of our people need the unequivocal assurance, demonstrated practically, that they continue to be blessed with the kind of ethical leadership they
have seen serving in our country's National Executive during
the last fourteen-and-half years.

Surely, as we sought to achieve what Nelson Mandela described as 'the RDP of the soul', as well as implement the Moral
Regeneration Programme, we have known that we must lead
by example, serving as role models in terms of the morality and
value system we have urged our people to respect!

I thank you most sincerely for the comradely manner in
which we have worked together in the National Executive,
the openness of our debates, the friendship among ourselves
we have enjoyed, and your firm commitment to the realisation
of the goals which our history and reality have dictated.

I wish you success in all your future endeavours, convinced
that you constitute a corps of patriots on whom the masses of
our people can continue to count as their reliable and selfless
leaders, regardless of whether you occupy positions in organs
of state or you do not.

You, an outstanding and immensely talented collective
of patriots, have, during the years we have worked together,
placed and demonstrated confidence in me as the leader of the
National Executive.

Please accept my humble thanks to you for this, as well as my
apology that it is only now, as I leave government, that I convey
this sentiment to you. However, in this context, I would like to
assure you that I am fully conscious of my responsibility to you,
at all times to honour your confidence and respect.

This has told me that I owe an obligation to you and the
masses of our people at all times to remain loyal to the morality of our revolution.

It has told me that I must always strive to serve the people.

It has told me never to betray those who are my comrades-in-arms, committed to achieve agreed common objectives.

It has told me never to dishonour the revolutionary democratic cause, by allowing my personal desires to assume precedence over the interests of the masses of the people.

As we part, I would like to assure you that I am determined to respect and act in accordance with the value system I have just described.

Today is Heritage Day. It may therefore be appropriate that today this outstanding collective of South Africans, the National Executive, should make a commitment to hand to our people, as part of their heritage, a tradition of honest government which is firmly opposed to corruption, duplicity and disrespect for principle.

I trust that, in time, history will hand down the judgement that when we, as our country's National Executive, were given the opportunity, we lived up to the expectations of the masses of our long-suffering people to serve them as honest and selfless leaders – men and women of conscience.

Please convey my humble thanks to your families that they released you to enable you to perform the outstanding public service for which I sincerely thank you.

I bid you a fond farewell as a member of the National Executive.

Because we are, or have become comrades, friends and partners in the pursuit of a common cause, I trust that it will be possible for us informally to continue talking to each other and one another, concerned, still, together to serve the peoples of South Africa, Africa and the rest of the world.

Yours sincerely,
Thabo Mbeki.

Having reread this letter many times, I must say that South Africa and the world have been robbed of the best message we have ever had on leadership, integrity and selfless service as this is a document that was not widely publicised. It would help the nation and the leadership of the country if the contents of this letter were to be made available again to relearn about revolutionary leadership and integrity.

The reading of this letter to cabinet was moving. Unfortunately, even when minutes are one day declassified, the emotions which filled that cabinet room will not be revealed, since emotions are not captured in minutes. So the nation will never know the feelings and responses of their cabinet to such a moving farewell letter. It was departure with grace 'without resistance or rancour' in 'the interest of the masses of our people', as Mbeki has said in the letter.

The meeting was updated about the appeal against the Nicholson judgment. Papers had been served and it was understood that the matter would be pursued despite Mbeki's resignation.

Finally, cabinet members were given the opportunity to designate one of their own to act as president during the hiatus between the resignation taking effect and the swearing in of the new president. Matsepe-Casaburri's appointment was announced before midnight on the Wednesday, for the comfort of the nation.

After the cabinet meeting all the cabinet ministers and deputy ministers who had not resigned, including their officials, had to catch late-night or early morning flights to Cape Town, in order to be in parliament for the election of the president. The pain of parting from the man who would by the next morning no longer be our president was written on the faces of many of us. Those who had resigned in solidarity remained behind with him, but for those who had not resigned but still had great respect for him and the service he had rendered to the country, the African continent and the world, it was a painful farewell. Many shook hands with him, others hugged him and some wept openly, while others battled to hide their tears. Their contorted faces told it all. They then hurriedly left him behind, to catch their flights.

I waited until everyone had paid their respects and left, including the ministers and deputy ministers who had resigned, and then walked with him back to his office. It was at this moment that my multifarious roles came together – I was pastor and comrade, director-general of the presidency and secretary of the cabinet. Never had I felt so great a tension between my personal position and my official duties. As a pastor, I felt I needed to be with Mbeki, which would have meant remaining behind. My ministry would just have been my presence. As a comrade, I felt that staying to express my solidarity was appropriate. But my official duties required me to leave for Cape Town immediately – the orchestration of all the events that would unfold the following day in parliament and Tuynhuys (the office of the president) was wholly or partly my responsibility.

In this interregnum the role of cabinet secretary was the most vital, as Trevor Fowler had argued. Everything that had to do with the executive hinged on me. I was in command of the troops in Cape Town who were preparing for the swearing in of the new president, once elected by parliament. Our staff had to work closely with the parliamentary staff to ensure that the election of the president (which is a responsibility of parliament) and the swearing in of the president (which was the responsibility of the presidency) were well coordinated and seamless.

Could I, like some ministers and deputy ministers, have resigned? The answer is categorically no. No matter how much I loved the president and how loyal I was to him – as president, as a person or as a comrade – as director-general in the presidency, secretary of the cabinet, secretary of the NSC and chairperson of the NSC DG's committee, I had a crucial responsibility to ensure that there was stability during this transitional period, as the president had commanded, and that the transition was managed as efficiently and sensitively as possible given all the challenges of the time, views and feelings.

I also had to set an example to the other directors-general whom, as chair of FOSAD, I had asked to remain in their posts to ensure that there was stability, especially for those heads of departments whose ministers had resigned. The message to the directors-general, especially those who were responsible for the security of the state and the people of South Africa, was clear: 'the stability of the country rests entirely on you as heads of department and other state institutions at this critical moment in the history of the country'. In the absence of ministers they had to run government.

The president also understood that, unlike elected office bearers, I, as a public servant, had a responsibility to the state and not merely to the leadership of the party in power, and my loyalty had to be to the state which superseded loyalty to individuals. I also had to be loyal to any constitutionally elected president of the country as long as I was the secretary of cabinet or head of the presidency.

When I left for Cape Town, Thabo Mbeki was still president and commander-in-chief of the armed forces. Accordingly, I was also still under his command until midnight on the Wednesday and had to ask his permission to leave him to go to Cape Town. Graciously he granted it. I shook hands with him, assuring him that we would have time for further discussion when I returned the following day, since my office was also responsible for former presidents and I would thus still be responsible for Mbeki the following morning, in his new status. I also confirmed that the farewell function had, with Motlanthe's consent, been set for the Friday.

I left the Union Buildings to catch a late-night flight to Cape Town, arriving in my official apartment at about the time that President Mbeki's presidency ended. I resisted the urge to call him. It was midnight and I felt we should let him rest after such an intense and emotional week. From then until Thursday afternoon, I was under the command of Acting-President Matsepe-Cassaburi.

CHAPTER 4

Putting Motlanthe in Power

Wednesday, 24 September 2008

Before that final cabinet meeting I had briefed Motlanthe about the preparations for the swearing-in ceremony. If he had not been a member of cabinet I would have been constrained about revealing details of the last cabinet meeting and the plan to designate one of the ministers to act as the president, and would have limited myself to preparations for the swearing-in ceremony. My task was made easier by the fact that he was part of cabinet and was aware of all the developments related to cabinet business and the executive of government.

I also had to find out whether members of his family would attend, so that we could make the necessary arrangements to take care of them and whether he wished to invite any guests. The answer to both questions was no. His response suggested to me that he felt that the circumstances were so difficult he did not believe the ceremony should be celebratory. His task was to manage government and ensure that there was no disruption of its work during the period leading up to the next elections, due in seven or so months.

Some people have asked why we did not have the type of inauguration ceremony that had become traditional since April 1994 and whether or not this was an expression of a particular attitude by government. The answer to this question is a categorical no. Apart from the fact that the circumstances of Mbeki's recall left no time for elaborate arrangements, the ruling party understood that the urgency of the transition processes did not allow for such a ceremony. What was critical was to ensure that there was stability. In any case, Motlanthe himself did not even have such an inauguration in mind, as indicated earlier.

Thursday, 25 September 2008

On my arrival in Cape Town on Thursday morning, I found myself in an unusual quandary, assisting one president I had such great respect for to leave office under difficult circumstances and managing the assumption of office by another, who was also my comrade. But the office I held required me to do it. I immediately linked up with the command structures to get reports of progress made in preparation for the election and swearing in of the new president. Staff reported that despite the difficult environment and new dynamics in the relationship between the presidency and parliament, all the necessary arrangements were in place.

The mood in the presidency in Tuynhuys was sombre. Staff that had not been at the Union Buildings were still shocked by the unfolding events and the speed with which the changes were happening. They would have liked to have had a briefing to help them understand what was happening but there was no time for one. They had to execute their responsibilities as professional public servants, even if they did not understand much of what was happening or why.

Whatever their personal views, their first task was to execute their responsibilities as loyal and professional public servants who serve the state irrespective of who was in office. This had already been discussed with them and drilled into their minds in preparation for the transition that had been expected in seven months' time.

One critical call I received that Thursday morning was from the acting chief of the South African National Defence Force (SANDF) – the chief of the force was out of the country. The fact that the chief of the SANDF was not instructed to return home during this time of crisis was testimony to the strength of our democracy, which separated political democratic processes from military matters. The acting chief asked two questions. The first was who the commander-in-chief was, since it was no longer Mbeki. It seemed to be a strange question in view of the fact that the announcement about Matsepe-Casaburri's selection as acting president had been made the night before, but it transpired that it was necessary for the acting chief to be informed officially and not obtain this information from the media. We had erred in not officially notifying him, assuming that this would be done by the minister of defence. However, our meeting had ended late on the previous day and the minister's resignation was effective from midnight.

A lesson we learned was that it is not sufficient to announce the appointment of an acting president via the media. A formal official communication should have been sent to all relevant state entities, especially the armed forces, as is the case when the national flag has to be flown at half mast. We should also have taken this more seriously, especially because the president had resigned.

I assured the acting SANDF chief that Matsepe-Cassaburi had been appointed acting president and was, constitutionally, the commander-in-chief. I also had to inform her accordingly.

The acting chief's second question related to the resignation of the minister of defence. Normally, when the minister is out of the country or unable to discharge his or her responsibilities an acting minister is appointed, but this had not happened. In the absence of an acting minister of defence to authorise the normal business of the force – which is the responsibility of the minister, not that of the commander-in-chief – it was felt that it would affect the functioning of the SANDF.

After an election ministers remain in office until the president-elect is inaugurated, but this was not an election and some ministers resigned. With hindsight, I realised that the acting president should have been advised to appoint acting ministers to replace those who had resigned, because 24 hours was too long for departments to function without a minister. However, given the fact that it was now only a matter of hours before the new president was to be sworn in, I advised the acting chief not to worry – a minister would be appointed within the next 24 hours or so. In jest, I suggested the armed forces take leave for a day, after which they would have a minister. I also implied that everything was under control and there was no need for any action from the military.

In parliament, the election conducted by Chief Justice Pius Langa went off without any notable problems. The next step was the swearing-in ceremony, for which I had to take responsibility. I received the chief justice and ushered him into the usual holding room, where he put on his robes. We went through the ceremony together as we normally do, and when he was ready I went ahead of him to ensure the president-elect was also happy with the script.

Invited guests were already seated in the cabinet room, where the ceremony would be conducted.

I took the podium and announced the arrival of the president-elect and the chief justice. This, as one would expect, was emotionally difficult. But I put up a face and did it. After welcoming the guests I handed over to the chief justice, and once the ceremony was over I led the president to his office. This was another very emotional moment. I had just concluded the process of helping Mbeki to leave, and now I had to manage the induction of Motlanthe, leading him into the office his predecessor had had no time to clear.

The depth of the emotions in this moment was well expressed by one staff member who saw me leading President Motlanthe into what was still considered Mbeki's office. It felt, said the staff member, like a *coup d'état*. If it wasn't that, it was certainly a *coup de théâtre*. She further said that my walking Motlanthe to Mbeki's office seemed like I had been frogmarched or commanded at a point of a gun to do so. Having witnessed this sight, the staff member took refuge in one of the offices in Tuynhuys and wept bitterly. When this was reported to me I called her and asked what the problem was. The response was that it was not only the pain of seeing Mbeki's office occupied by another in the way it happened; it was also 'feeling for you', meaning 'feeling for me': 'How could they make you do this?' This was not the only staff member I was required to counsel while at the same time managing my own emotions and pain.

Mbeki's immediate staff were the most affected, as they had to receive the new president and assist him immediately. Fortunately, because President Motlanthe had been minister in the presidency, members of his staff were already part of the private office of the president and therefore immediately available to him. They worked together with the rest of Mbeki's staff in a seamless manner, as they were under the same command. Some of the staff were set aside to continue serving Mbeki, in terms of the provision for privileges of former presidents.

The trauma that staff were going through was not related to President Motlanthe; rather it related to the speed and manner in which Mbeki was removed from office and the sudden reality that they had to work with another president. It was too sudden and shocking, and they had not been allowed time to internalise it. The trauma had to do with their feelings for Mbeki, rather than feelings against Motlanthe.

The president's immediate task was to address parliament. For the first time the president made a speech I had not seen, as it was prepared with the party at a party level. But the speech was states-manlike, focusing on the need for stability and a seamless transition which would have no negative impact on service delivery, especi-ally for the poor and disadvantaged. He emphasised that the policies of government would remain the same, since these were products of a collective rather than an individual.

He said: 'We are able to make such pronouncements with neither hesitation nor doubt, precisely because the policies we are charged to implement are the policies of the African National Congress.' He further said: 'Mine is not the desire to deviate from what is working. It is not for me to reinvent policy. Nor do I intend to reshape either cabinet or the public service. We will not allow that the work of government be interrupted. We will not allow the stability of our democratic order to be compromised.'

The speech reassured the nation, the government and the in-ternational community that he would perpetuate Mbeki's themes – stability, peace and service delivery. He also took the opportunity to announce new members of cabinet to replace those who had resigned, again to give assurance that the transition was being man-aged effectively.

Once President Motlanthe was settled in his office we had to discuss his plans for the swearing in of the new ministers and deputy ministers, which we had already anticipated. Invitations were extended to the appointees and their families for a swearing-in ceremony on the Friday afternoon. The command system for arranging swearing-in ceremonies was triggered and, having completed the plans, I had to leave for Gauteng as the next day's activities would take place at the administrative seat of government in Pretoria, Tshwane.

Friday, 26 September 2008

It was a week since the series of dramatic events had been set in motion. My adrenalin levels were low and my energy levels almost zero. I had to pull myself out of bed and resume my management of this difficult and deeply emotional transition.

Two major events were scheduled for the day. The first was the farewell function – scheduled for lunchtime – for former President Mbeki, former Deputy President Phumzile Mlambo-Ngcuka and former Minister in the Presidency Dr Essop Pahad, who had also resigned. The second was the swearing-in ceremony for new members of the executive, scheduled for the afternoon.

At my office in the Union Buildings, I started with briefings about the state of preparedness for both these events. One of the challenges relating to the swearing-in ceremony was the situation of ministers who had initially resigned and later rescinded their resignations, and of those who had resigned and now been reappointed. The legal unit was assigned to deal with these matters to ensure that the ceremony met all the legal requirements.

The farewell function was held at the Bryntirion Estate, of which Mahlamba Ndlopfu is part. All the presidency staff, including those deployed in Cape Town, were invited. Other invitees were top personnel in other state organs, individuals who worked directly with the presidency and members of the executive. The new president had intended to attend but urgent matters of state made it impossible for him to do so, and he apologised and wished us and Mbeki well.

As head of the presidency I had to be the host of the function and, in terms of protocol, I had to be at the marquee before the guests of honour arrived. First, I had to meet the staff, who were already in the marquee, many of whom I had not seen since the recall of the president. As I walked towards the marquee I was greeted by weeping staff members. Some hugged me and others just looked at me and turned away to hide their faces, contorted by pain and grief.

The mood was sombre with sadness written on the faces of the guests and many with tears flowing. Once more I felt that I was attending a mourning vigil. Despite my exhaustion, I had to try to behave like a commander, but the grief written on the faces of so many broke me and I battled to prevent myself from weeping too. I couldn't give in though, and I picked myself up, contained my tears and went out boldly to receive the guests of honour at the drop-off point.

The first to arrive and be welcomed was Essop Pahad, followed by Phumzile Mlambo-Ngcuka and then by the former president and Mrs Mbeki. The response of the staff and the other guests was mixed. Some ululated, showing respect, support and appreciation; others just cried. It was a difficult moment. Although one of the senior members of staff was designated as the programme director, in the end I presided because of the difficult circumstances. My introductory remarks were not easy, as one could not go into detail about what happened, since that would have taken us to the party political arena, inappropriate for a farewell function with public servants. In the speeches it was easier to talk about the 'former' minister and the 'former' deputy president, but it was difficult to refer to Mbeki as 'former' president. In an attempt to make light of this I proposed that we assume the culture of the USA, where the president retains the title of president after leaving office.

Speaker after speaker expressed appreciation for the leadership Thabo Mbeki had given to the country and the continent, but some broke down before they could make any speech. The speeches were punctuated with words like wisdom, commitment, service, sacrifice and leadership, and there were special thanks for his commitment to ensuring stability during this period of transition. In response, Mbeki urged the staff to remain as loyal to the state and the new president as they had been to him.

When the announcement was made that lunch was served, I had to be excused together with a few critical staff who were involved in preparing for the swearing-in ceremony that afternoon. The president understood this and accepted our apology for breaking protocol. We bade him farewell and left. We found this moment of leaving him in the middle of his farewell function very difficult and emotional, as it was the first act which brought home the reality that he was no longer the president!

At the Union Buildings, where the swearing-in ceremony was to be conducted, I found staff at work who missed the farewell function to ensure that the swearing-in ceremony was well prepared for. I had to make the final decisions about the legal complexities regarding ministers who resigned but then withdrew their resignations, and protocol issues. The ceremony was concluded late that afternoon, so by the time the dramatic week ended the country once again had a full cabinet. The cabinet secretariat gave each minister and deputy minister their induction files, which contained all that they needed to know in terms of their appointments, and then handed them over to the officials of the relevant departments.

After the ceremony I accompanied the president back to his office, as I would normally do, to evaluate the ceremony and then deal with whatever matters that required our immediate attention. The first was his diary and the challenge here was to integrate his with that of Mbeki, to make sure that essential engagements did not fall through the cracks. The staff had selected the most critical engagements that had to be honoured, and those which could be postponed. Others just had to be cancelled.

It was agreed that special briefing sessions would be arranged for Motlanthe to cover those areas that were the direct responsibility of the president, including security-related matters. There was also an immediate need for him to meet and address the directors-general who would be convened through FOSAD to reassure them and keep them in their posts. We also dealt with personal issues such as moving house and staff support.

At the end of the discussion I asked President Motlanthe to release me to visit former President Mbeki, to deal with matters related to his departure from office. The irony of all this is that, in terms of the regulatory framework, I, as head of the presidency, was responsible for both serving and retired presidents and deputy presidents – an invidious situation in this case, to take care of a president who had been recalled by his party under very controversial and emotional circumstances and at the same time to serve the new president the party had nominated and parliament voted into office. I had to be loyal to the new president, even as I offered services to the old one. The risk of being misunderstood was very high and the situation was likely to cause ill will, bad feelings and resentment, with questions of divided loyalties and trust.

Fortunately, Motlanthe was above such petty issues. His trust in me was never shaken by these challenging circumstances. Instead he focused more on the broader responsibilities with which he was

82

entrusted – the management of government during the transition period leading to the next elections. He was focused on the stability of the country and a smooth transition from Mbeki's administration to his. He also understood my role well and released me to discharge my responsibilities to the former president.

In the early evening I arrived at Mahlamba Ndlopfu and found the former president with his special advisers, Mojanku Gumbi and Titus Mafolo, and the staff we had deployed to continue serving him, all of whom were still my responsibility. In terms of the law, special advisers to political office bearers remain in office for a month after their principal has left office. This was useful, as it made Mbeki's advisers available to assist the former president in packing and preparing to leave his official residences.

Friends and family had gathered to express solidarity. After greeting them we retreated, as usual, to the historic lounge where most decisions were made and went through all the issues that affected him and the family in relation to the end of his term. These ranged from staying in Mahlamba Ndlopfu for 60 days while preparing to move, releasing the Cape Town house – that is, Genadendal – as soon as possible, keeping or appointing two secretaries and researchers, securing a 120 m^2 office with telephones and furniture, and so on.

Fortunately, Mr and Mrs Mbeki had already secured a house for themselves, which was being prepared for occupation by April the following year, but it would be almost impossible to fast-track by several months the completion of the renovations. They had to brace themselves for the reality that they might have to move in before it was ready.

Meanwhile, an overenthusiastic public works department staff member planned to have Mbeki leave Mahlamba Ndlopfu before the stipulated time, arguing that the new president needed to move in immediately for security reasons. This was disturbing, as it was against the rules and regulations, especially since he claimed that he was acting on instructions from the minister of public works and with the consent of the president. I suspected that this could not be correct and I checked with the president and the minister, both of whom confirmed my suspicions, thus stopping him in his tracks. The only way to explain this behaviour was that the official wanted to reserve a place in the good books of those who were taking over government.

The greatest challenge we faced was the handling and management of classified documents from Mahlamba Ndlopfu and Genadendal. A team vetted for 'top secret' from the private office of the president was deployed to go through the offices and studies, separating classified documents from the others. The latter would be returned to the Union Buildings for filing and archiving, while the former were to be sealed and passed on to my office to be properly secured for further assessment.

It took me two weeks, with the help of the secretariat of the NSC, to assess the documents, secure those which had to be secured, return some of the more sensitive ones to the intelligence services, and dispose of those which had to be disposed of or were supposed to have been disposed of in terms of the law. This was done in consultation with the National Intelligence Service (NIS) and I reported to President Motlanthe on all actions taken, while Mbeki assisted in clarifying some of the issues and helping to decode others which he understood better.

The next step was to hand over the key sensitive areas and facilities that are the direct responsibility of the president. Since President Mandela had managed the handover to his successor gradually before he retired, this was the first such formal handover since the democratic elections in 1994 and procedures and regulations had to be developed and put in place in consultation with all affected departments and the president.

At the end of the two months the former president had to leave Mahlamba Ndlopfu and move into his new home before it was ready and at the same time his office, which was the responsibility of the government, was also not ready. All this notwithstanding, he had to move and he did so with grace.

CHAPTER 5

Filling Mbeki's Shoes

President Kgalema Motlanthe, then secretary-general of the ANC, first came to government in July 2008, as an unwilling minister without portfolio in the presidency. He was selected by the post-Polokwane leadership to take care of their interests because some deeply distrusted Mbeki. For them, Mbeki should have been removed as president immediately after Polokwane.

There was no clear indication of what these interests were. The reality is that Polokwane did not radically change the policies of the ANC relating to governance issues. The traditional ANC language of 'change and continuity' was used at the Polokwane conference to indicate that the overall thrust of the policy was unaltered. The only changes related to aspects that would enable the government to better achieve the broad objective of the ANC, which was to better the lives of the people.

An analysis of Polokwane shows that it was more about the removal of Mbeki than about a change of policy. In fact, those who were at the conference to make sure Mbeki was not re-elected as the president of the ANC did not focus on policy issues. All that was important to them was the implementation of their strategies to make sure Mbeki was not re-elected.

For instance, in the policy development commission in which I participated, some used every opportunity to criticise Mbeki rather than to discuss policy issues and much of the time was wasted by people making extraneous statements that were irrelevant to the issues under discussion.

Some, of course, primarily members of the Congress of South African Trade Unions (COSATU) and the South African Communist Party (SACP), believed that the removal of Mbeki as president of the ANC meant that there would be changes in the ANC's policies, because they saw Mbeki as the major barrier to the advancement of the policies they espoused. The mistake they made was that if no policy changes were made at Polokwane, they would have to wait for another conference to change radically policy in the ANC. History shows that indeed they were unable to achieve their objectives. This explains some of the rumblings that keep coming from those quarters.

Those who were thinking in strategic terms believed that it would be easy to influence the post-Polokwane leadership to change policies midstream. However, they failed to take account of the fact that the party's policies could not be changed without the approval of a national conference. There was also a miscalculation about or a lack of understanding of the dynamics of forces within the ANC, which would make such decisions more complicated than people believed. It is just such a failure to assess the balance of forces that led to the tensions that emerged between the ANC and COSATU soon after Polokwane.

It also did not make sense to deploy Motlanthe to keep a watch on cabinet's implementation of the policy decisions taken at Polokwane. Cabinet members and deputy ministers were disciplined members of the ANC, many of whom were re-elected at Polokwane as members of the NEC and would as a matter of duty have ensured that the interests of Polokwane were taken care of. Some of the vociferous campaigners against Mbeki were also members of the cabinet.

In his position as secretary-general of the ANC, which he had held for ten years, Motlanthe was the person best informed about the policy development processes within the movement and the person who ensured that the ruling party implemented the decisions of the conference. There should not have been any doubt that these could be monitored effectively from the secretary-general's office.

A crude and debased view was that there might be 'looting' before the then government left office. Again, given the number of ministers and deputy ministers in cabinet who supported the Polokwane project, this made no sense and was not based on reality. Clearly, this view was initially intended to legitimate the takeover by presenting the Mbeki government as corrupt, which was unfounded. This view was also held by those who believed that Mbeki's cabinet consisted of enemies of the Polokwane crusade. At least one cabinet member, shocked at such allegations, believed the intention of those who espoused that view was to insult and hurt, rather than to deal with a particular reality.

The hurt inflicted by the events at Polokwane was indeed deep, with relationships within the ANC deteriorating after the conference to the level of dog eats dog, causing harm that destroyed the comradeship among people who had spent a large part of their lives in the trenches together.

The fact is that Mbeki's cabinet had been appointed (in consultation with ANC officials) on the basis of the principle of clean government, and its sole objective – as reflected in the party's slogan

'A better life for all' – was to better the lives of the people of South Africa, particularly the historically disadvantaged. The integrity of individuals in cabinet was critical and any indication of corruption was dealt with immediately. Ironically, it is for this very reason that Mbeki had relieved Jacob Zuma of his responsibilities, paying dearly for this action by losing his presidency at the height of its glory seven months earlier.

Clearly none of the reasons stated above make any sense. The question then is why? One has no answer for this question but it would appear that there were other interests at Polokwane, which were outside policy issues and were not clearly articulated.

History will show that Mbeki carried the flag of success and was tripped just before he crossed the winning line because of internal party dynamics and not governance or policy issues. When the dust has finally settled I believe that the valley of the shadow of Polokwane – that dark cloud – will not forever cover the hills of success Mbeki scaled. The time will come when these successes will be celebrated. However, to date he has not been able to celebrate these successes, nor were those he served given the opportunity to do so.

There are striking similarities between Mbeki's case and that of Kwame Nkrumah of Ghana, whose life and successes were only celebrated in his country many years after he was deposed as president and left to die in exile.

A more rational and publicly articulated reason for deploying Motlanthe was the need to understudy the government, to ensure a smooth transition to the next administration, but even this reason suggested that the handover of power would be from one hostile party to another, with the entire government, including senior public servants, being removed and replaced. If this were to happen it would indeed erase any institutional memory and destabilise the government. Another problem with this perspective is that it

assumed that all those who were deployed in government were enemies of the post-Polokwane ANC. It is this spirit that has turned
a substantial number of comrades who were in government before
Polokwane into targets of the government that came into power
after the 2009 elections.

This story of purging, which has not yet been told, reflects an organisation that began to feed on its own. Solid cadres of the movement were either moved from positions in which they served with
excellence to other positions that made no sense in terms of their
skills, experience and capacity, while others were dumped from the
public service in an unceremonious way without appreciation of
the services they had rendered. An unpleasant example is that of
police, particularly members of the VIP Protection Unit, who were
totally loyal to the state but happened to have been deployed to
serve political principals who were either removed from office or
had resigned. They were treated like disloyal police who were regarded as suspects, and many of them were moved to senseless jobs
which had nothing to do with their rank or profession.

The reluctant minister

It is common cause that Motlanthe did not believe in any of these
arguments and that it took almost six months to persuade him to
join the cabinet. In my discussions with him before he joined, it
was clear that he was unenthusiastic. Maybe it is in the nature of
true cadres of the movement not to crave positions or even to show
personal interest. Unfortunately, this character trait of the movement was damaged beyond repair, as the organisation moved from
a liberation movement to a governing party.

A further complication was the feeling that some party members favoured the deployment in order to remove Motlanthe from Luthuli House, thus reducing his influence and paving their way to the presidency once Jacob Zuma had served his term. Considering Motlanthe a threat, such people wanted to keep him busy with governance issues while they furthered their personal ambitions. Some even wished the corruption case against Zuma to succeed, to open the space for them to assume the presidency of the country after the April 2009 elections. These increased tensions within the post-Polokwane leadership apparently delayed the deployment of Comrade Kgalema.

Whatever the original intentions, Motlanthe's deployment turned out to be something of a blessing. When he was abruptly thrust into the position of president of the country he was able to draw on his experience of the workings of cabinet to manage the transition seamlessly. The issues he had to deal with were already familiar to him so he hit the ground running.

A new form of transition

The events leading to Polokwane and their aftermath changed the emerging culture of the ANC in terms of managing the transition from one presidency to another. The transition from Mandela to Mbeki in 1999 had been well managed, with Mandela deciding early on to transfer certain responsibilities to Mbeki, who was deputy president. He had already done so as early as October 1995, when I was persuaded to join the presidency, about eighteen months after Mandela took office.

The plan was very clear: Mbeki would deal with the transformation of society and the economy, including the day-to-day running of the country, while Mandela dealt with the broader issues of reconciliation and the promotion of the unity of the people of South Africa, as laid down in s 83(c) of the Constitution. The preamble to the Constitution calls on the government to

- heal the divisions of the past and establish a society based on democratic values, social justice and fundamental human rights; and to
- build a united and democratic South Africa able to take its rightful place as a sovereign state in the family of nations.

It was these injunctions on which Mandela focused so successfully. For this he has been honoured at home and abroad as a nation builder, a uniting force, a reconciler and a magnanimous leader with an extraordinary heart, who made a point of reaching out to his adversaries. This, contrasted with his 27 years of incarceration, pain and suffering, made him look like a saint, deserving a day in the international calendar set aside as 'Mandela Day'!

While Mandela was dealing with the broader issues of national unity, Mbeki was in the engine room of governance and transformation. My task in this engine room was to create capacity to manage government and to develop policies, as well as monitor their implementation. The major entity created for this purpose was the Policy Coordination and Advisory Services (PCAS), of which Joel Netshitenzhe later became the head.

Eighteen months before the general election of 1999, Thabo Mbeki was elected president of the ANC at the Mafikeng conference, making him the preferred candidate for president of the country. Famously, when he was asked whether he was ready to step into Mandela's shoes his response was, 'I don't want Mandela's shoes. Mandela's shoes are ugly.' Although this was said in jest and elicited laughter from many of the delegates, it was open to misinterpretation and some considered him to be mocking Mandela.

What Mbeki intended to indicate is that it was impossible to fit into Mandela's shoes; that he could never be Mandela however hard he tried. In any case, to be a Mandela one would need, among other things, to have gone to jail for 27 years. Mandela and Mbeki were different personalities and Mbeki just wanted to be himself. Those of us who worked with Mbeki as deputy president in the run-up to the 1999 elections will recall that this was the season of a barrage of questions about what would happen 'after Mandela'. The inference was that there would be a huge gap 'after Mandela' and that 'another Mandela' had to be found to succeed him.

Interestingly, this question was asked, in the main, more by foreigners and white South Africans than by blacks, for obvious reasons. Mandela was seen as the only embodiment of the policies of reconciliation, peace and nation-building, as the only person within the ANC who was ready always to walk the extra mile to accommodate the interests of whites. His protestation that the policies he followed were the policies of the ANC fell on deaf ears among those who believed he was the odd man out in the party. Indeed, Mandela was different and unique, but he always pursued his vision of a united and reconciled South Africa within the policy framework of the ANC.

Mbeki knew he was not and never could be a Mandela, and indeed he had no wish to be one; he was his own man. The path he took established an Mbeki legacy that was totally different from that of Mandela, although it, too, fell within the policy framework of the ANC, thus proving that very different leaders may pursue identical policies.

Whatever the case, the handover from Mandela to Mbeki was managed effectively. Six months before the June 1999 elections I was asked to prepare for the transition processes in consultation with the director-general in the president's office, Professor Jakes Gerwel. The directive was very clear: to plan for the integration of the offices of the president and the deputy president into one presidency, which would come into operation immediately after the presidential inauguration. In line with the recommendations of the Presidential Review Commission (PRC) published in 1998, Mbeki felt that an integrated presidency would be more effective as well as easier to manage and coordinate.

The 1993 Interim Constitution, which had provided for the establishment of a Government of National Unity (GNU), had created two positions of deputy president – one for the majority party, the other for the largest opposition party, then the National Party. When the National Party withdrew from the unity government, Deputy President F.W. de Klerk's office was closed.

The 1996 Constitution made no provision for a GNU. Section 91(1), (2) and (5) provided that the cabinet should consist of 'the President, as head of the Cabinet, a Deputy President and Ministers'; that the 'President appoints the Deputy President and Ministers, assigns their powers and functions, and may dismiss them'; and that the 'Deputy President must assist the President in the execution of the functions of government'. This suggested a different way of structuring the presidency and was also in line with the PRC report. Details were developed for this integration, including the integration of the staff, systems and institutions of the two offices. For those of us who had to manage this integration, it felt like managing the merger of two large companies.

Because the transition from Mbeki to Motlanthe was abrupt and unexpected, no plans had been put in place for such an eventuality, although preparations were already under way for the routine transition that had been expected to take place in April the following year.

It is surprising that there was any question in the ANC about who should be appointed to hold the fort until the 2009 election. The decision that the president of the ANC would not make himself available for election as president for the interim period should have made deputy president of the ANC Motlanthe the natural choice. Still, the matter was fiercely debated, with other members of the NEC believing they were the appropriate candidates. Finally a decision was made that Motlanthe would be the interim president until the elections in 2009.

Motlanthe had a very clear understanding of his role when he took over from President Mbeki. He had to ensure that there was a seamless transition that would not negatively affect the government's delivery programme and he had to complete the work started by Mbeki's administration and advance the policies of the party, whose achievements were crucial for the next election. Because of the urgency involved, there was no time for Motlanthe to find and test his own shoes; he had to step into Mbeki's to complete his mission, which was the party's (ANC's) mission.

Because his was a holding operation, he focused on delivering services to the people rather than wasting time on activities intended to profile him as a possible alternative for president of the country in April 2009. He presented himself as a classic cadre of the movement – he was about the people rather than about himself, his friends or his family.

Initially, he was briefed about the immediate matters he had to attend to as president, among them outstanding cabinet business. Regionally, he had responsibilities as chair of the Southern African Development Community (SADC) and a member of the SADC troika on politics, defence and security, which made him directly responsible for Zimbabwe. And then there was the imminent African Union Conference on the African Diaspora.

I was astonished at the speed with which he mastered his role as chair of SADC and immediately provided leadership in relation to the complex and controversial matter of Zimbabwe – he operated like a twin brother to Mbeki. The Conference on the African

Diaspora, however, had to be postponed, as it was felt that the political climate was not conducive for holding it in South Africa.

The first tricky domestic matter on which he showed his leadership qualities and ability to function under pressure related to an important telecommunications issue – the question of the parastatal, Telkom, relinquishing its 50 per cent stake in cellphone operator Vodacom, a textbook case of the state mediating conflicting interests within and outside the party and determining what was good for the country.

The fact is, though, that in relation to these issues it did not matter who the leader was if he or she was a genuine ANC cadre. Responses were driven by the culture and traditions of the ANC and the line was always very clear – justice had to be done as well as to be seen to be done, irrespective of the power dynamics within the country (and the ruling party), in the international community and the international governance system. In this tradition, justice was indivisible and the same for everyone – rich or poor, powerful or weak.

This tradition is, naturally, the antithesis of the logic of the international governance system such as the UN Security Council which defers to power even where it tramples on the weak and distorts the course of justice. The ANC culture and tradition was also in line with the desire of Africans to exercise their right to determine their own destiny rather than be dictated to by others. There is a strong feeling which is lately expressed more boldly that the days when Africa was used as a battleground to achieve the global interests of others at the expense of those of the African people are past. Africa has to be left to solve its problems in the way in which it would serve the interests of its people rather than those of other powers.

The SADC perspective on Zimbabwe was a classic case. SADC was totally opposed to the policy of undemocratic 'regime change' advocated by some of the major Western powers. Notwithstanding the view that Zimbabwe may have made mistakes or have approached certain matters in a way that exposed it to attack, an undemocratic regime change would not be allowed in the region, especially when it was driven by the major Western powers.

SADC determined that if this was allowed to happen in one country it would then be used in another until all governments of which the Western powers disapproved were removed from power. The key principle was that no foreign power should be allowed to determine who the leader of another country should be – that should be the sole prerogative of the citizens of that country.

All these matters fitted perfectly within the policy framework of the ANC, whatever the noises from its alliance partners in this regard. The unfortunate thing about these noises, though, was that they tended to coincide with those of Britain and the United States. On his part, Motlanthe remained faithful to the policies and traditions of the ANC and those of his African brothers and sisters.

My relationship with Motlanthe

Apart from the mad moment of the hoax e-mails, which falsely alleged a plot by senior party members against then deputy president of the ANC, Jacob Zuma, my relationship with Motlanthe (as a comrade in the struggle) was entirely positive. I had come to know Comrade Motlanthe when he was released from Robben Island in 1987, at a time of heightened levels of our struggle. He was employed by the National Union of Mineworkers (NUM) and later became its general secretary at the time when I was general secretary of the South African Council of Churches (SACC). I come to know him better when we were elected as NEC members and he became the secretary-general of the ANC.

Motlanthe's role as general secretary of NUM not only prepared him for the position of secretary-general of the ANC, but positioned him strategically to assume the role of president of the country.

One of the incidents that brought us even closer during his time as secretary-general was the crisis occasioned by the trial on charges of corruption of then deputy president Jacob Zuma's former financial adviser, Schabir Shaik, which allegedly implicated Zuma. The trial created destructive, though suppressed, tensions between President Mbeki and his deputy, particularly the decision of Mbeki to dismiss Zuma as deputy president.

Some within the ANC believed that Zuma had been falsely accused and was thus a victim of state institutions, including the National Prosecuting Authority (NPA), which were pursuing the case. In some quarters 'institutions of state' was translated as President Mbeki. For them a 'state case' against Zuma meant Mbeki's case against Zuma. Others believed that the target in this case was not Shaik but Zuma himself, and yet others believed that the case was not serious enough for Zuma to be charged. There were those who could not understand why Mbeki allowed the case to continue, believing that, as president of the country, he could stop it. Cases in Britain and France were cited in this regard. A later view about the removal of Zuma as deputy president of the country was that the case was orchestrated by Mbeki to stop Zuma from becoming president.

The surprising aspect of this tension was that President Mbeki and Deputy President Zuma had been long-standing friends and comrades who had worked together in exile for many years and had, while in exile, been central to the initiation of the formal talks between the ANC and the apartheid government following the 'talks about talks' which were led by Mbeki. The formal negotiations led to the release of political prisoners and the unbanning of political organisations, opening the way for negotiations out of which the democratic South Africa had been born. Given their role together it was difficult for comrades to understand the conflict and enmity that had developed between them.

What made it even more difficult for the leadership of the ANC, particularly the NEC, was that both denied that there was any tension or problem between them, expressing this denialism individually and collectively in joint statements presented to NEC meetings at which the matter was discussed. Notwithstanding their denials, the tensions were palpable and affected everything the ANC was doing at the time.

It was during this difficult period that my relationship with Motlanthe deepened. We had a common challenge. His was to deal with a president and deputy president of the ANC who denied there was a problem when reality suggested otherwise, while I had to deal with the same principals in the form of the president and the deputy president of the country. As we were both members of the NEC, we agreed to work together from our different vantage points to try to resolve the problem. At the height of the tensions we met from time to time to discuss the matter and to strategise about ways and means of assisting the leaders to deal head-on with the negative relationship that was developing and reaching destructive proportions, threatening the unity and cohesion of the movement.

The crisis deepened in May 2005, when Zuma was relieved of his position as deputy president of the country. Although Mbeki took this action only after broad consultation, which involved the party, the leagues and alliance partners, aggrieved and disgruntled members of the ANC rallied around Zuma and targeted Mbeki as their common and singular problem.

What followed were tense meetings of the NEC, leading to a highly charged National General Council (NGC) in July, where lines were drawn and divisions clearly defined. This was the first NGC meeting at which I experienced behaviour that was totally alien to the ANC I had known for so many years. The language used was uncomradely, people were behaving like enemies rather than comrades-in-arms, and there was a readiness to lie or to support positions which were clearly illogical or ideologically irrational. I even heard swear words and abusive language by younger comrades against veterans of the movement, which I had never heard before. It was shocking.

This opened the floodgates for the behaviour we are witnessing today, where the language of political discourse has become disrespectful and vulgar. In this regard one just has to revisit the statements of the ANC Youth League (ANCYL) and the Veterans League about Comrade Kader Asmal in 2009. The same can be said of statements about the leader of the opposition, Helen Zille, relating to her predominantly male provincial executive council in the Western Cape. When the language used by comrades becomes so pornographic that one can no longer watch or listen to news bulletins with one's children, people are bound to stop and wonder what has become of their movement. Even reading a newspaper has become a problem, as the children ask about the screaming headlines of abusive discourse and immoral behaviour. The more vulgar you are, the more popular you are. In Sesotho it would be said about those who use such language that *ha ba hodiswa hantle*. A translation would be that 'these people were not brought up properly'.

The determining factor in debates within the organisation became less consideration of matters that were on the table than support for one person or another. Many began to operate as if they belonged to different parties within the same party, scheming and strategising against each other, and were prepared to lie or to distort facts as long as this advanced the cause of their faction.

One of the greatest lies told at the July 2005 NGC meeting was that the council had reinstated Zuma in defiance of the decision of the NEC. The reality is that Comrade Zuma voluntarily offered to stand down as deputy president of the ANC, at least for a while, to give himself a chance to focus on the case against him. My recollection is that the NEC reluctantly accepted his decision, after a meeting which continued into the early hours of the following day. In any case, there was no way in which the NEC would have made such a decision without following due process prescribed in the constitution of the organisation. During one of the breaks at the NGC meeting one person who had attended a caucus meeting, expressed his disgust to me about the level to which comrades had sunk – agreeing to reinforce the lie that the NEC had suspended or removed Zuma from his position despite the fact that they knew very well that this was not the case. They had agreed that one of them would take the platform and call for Zuma's reinstatement and that Comrade Zuma would be asked to respond. And that is exactly what happened – like a well-choreographed performance. Regrettably, the chairperson allowed it to happen and not one member of the NEC was bold enough to stand up and challenge the lie, nor did any of the officials do so. Everyone froze on the stage, while those behind the performance celebrated as the lie became the truth.

The aftermath of this NGC meeting was more challenging than ever for me as director-general in the presidency and for Comrade Kgalema as the secretary-general of the ANC. The crisis necessitated that he and I meet urgently, which we did in August, spending two difficult hours together attempting to find a solution.

The one thing we agreed upon was that the issue which had brought the ANC to this desperate point related to the corruption allegations and case against Jacob Zuma, which could potentially wreck the ANC and have a negative impact on the country. We also agreed that it would be a tragedy and cause incalculable pain if Zuma were to be found guilty and to suffer imprisonment as he had during the struggle. If we could possibly help it, we would not wish to see him in prison.

The question was how to achieve this objective and thereby to reduce the challenges facing the ANC. Was there a way in which we could ensure that Zuma did not end up in prison without violating the law or interfering with the course of justice? Could the president intervene and stop the trial? The answer was no. Our constitutional democracy would not allow it.

Some people later referred to cases in the US, the UK and France where there was intervention by the president or prime ministers or some organ of the state, arguing that the president could do the same. The problem with this analogy was that this was tantamount to comparing apples with oranges. The reality is that our Constitution does not allow the president or executive to intervene in processes which are already in court. At best, Mbeki could consider pardoning Zuma at the end of the trial if he was found guilty. Having considered this option, we agreed that we did not have the luxury of time to wait until the end of this trial.

Another possibility was to enter into a plea-bargaining agreement which would end the trial without going through the pain. This seemed to be the best option, as it could be done within the law. The challenge here was that there was no guarantee that such an arrangement would not still result in a prison sentence. There was also the concern that a term in prison without the option of a fine would disqualify Zuma from being elected to parliament. This would make him feel that those who did not want him to be president had achieved their objectives. At the time, I had not known that such a matter was considered earlier, when Schabir Shaik was charged, and that it was rejected.

Whatever the challenges and options, we agreed that Comrade Kgalema was the only one who could engage with Comrade Zuma on such matters and find possible ways to resolve or settle this matter. We agreed to leave the matter with him.

In our discussion we also spoke about older comrades who could assist us to deal with the destructive negative relationship between the president and deputy president, which was threatening to destroy the ANC. We lamented the fact that people such as Oliver Tambo, Govan Mbeki and Walter Sisulu, to whom both Mbeki and Zuma might have listened to, had passed away. The only person who was still available and could make a difference was Nelson Mandela. We were worried about his age but felt that we had no choice but to ask him to assist us.

We discussed ways in which we could reach out to him as he was out of the country at the time. A special operation was set up which would be triggered by Comrade Kgalema to reach Mandela where he was. But unfortunately, the hoax e-mail saga hit us like a bolt from the blue, making it almost impossible to pick up the pieces.

Whoever was responsible for producing and disseminating the e-mails achieved their objective of sowing even more distrust among ANC members and further deepening divisions. They also succeeded in inserting a wedge between me and Comrade Kgalema, thereby making it impossible for us to continue to try to find solutions to the greatest challenge that had ever faced the ANC, one that threatened not only the future of the ANC but the country as well.

The hoax e-mails were a classic intelligence project which involved false e-mails in the names of some comrades suggesting a conspiracy against Zuma and other ANC leaders. The false e-mails also made use of the negative media reports about Sandile Majali, a businessman, and Motlanthe in relation to an oil deal pursued by Majali. In the light of the tensions that had developed between the president and deputy president of the ANC, Comrade Kgalema as the secretary-general of the organisation became the critical person around which the ANC was able to hold together.

For this reason it is not surprising that Comrade Kgalema Motlanthe was made a priority target of all these schemes with the view of disrupting his stabilising efforts – to make him a victim as well and to try to cause him take sides in the conflict. The objective was to make it difficult for him to continue dealing with these debilitating tensions from an objective position.

I interacted with Comrade Motlanthe twice before the November 2005 NEC meeting, to show how false the e-mails were in my particular case. The language used in my name in official communications was so outrageous that no one could ever believe them. A sophisticated intelligence project would have taken time to study the language I use in informal and formal communication, the way I sign letters, what I communicate by telephone, formal letter or e-mail and with whom, my style of writing, form, structure, and so forth. This was not done and if it was then it was a hopelessly amateurish work. Whoever produced the e-mails also mixed up historical facts and events, suggesting that he or she worked from scripts and had no personal knowledge of the events. In fact, the e-mails were like cut-and-paste texts. These discussions unfortunately resolved nothing, given the prevailing climate.

I also sent a formal letter to all the officials of the ANC to raise my concerns, but to date there has not been any acknowledgement or response. Instead, the matter of the false e-mails landed at the door of the NEC, bedevilling relationships and making it more difficult to resolve problems. Indeed, history will show that those who ran this intelligence project achieved their objectives. But what is more important is that with the passing of time we will come to know who planned this intelligence project, who implemented it and who were its beneficiaries. The Biblical saying that 'there is nothing concealed that will not be disclosed or hidden that will not be made known' will be proved true.

Transition and contracts of DGs

Among the urgent matters President Motlanthe had to deal with immediately after assuming office was the question of my contract, which was due to come to an end the following month (October 2008). Motlanthe took the same position as Mbeki, asking me to change my mind about not extending it beyond the end of October. After I painstakingly explained my reasons for not wanting to renew the contract, he accepted my decision reluctantly, as had Mbeki.

In the interests of stability and a smooth transition, he also accepted my alternative proposal that I stay on a new short-term contract to assist in the management of the transitional processes leading to and after the elections. This was to avoid a long-term contract, which would have kept me beyond the elections in 2009.

President Motlanthe was also briefed about the contracts of directors-general, which were due to expire during the transition period – that is, January to August 2009 – and how the management of these contracts could affect the performance of government.

The standard approach to such matters was that in our system (which is different from the presidential system of the USA and from the Commonwealth system in its traditional form), the contracts of directors-general were not linked to the term of office of the political office bearers – that is, ministers, deputy presidents or even the president. In this regard the renewal of these contracts was based on the needs of government and on the performance of the particular director-general. Having considered this matter carefully, President Motlanthe decided that the contracts would be dealt with in the normal way without being influenced by the transitional processes, to make sure that government was not destabilised.

This, of course, did not endear Motlanthe to some quarters within the ANC, who called for a moratorium on the appointment of new directors-general and other senior officials. The moratorium, they argued, must include the extension of contracts. Some called for a moratorium on all appointments until the new government was in place. Interestingly, these positions were never translated into the official position of the ANC, remaining views rather than policy. But they nevertheless had a great impact on the decisions of provincial governments, the national executive (cabinet) and the leadership role of the president during this transitional period. Every appointment or renewal of a director-general's contract was seen as an act of defiance against the positions of the 'party' or the spirit of Polokwane. Facts here did not matter. What mattered were feelings and emotions.

In reality, though, whenever the contracts of directors-general were extended Motlanthe kept Zuma informed. Once the election dates were announced and party candidates declared, formal consultative processes relating to transitional matters were established. This enabled the presidency to understand as well as to anticipate the changes which might be made if the ANC, or any party for that matter, won the election.

CHAPTER 6

Attacks on Motlanthe

It did not take long (a mere three months) after Motlanthe's election as president for him to become the target of vicious attacks, both political and personal. The attacks came from several quarters: from unnamed leaders of the ANC and unknown 'sources', on which the media relied for their stories. Quoted repeatedly by the media, these faceless leaders and sources began to assume a level of authenticity and authority. In using these sources and being ready to believe them, the media also began to be seen as part of the strategy of attacking the integrity of the president.

For some members of the media Motlanthe's sin was the fact that he did not take a different position on Zimbabwe from that of Mbeki. What they failed to understand was that, as chair of SADC, he was acting on behalf of and within the framework of SADC policy and plans, and that was the same basis on which Mbeki had operated. Secondly, the president was also working within the policy framework of the ANC and government, which had not changed. As has been said before, the removal of Mbeki from office did not result in change of policy within the ANC. The stand the media took demonstrates the weakness of the individualisation of politics, where presidents are regarded as individual politicians rather than as part of the collective leadership of the party.

In essence, the ANC model just does not fit in with the Western models of political leadership to which the media look for examples; in the ANC the party, not the individual, determines policy. The individual leader's strengths are critical but the policy remains the same unless it is changed by the party. The process to change policy is elaborate. It starts from branches through regions and provinces to the NEC and on to a national policy conference and, finally, the national conference.

The third quarter from which attacks came was voices among the alliance partners, who felt Motlanthe was not vigorously promoting or supporting the policy positions they had believed would be adopted if Mbeki was recalled. Again, this was not possible, as Motlanthe would have had to go to conference to change the policies.

The most difficult to understand were the voices from within the ANC itself, especially because it was they who had deployed Motlanthe as president. The party dynamics that produced these attacks on the president were crude and inexplicable and were clearly generated by some high-ranking party leaders. Those who participate in projects of leaking information, especially false information, about their own comrades to discredit them forget that their collaborators do talk about them in other forums.

It was clear that the growth in stature of the president, based on his effective execution of his responsibilities, including his management of difficult and challenging situations, worried some, especially those who had presidential ambitions. It appeared that those who thought that deploying Motlanthe in government would remove him from party activity had not achieved their objective. In fact, their strategy was working against them. There was a feeling that Motlanthe was using his office to promote himself and position himself for the presidency.

Some believed he was not fulfilling the mandate of Polokwane, others were incensed by the fact that he was no different from Mbeki, while still others were disappointed that he was not using his position to negate the legacy of Mbeki or to rubbish it.

The reality is that there was no way in which Motlanthe could have negated what Mbeki was doing. The incumbents in government who had been deployed by the ANC had developed an elaborate Programme of Action (POA) based on the party's policies and its election manifesto. The intention was to ensure that all the commitments made at the last elections were met before the end of the term of the government. It was also designed to produce maximum effect before the next elections. There was also the psychological milestone of fifteen years of ANC government, which had to show results, and preparations were being made to celebrate this moment.

It must be said here that Mbeki, wanting to leave a legacy of an effective and efficient government, had focused on ending his term of office having achieved all the objectives that had been set, notwithstanding the political climate which was developing.

The events leading up to and following on the Polokwane conference were disturbing, but they did not alter his course or deter him from pursuing this ideal. One might even say that he discounted the events of Polokwane and concentrated on completing his term with resounding success. Unfortunately, his premature removal robbed him of the opportunity to complete his mission and hand over government with honour.

The POA was so clear and so firmly based on the policies of the party that it was not possible for Motlanthe to deviate from it in the name of just being different. But this is exactly what made him a target of the attacks from faceless opponents in the leadership of the ANC.

For a month or so, from mid-December to January, a vicious and obviously orchestrated campaign was unleashed against the president, focusing mainly on his personal life, which he had always endeavoured to keep private. It questioned the fact that he had not been seen in public with his wife and children and speculated about the apparent estrangement between him and his family.

The media went as far as camping at the house where they thought Mrs Motlanthe stayed. By mid-January 2009, the attacks were intensified by allegations that Motlanthe was involved in an ongoing affair with a woman who worked at ANC headquarters and that he had fathered a child with a much younger woman. At this point the reporting deteriorated into gutter journalism and gutter politics. By the end of January 2009, when the attacks became really outrageous, the ANC intervened and expressed its support of Comrade Kgalema.

By mid-January the attacks targeted some who had worked with Mbeki and were still in the presidency. Strangely, Advocate Mojanku Gumbi was included in these attacks, although she had long left the presidency having served her one-month notice after the removal of Mbeki. We were accused of influencing or misleading Motlanthe, or advising him in a manner that led him in directions which were outside the wishes of those who believed that the removal of Mbeki would lead to a radical change in the policies of government.

On my side the pain was deep. As director-general in the presidency and secretary of cabinet I had managed the transition from Mbeki to Motlanthe as professionally as I could, avoiding expressing my views and feelings and behaving as a classic loyal public servant. Together with my team I made sure that the transition was as seamless as possible and there were no disruptions in the services government offered to its citizens. I had been asked by President Motlanthe, I believe with the consent of the leadership at Luthuli House, to remain in office to do exactly that.

The ANC had removed Mbeki, who they had originally voted in, replacing him with their preferred alternative, Motlanthe. So, we could not understand why because some within the party had begun to differ with him, it was we who had become their targets. What shocked me most was that no official of the party came to our defence or denounced these faceless 'leaders of the ANC' or 'ANC sources', as the media called them.

I discussed the matter with the president, who was as surprised as I was. By January 2009 he was convinced that, for whatever reason, there were people who were determined to cast aspersions on his integrity. He indicated to me that he would deal with the matter within the ANC.

As this matter, like that of Mbeki, was a party matter I decided to deal with it at a party level and wrote a letter to the secretary-general of the party, Comrade Gwede Mantashe, not in my capacity as a government official but as a member of the ANC, expressing my concern about these attacks on us and on the president. I indicated that I was terribly aggrieved that my own organisation had attacked me and my colleagues for no apparent reason other than the fact that we were serving our people – the people of South Africa – to the best of our abilities.

I raised with him the fact that I had not applied for the job in 1995; that in fact I had been reluctant to accede to the pleas of Mandela and Mbeki to take it on; that I had believed then, as I believed now, that my calling was to be an advocate for the cause of the poor and oppressed rather than a civil servant. I also informed him that I had appealed to both the secretary-general (then Comrade Motlanthe)

and the deputy president (then Comrade Zuma) of the ANC between 2003 and 2004 to plead with President Mbeki on my behalf
to release me from my job as I believed that I had discharged my
responsibilities but that they had failed to convince Mbeki to do so.
Now I was targeted because I had worked with Mbeki and because
I was working with Motlanthe.

Comrade Mantashe's response was rapid. He immediately offered to meet me. He went out of his way to come to my home
in Soweto to discuss the matter. I expressed my appreciation for
the trouble he had taken to come to my home. In presenting my
concerns to him I was trying to understand how the organisation I
had worked with for so many years could make me a target of attack. What had I done to deserve this, especially after making such
sacrifices for the liberation of the people and the transformation of
our society after 1994?

He responded in language that was typical of him: *'Wena Mfundisi,
awenzanga luthu, Uyabethwa nje … uyabethwa!'* This is difficult to
translate. Literally it means: 'You, Reverend, you have done nothing. You just get beaten for no reason.' In its deep figurative sense, it
means that I was a victim of circumstances. In Setswana they say *o
tshelwa ke madi a kgofa*, to convey that when they beat someone, an
Mbeki or a Motlanthe, their blood splatters on you because of your
proximity to them.

I have always understood that if you worked with the president
you were likely to be hit along with him or her when he or she is
under attack. As a cadre of the movement I knew that I would have
to put my body between him or her and the line of fire. But what
I did not expect was that the fire was going to be coming from my
own comrades.

It is now history that we became a punching bag for anyone who
felt like punching us, to achieve objectives which were unrelated to
what we were doing. If it was not *madi a kgofa*, we should have been

told what it was. One-on-one discussions, which I held with almost all the officials of the ANC, could not produce one reason, at least not at an official level, why we deserved to be attacked.

At our meeting Comrade Gwede promised that the ANC would do something about the attacks. I indicated to him that the least the organisation could do would be to denounce the faceless 'ANC leaders' and 'sources' who had made such statements. In the event, I am unaware to this day of any such statement being made by the ANC.

Comrade Gwede's observations took me back to the days of the Polokwane conference when a number of comrades had come to me, individually and collectively, to ask what I had done to deserve the vicious attacks on me by comrades who were campaigning against Mbeki. They told me that the portrait that was being drawn of me was a caricature that was totally unlike me. It was also clear that there was a script which comrades were following, which suggested a well-organised campaign to rubbish us so they could get more votes.

Interestingly, even those who were involved in the campaign against Mbeki, mainly comrades from Limpopo and the Northern Cape, ridiculed these attacks, calling them unhelpful. They were as shocked as I was at the level to which some of our comrades had sunk in pursuit of their goal, whatever it was.

The dissatisfaction with Motlanthe reached such a level that members of the ANC began to treat him as they had treated Mbeki. For instance, after the Polokwane conference a huge effort had been made to limit Mbeki's role in government, although this proved to be very difficult to achieve. The intention behind the move was to turn him into a lame duck and to diminish his stature. Some could not live with the fact that Mbeki continued as president of the country after Polokwane and that he was continuing with his international programme which was raising his stature even further.

An example of these attempts was the state of the nation address, traditionally delivered annually in February at the opening of parliament. In an effort to prevent Mbeki from delivering the address in February 2009, an attempt was made to bring forward the election date to ensure that there was no state of the nation address. Efforts were also made to ensure that he was no longer president by the time Freedom Day was celebrated in April. Of course, by then events had taken the dramatic turn that saw him recalled from office before either of these occasions was celebrated. The story with Motlanthe was similar but in his case the attempts failed.

My respect for Motlanthe grew as I observed that he refused to allow himself to be distracted by the vicious and personalised attacks against him. He held his head high and focused on the tasks at hand to ensure stability in government, continuity, improved service delivery and an orderly transition through to the coming election. His task was to complete Mbeki's term and he did so with dignity. But this was to be his Achilles heel, angering those who wanted Mbeki and his legacy obliterated, buried and forgotten.

The problem with these angry voices is that they missed the point that obliterating the legacy of Mbeki would obliterate the track record of the ruling party in government, which would work against the ANC's election strategies. In fact, during the elections the messaging eventually did change from 'Mbeki has failed to achieve the objectives set out in the party manifesto' to 'the ANC government achieved the objectives set out in the party manifesto'. Even if Mbeki's name was not mentioned, his work was acclaimed and used to further the ANC's election objectives.

Once the date of the elections was announced, on 10 February 2009, the leadership role of the president came under even more pressure and his authority was eroded with every passing day. Almost every decision he made had to be made in consultation with Jacob Zuma, as president of the ANC. Although it was Motlanthe's role to manage the transitional process, a committee was constituted at Luthuli House and the changes the new government intended to make were managed from there.

The government's preparations for the management of the transition reached their climax in February 2009, when the cabinet memo on transitional management was processed and the dates of the election, the dissolution of parliament, the constitution of the new parliament, the election of the president and the inauguration ceremony were all set. Because there had been three such transitions (in 1994, 1999 and 2004) since the dawn of democracy, the process was familiar and only required perfecting. It was agreed that it was now time to document the process in the form of a manual, to avoid future governments reinventing the wheel and wasting state resources.

Interestingly, the greatest challenge proved to be the inauguration ceremony, which was fixed for 9 May 2009. In a normal democracy public servants prepare for such ceremonies according to a prescribed manual, without knowing who will be elected. But once the prospective presidents are nominated the state begins to consult those who have the greatest chance of being elected president in order to determine their interests, their wishes, the special guests they would like to have at the ceremony, and so forth.

In this case, and understandably so, the ANC leadership at Luthuli House was more focused on preparations to take over government than on ceremonial issues. The transitional team appointed to undertake this task dealt with proposed structural and institutional changes relating to the cabinet and cabinet portfolios, parastatals and their management, and so on.

With regard to the inauguration ceremony, the president kept the president of the ANC informed and consulted him about matters which affected him or might be of interest to him. The transitional team at Luthuli House only looked at the ceremonial issues about three weeks before the date of the ceremony, which was perfectly normal, as parties do so in the main only after winning an election.

There were three areas of interest. The first was invitations to international guests who were close to the ruling party and local guests who had supported the party during the election. The second was seating arrangements and protocol matters, and the third was the 'interfaith prayers' section of the ceremony, which had become a unique feature of major state ceremonies in democratic South Africa.

Apart from problems of time constraints and international protocol issues, including normal diplomatic sensitivities, the matter of the invitations was dealt with without any major challenges. I was surprised, though, when interfaith prayers became an issue.

Standard arrangements were made to have all the major faith communities represented in the panel of leaders who were to say the prayers. The National Religious Leaders' Forum (NRLF), which represents most of the faith communities in South Africa, was asked to provide names. The panel included one person from each of the faith communities: African traditional religions, the African indigenous or independent churches, the traditional mainstream Christian churches, Hindu, Islam and Judaism. Care is taken to ensure that there is rotation from one inauguration to another among the different traditions and within each faith stream. Although each person who is selected to say a prayer has the freedom to pray in the way in which they do it within that faith community, the prayers are ultimately choreographed to fit in with the protocol arrangements for the ceremony.

The first message, which purported to come from the leadership of the ruling party, said the panel should be changed as it was not representative of the religious traditions within South Africa, an assertion that made no sense. The panel was as representative as was possible given the complexity and plurality of the religious expressions in this country. It turned out that the issue was more about the individuals who were to say the prayers rather than the matter of representivity – the people who were wanted were those who had supported the party's election campaign. This request created problems for us, as the arrangements had been made well in advance and had involved consultation with the institutional structures representative of the faith communities within South Africa.

At the level of the state, it was problematic to remove the names of panel members because they had not publicly supported a particular party, especially because they had already been informed of their participation. We referred the matter to the president, who, as deputy president of the ANC, said that he was not aware of such a decision within the party. In fact, the ruling had come from some members of the religious desk of the ANC rather than from the leadership, a situation that was untenable. The reality is that the party requires the support and cooperation of all the institutions and organisations of society, regardless of which party they support, if it is to govern effectively.

It was agreed that the panel should be left as it was to avoid alienating these established institutions and that the party should find other ways of rewarding those who supported it publicly. This was a strategic revolutionary perspective which recognised the complexity of the South African society and the need to mobilise every South African, irrespective of race, colour, creed or gender, to support the project of transforming the country for the better.

The matter of seating arrangements for former presidents raised some interesting issues of protocol, with protocol staff having to deal with the presence of former president Mbeki. This was not as simple as one would have thought. It had not occurred to those who had removed him from office that he was, nonetheless, a former president in good standing and was due all the privileges attendant on that position.

The Constitution specifically deals with the status of presidents who are removed from office either because of 'a serious violation of the Constitution or the law' or for 'serious misconduct' (s 89[1][a] and [b]). Such presidents are not permitted to 'receive any benefits of that office' and may not 'serve in any public office' (s 89[2]). President Mbeki, however, had not been removed from office in terms of s 89. In fact, he was not removed from office at all. He resigned after his party recalled him.

He also did not resign because of a motion of no confidence in him by parliament in terms of s 102 of the Constitution. He had not only executed his presidential responsibilities strictly in terms of the Constitution and the law but upheld, defended and respected the Constitution (s 83[b]). This meant that Mbeki had the right to be treated in the same way as all former presidents are treated in terms of the protocol system of the country. When questions were raised about this, President Motlanthe was adamant that the normal protocol had to be followed, whatever the feelings about the matter.

Following a discussion between Motlanthe and President-Elect Zuma, a decision was made which had an enormous impact on the country and on the international guests who attended the ceremony. The decision was to put all the post-apartheid presidents on the stage together with President Motlanthe and President-Elect Zuma. This meant that former presidents Mandela and Mbeki would be on the stage together.

This gathering of all four presidents on the podium sent a very positive message to the country and to the world. Firstly, it demonstrated the maturity of the ANC in dealing with difficult circumstances which might have destabilised the country. Secondly, it reassured South Africans and the world that the removal of Mbeki would not lead to instability or chaos. Whatever the anger and unhappiness on both sides, the leadership took a stand beyond their personal interest to assure the country of their commitment to peace and stability.

A very telling observation was made by one of the African heads of state following the ceremony. The conferring of the Order of Mapungubwe by President Motlanthe on President Zuma as part of the handover ceremony symbolised to him the model of a peaceful handover ceremony, which did not happen in many African countries. He said that in many African states 'no president who has been in power for only seven months hands over power like that'. Instead of conferring an Order 'they would shoot you'. He also pointed out that the presence of three former presidents and the new president together on the stage was also unique. 'It could only happen in South Africa,' he said, pointing out that few African countries have former presidents: 'Either they are dead or, if alive, are in exile!'

These comments made me appreciate the remarkable event we had just witnessed. In the midst of the pain an extraordinary message was sent to the world: it is possible, against all the odds, to maintain peace and stability in the country. What was critical, though, is that the leaders on the stage had to move beyond their self-interest and personal feelings in the interest of the common good of all South Africans, of humanity.

Just as Mbeki had been prepared to leave office without any re-sistance, Motlanthe was ready to leave the stage without returning to Mahlamba Ndlopfu. As had been the case with President Mbeki after his resignation, some overzealous officials had determined that President Zuma needed to move to Mahlamba Ndlopfu immedi-ately after the inauguration ceremony. The reasons, they said, related to 'security'. The 'security reasons' for making such an unreasonable demand on President Motlanthe were a flimsy excuse. There was no reason why the security establishment of the Republic of South Africa would fail to secure the new president for a few days, until his predecessor was able to move from one of the official residences.

By the time the message reached our protocol team and the presidential protection unit, it had also been conveyed to Motlanthe, who was quite prepared to accede to the demand until we intervened, indicating that it was irregular and unacceptable. For me this was one of the most shocking acts by comrades in government, to even conceive such a callous and inconsiderate plan. What is even more shocking is that they had the audacity, what is called *sebete* in Sesotho, to face the president and tell him that he can dress up in his official residence but cannot come back to it after the inauguration. I do not know where they got *isibindi e singaka* ('this type of courage').

All this proved that we had the wrong people in all sorts of positions of responsibility, who were not worthy of the jobs they had been given. It also became clear that a country could be destabilised simply because of overzealous officials who wanted to ingratiate themselves with new incumbents, to their personal benefit.

My role as director-general became, as they say in Sesotho, a *thibang thibang* function – an attempt to prevent comrades who had fought in the trenches together from causing their own leaders pain because of political differences or sensitivities. The concept of *thibang thibang* is very difficult to explain in English. The fact is that one spends a great deal of time ensuring that comrades, whatever their differences and political standpoints, do not execute irregular operations that would cause enormous pain and hurt to their fellow comrades or leaders.

It was clear to me that many people behaved as they did in the hopes of getting into the good books of those they believed would secure their future or interests – taking out a type of insurance for the future, with no regard for the consequences of their actions. With hindsight I now suspect that it might have been *thibang thibang* that put me in the bad books of those who have since chosen to block my career even outside the public sector and the political sphere.

The rules about housing for presidents, especially during the transition period, are very clear. The outgoing president has 60 days to clear up and move out of the presidential residence. Normally the president releases one of the residences (Cape Town or Pretoria) while using the other until the end of the two months.

It is interesting, though, that both President Motlanthe and President Zuma disapproved of these acts which were executed in their names during the September 2008 and the May 2009 transition periods. Nevertheless, it is alarming that officials could use the names or the authority of leaders to execute outrageous operations without the knowledge of the leaders themselves.

The situation with regard to the official residences made me think about other jurisdictions and the way in which they handle transition. In this regard, the America system is interesting. The election is held at the beginning of November but the new president is only sworn in towards the end of January, more than two months later, thus giving the outgoing president sufficient time to make the move without pressure.

Another reason for prescribing a particular period is that it makes it possible for the president-elect to be briefed before he or she takes over. Our system does not provide for this handover period. As a result, a few months later I was still running between President Motlanthe and former president Mbeki to assist them with the handover process. While I cannot elaborate on the details because of the sensitivities involved, suffice it to say that we need a better system to manage the transition from one president to another.

By the time I left government I had started to document the challenges and to suggest ways in which they could be dealt with. It was my hope then that my successors would take these matters further.

One other unique thing that happened during this transition from one president to another is the fact that a president who was in power for seven months was ready peacefully to hand over power to another and then become his deputy president. President Motlanthe knew as he was sworn in as president in September 2008 that he was going to be a caretaker president until the elections in April the following year. He also recognised the seniority of the president of the ruling party, as he was his deputy. He executed his responsibilities as president until the new president was elected and sworn in.

This may look ordinary but it is almost unheard of that a president of a country accepts so easily a change of roles, where he or she becomes the deputy to the new president.

PART TWO

Understanding Mbeki's Removal

CHAPTER 7

Dark Clouds Gather

The fatally flawed Nicholson judgment that was later dismissed by the judges of the Supreme Court of Appeal (SCA) was the trigger to the removal of Mbeki from office. Clouds had been gathering for some time but by the week of 12 to 19 September 2008, those occasioned by the Nicholson judgment were ominous and began to suggest that Mbeki could be removed from office.

Waking to a storm: The Nicholson judgment

Mbeki returned from Zimbabwe in the early hours of Friday, 12 September, after an extraordinary success. As the facilitator of the Zimbabwe Dialogue between the three main political parties in Zimbabwe, he had just got them to initial an agreement, with a formal signing ceremony on Monday, 15 September 2008. With this mission accomplished, he headed for Harare International Airport, elated that at last an agreement had been reached to resolve Zimbabwe's seemingly intractable problems, following some eight years' effort to reach settlement among the conflicting parties. The excitement of the facilitation team could not be suppressed as we swept through the empty streets of Harare for the airport in the early hours.

In the presidential plane we reminisced about the events that led to the agreement and the pain we had gone through to achieve this feat, and a feat it was, worthy of celebration. Everyone felt that the troubles we went through were worth it if they would guarantee peace in Zimbabwe. We also knew that as we celebrated there were superpowers out there who would be terribly disappointed that we had succeeded, as the agreement would not serve their national interests and strategic objectives. We also knew that efforts would be made to reverse this agreement or cause it to collapse, so that a way could be found to achieve the objective of 'regime change' to secure and guarantee their own interests at the expense of Zimbabweans.

On his arrival at home Mbeki went straight to rest after many days of hard work and sleepless nights in Harare. But instead of waking up later in the day to announce this extraordinary achievement in Zimbabwe, he awoke to the Nicholson storm, with news headlines that totally overshadowed the good news from Zimbabwe. It was as if it was planned to produce such an effect and rob Mbeki and his team of fully enjoying their success.

The facilitation team, consisting of Minister Sydney Mufamadi, Advocate Mojanku Gumbi and myself, were up and going before him and were alarmed by the judgment as it was presented in court. It felt more like a political statement than a legal judgment. It just did not make sense in law, especially regarding Judge Nicholson's comments about the president, his cabinet and the cabinet secretary.

Nicholson ruled that the decision to charge Jacob Zuma with corruption and fraud was invalid because the National Directorate of Public Prosecutions (NDPP) had not given him a chance to make representations before deciding to charge him. This part of the ruling was not alarming as it was the subject of the appeal and was based on procedural legal matters that the National Prosecuting Authority (NPA) had to apply their minds to. What was alarming, though, were the inexplicable, damning comments Nicholson made about Mbeki and others who worked with him, including his cabinet and myself.

Nicholson ruled that the applicant (Zuma) was correct in averring political meddling in his prosecution. Such allegations had been made during the campaign to support Zuma as he progressed through the corruption and fraud case, including the appeals he had made every step of the way, but there was no evidence to support this. It all remained in the realm of speculation, conjecture and angry emotions. Nicholson gave these speculative, conjectural views and angry emotions a veneer of a court ruling. This became the 'evidence' which was so desperately needed by some to remove Mbeki as president of the country. The 'evidence', though, would not pass muster in the SCA. The SCA ruled that the remarks made by Nicholson about Mbeki and those who worked with him had no basis and were extraneous to the case before him. The reality is that none of the persons referred to above were given an opportunity to defend themselves.

Those who wanted Mbeki to be removed immediately after the Polokwane conference found in Nicholson's judgment a useful tool to leverage their argument. The judgment was just what they needed and it was harnessed to achieve their objective of removing Mbeki before his term came to an end.

The judgment gave those who wanted Mbeki to leave *ngoko* ('now') after Polokwane a potent and emotive reason and tool to precipitate his removal from government, which they had no basis for prior to the Nicholson judgment. They felt that *uyababanbezela* ('he was delaying them'), they chanted the slogan and sang the song '*Uyangibambezela*' ('You are delaying me'), but could not do much about it until Nicholson (inadvertently) gave them ammunition.

For those who were tasked with the project of making Zuma's case go away, the Nicholson judgment was also like a godsend. The challenge, though, was that the basis on which Nicholson made his determination could conceivably be reversed on appeal. It is for this reason that major battles ensued to ensure that none of the affected parties (President Mbeki, cabinet ministers and the secretary of cabinet) and the NPA appealed against the judgment.

On retracing my steps to the moment when announcements were made by ANC Secretary-General Gwede Mantashe, accompanied by his deputy Thandi Modise and the spokesperson Jessie Duarte, it is clear that the issue was not any of the host of reasons given for the removal of Mbeki from office. The key issue was the case against Zuma. The Nicholson judgment was the best instrument to kill the case once and for all and nothing that threatened this victory could be allowed.

In the words of Mantashe at the press conference following the decision to recall Mbeki: 'The *biggest worry* for us is the question of the *reversal* of the possible closure of this chapter' (my emphasis). In the ANC's view, Mantashe said, the case 'is not in the public interest. If the case is pursued, it will continue to be a point of division in the ANC. *That is the main issue*' (my emphasis). The removal of Mbeki *ngoko*, rather than later, was related to this matter. They could not let him continue as president if he was likely to disturb this project or obstruct attempts to interfere in the judicial processes.

In order to conserve the ammunition given by Nicholson, a project was unleashed to prevent any appeal, causing further divisions within the ANC. Some felt that whatever damage the judgment had caused to the integrity and person of Mbeki and his cabinet should be left as it was and that they should live with the negative imputations to save the party and its president, Jacob Zuma. But Mbeki and the others fingered in the Nicholson judgment had been done the worst injustice and believed they had a right to clear their names. A failure to appeal would be construed as an admission of guilt.

These contradictory positions presented the ANC with a dilemma. Officially the party could not instruct Mbeki or cabinet not to appeal, as this would be to deny them rights that are enshrined in the constitutions of both the ANC and the country. Some of the party's leaders felt he should not pursue the appeal route but could not face him and tell him that. Instead efforts were made on the sidelines to influence anyone who mattered, unfortunately including me as the cabinet secretary and director-general in the presidency.

The group constituted to make Zuma's case 'go away' found itself in a difficult situation – any decision taken by the party would have to come down on the side of one of its two leaders, thereby violating the other's rights. Another factor was that Zuma had had the support of the party at every stage of his case. After Polokwane, the position was now even clearer: the party was on the side of its president against Mbeki. Nevertheless, it was still difficult for the party to be seen publicly to violate one of its own members' rights.

Under normal circumstances, the NPA could have appealed against the Nicholson judgment on behalf of the state and the case of the cabinet and the president would have been joined together with it. But because of the accusation that the president and members of the cabinet influenced the NPA, cabinet and the president decided to appeal on their own. The appeal would be lodged irrespective of whether or not the NPA lodged its own. In fact, they believed that, in order to avoid confusion, their appeal should have nothing to do with that of the NPA – the grounds were, in any case, very different.

As secretary of the cabinet, I was asked by the lawyers contracted by Mbeki (as president) and by government to sign an affidavit to confirm that cabinet had taken a decision to appeal, which I did. This was a normal and regular responsibility of the cabinet secretary. But this cost me dearly as some comrades felt that in doing so I was acting against the president of the ANC and supporting an 'inappropriate' decision of the cabinet. Some felt that I had defied the ANC or had acted against the directives of the ANC. Firstly there was no formal or official directive about this matter, but even if there was it would have been inappropriate and irregular.

The media made much of the fact that I had made an affidavit in support of Mbeki's case against that of Zuma, without pointing out that I simply carried out my responsibility as cabinet secretary to confirm a decision of cabinet in a court case that had nothing to do with support for one or the other. The ANC leadership did not take the trouble to explain this to its members or to disabuse them of the incorrect perspectives some held about me. Instead, I was confronted by third parties who demanded that I explain my position, which I had communicated officially through the minister of justice.

Later, efforts were made to change the decision of cabinet to appeal but no one was bold enough to introduce the item directly for discussion. Questions were raised as to whether or not cabinet made such a decision. Some even tried to influence the wording of the cabinet decision after the fact and attempts were made to put pressure on the cabinet secretary in this regard, which was of no avail since the cabinet secretary could not change or temper with decisions of cabinet.

For me the matter was simple and could not be coloured by the political discourse and contestations of the time and had nothing to do with sides people were taking for one or the other leader. As cabinet secretary I acted on behalf of the state and the battles within the ruling party thus had no bearing on my role. Indeed, if they were allowed to influence the position of the secretary of cabinet without it going through cabinet, it would be the beginning of the collapse of the democratic or constitutional state, the beginning of the corrosion of the integrity of the state.

The same applies to intelligence officers, the military, the police and the judiciary – siding with any party, even the ruling party or a faction thereof, is the ultimate threat to the integrity and security of the state. Any official decision made by the ruling party has to be filtered through parliament and/or the cabinet before the secretary of cabinet can act on it. This is a critical principle to preserve the integrity of the state and thereby the stability of the country. The quality and sustainability of our democracy depends in a large measure on the preservation of the integrity of the state as a constitutional state. In short, the secretary of the cabinet cannot act on instructions from the ruling party (or any other party for that matter) but only on those given by cabinet. Instructions from the president, which may come from the ruling party, must also be in line with decisions of cabinet. If they are not, it is the responsibility of the secretary of cabinet to advise the president that that is the case.

The NPA appealed against the Nicholson judgment and, in overturning it, the SCA was scathing about his findings, describing them as 'erroneous', 'unwarranted' and 'incomprehensible'. It remains puzzling to me that Judge Nicholson chose to make the comments he did, which in fact had no bearing on the matter before him.

The weekend before the SCA made its ruling on the Nicholson judgment there was restlessness and activity that suggested that some people had an idea as to what the ruling was going to be. Strenuous efforts were made to reach out to the leadership to do whatever was possible to stop or delay the ruling. This troubled me greatly, as it suggested that there were some among us who had no respect for the law or the Constitution, and that, for the sake of particular interests or causes, they would be prepared to break the law and violate the Constitution. During that weekend I felt that this was the stuff that dictatorship is made of. Once there is even a thought of interfering with or influencing judges, then we are at the door of dictatorship. That weekend we came close indeed. The good news is that we still had enough of our comrades who were bold enough to say 'no', 'no' and 'no' again.

Unfortunately, the ruling of the SCA was too late to save Mbeki, but it did clear his name and that of the members of cabinet and the secretary of cabinet. I do not remember anyone who had used the Nicholson judgment to remove Mbeki from office coming to Mbeki to apologise. He had been removed as president and this was not reversible.

The implications of the SCA ruling were more dire than the matter of the removal of Mbeki from office, as it threatened to open again the case against Zuma. The case was indeed reopened, and it is now history that classified material of discussions involving officials and former officials of the Directorate of Special Operations (DSO) and the NPA was used to get the case withdrawn.

The matter of the classified material used as a basis for the NDPP to withdraw the case remains a mystery to the public, as there has been no clarity about how this material was obtained, declassified and used in court. An investigation by the Inspectorate on Intelligence has shed no light in terms of what has been disclosed to the public. But the intelligence community and people in strategic places know exactly what happened, although I guess this will remain in the realm of classified information. Only time will tell.

My concern is that someone or some people broke the law and no one has bothered to investigate and act on it. Once we are ready to use stolen goods without asking where they come from, then we are on slippery ground, both in terms of the security of the state and in terms of our fight against crime and corruption. Once you freely corrupt state institutions or officials within those institutions, there can be no end but corruption of the whole of our society.

A storm on a perfect day

One thing many analysts and commentators missed during that testing week in September 2008 is that the crisis did not relate to governance issues. It was also not about service delivery, which was a burning issue at the time. It was a purely internal party matter triggered by challenges within the ANC. Some may argue that the crisis was triggered by the removal in 2005 of Jacob Zuma, then deputy president of the ANC, from his position as deputy president of the country. That is true. But the repercussions of his removal played themselves out within the party rather than at government level because the appointment or firing of members of cabinet is the constitutional prerogative of the president.

It is important to note that, at that time, the government of the Republic of South Africa (the 'Mbeki Administration', as the media termed it) was performing at its highest level, even with regard to controversial issues such as HIV and AIDS, where best-practice policy was in place, and Zimbabwe, where a political settlement had been reached. Government had also just launched a well-researched poverty eradication programme, which promised to deal once and for all with the problem.

The poverty alleviation programme, based on the outcome of research in Chile and Tunisia, was launched in July 2008, led by the country's deputy president, Phumzile Mlambo-Ngcuka, supported by the then minister in the presidency, Kgalema Motlanthe. The key element of the strategy was the collection of data about every poor family or individual in the country. Based on this information, customised solutions would be developed for each of them over and above the collective strategies to deal with poverty. It was found that when the challenge is reduced to helping a specific family escape the vicious cycle of poverty, the impact became greater and the results measurable.

The collection of the data required a visit to every poor family in the country, starting in the poorest areas. This strategy would obviously require hundreds of thousands of people to cover the whole country and would also rely on the participation and collaboration of all spheres of government (national, provincial and local), with local governments as the major players. It also required the involvement of various sectors of civil society, particularly community organisations, religious communities, labour and business. To achieve maximum effect the programme had to be driven by the presidency under the leadership of the deputy president.

One of the tragedies of political transitions – especially hostile or violent ones – is that even premier programmes like this suffer from delays or lack of focus or of consciousness about the critical importance of the programme. At worst, they are completely abandoned. Fortunately, notwithstanding delays occasioned by the transitional processes after the 2009 election, the government has picked up the programme and is doing whatever can be done to operationalise it.

With regard to HIV and AIDS, the policies and programmes that had been put in place had been commended by many, both locally and internationally. The July 2008 Joint United Nations Programme on HIV/AIDS (UNAIDS) country situational report said that South Africa had comprehensive policies and programmes to address the AIDS epidemic and the plan included management, treatment, care and support for those who had AIDS. The government had revamped its National AIDS Council into a multi-sectoral body providing for high-level leadership and coordination and developed a National Strategic Plan 2007–11.

In 2007 South Africa had 'the largest AIDS treatment programme in the world with approximately 370 000 people with ARV treatment in the public sector and an estimated 120 000 people in the private sector'. At the time, the country was spending more proportionally to combat the pandemic, including treatment and care, than many other countries. Its domestic resource commitment increased from US$479 million in 2004/2005 to US$878 million in 2009/2010.

So, if there was any debate about HIV and AIDS at all, it was more about the past than the present and was more an old and tired stick with which to beat Mbeki than an expression of reality. What is surprising, though, is that the critique intensified at the very time when South Africa had the best and most comprehensive programme in the world.

On the controversial issue of Zimbabwe, Mbeki, appointed by SADC to facilitate dialogue between the ruling Zimbabwe African National Union-Patriotic Front (ZANU-PF) and the two formations of the Movement for Democratic Change (MDC), had just achieved an extraordinary success in getting the three parties to sign the Global Political Agreement (GPA) to settle their conflict. The agreement had been reached at about midnight on 11 September 2008, the day before Nicholson announced his judgment.

As was to be expected, the Nicholson judgment overshadowed and crowded out Mbeki's triumph in settling the Zimbabwe dispute. What should have dominated the news in all the national and international media became like a squeak in a sea of Nicholson judgment headlines. By midday on the Friday, the Zimbabwe success story was dead, eclipsed by Nicholson's words.

And so, the people of South Africa and the international

community were robbed of the best news to have emanated from Zimbabwe for years. Despite this, no one could take away the positive experiences of ordinary Zimbabweans following the establishment of the Inclusive Government set out in the GPA. This account by one Zimbabwean sixteen months after the signing of the GPA is telling (e-mail dated 22 January 2010):

> I travelled home to Zimbabwe over the Christmas period, I was deeply moved to see God's hand over our motherland. I had been home last in Sept 2008, during which period one could not find a single item on the shelves of big supermarkets in Harare. This time the shelves were full, obviously that does not necessarily mean that everyone has money in their pockets to buy what their family needs. In 2008 even if one had money it was very difficult to get anything. Yes it's still a long road to get back to the quality of life of the early 90s but we have to acknowledge God's hand thus far and ask him to complete his work.

A response to this e-mail reads as follows:

> And I too went to Zim over the Christmas and was pleasantly surprised. God surely does answer prayer. It was good to see people excitedly shopping and enjoying Christmas with their families and loved ones. To God be all the praise.

To those both at home and abroad who were opposed to the political settlement in Zimbabwe, the Nicholson judgment was a godsend. Some thought that the gods conspired to use the judgment to obscure Mbeki's success in helping Zimbabwe find solutions to its challenges. Some believe it was a conspiracy hatched by the superpowers that were dead against the political settlement in Zimbabwe because it impeded their objective of 'regime change'. Whatever the thoughts and whatever people believed, the reality is that the Nicholson judgment totally overshadowed the Zimbabwe success story.

During our visit to Zimbabwe following the removal of Mbeki from office, ordinary Zimbabweans who met us in the hotel where the negotiations were taking place and some well-placed and connected leaders explicitly said that his removal had come as no surprise to Zimbabweans because the international forces that objected to his approach on Zimbabwe could not let him remain in power. Zimbabweans, they said, were aware that Mbeki had suffered dearly and paid a price for his stand on Zimbabwe and they would remain eternally grateful to him.

What made this perspective seem plausible to many are the vicious attacks on Mbeki over a sustained period of almost ten years for his handling of the Zimbabwe situation. This campaign was carried out mainly through the media, both in South Africa and internationally, and critical statements were made by officials in high places in both the United Kingdom and the United States.

During an unscheduled visit to South Africa by US Assistant Secretary of State Jendayi Fraser, she chose to denounce the Zimbabwe political settlement on South African soil – an unprecedented act. She declared the Zimbabwe facilitation led by former president Mbeki a failed process that had then run its course and this was just three months after the agreement was signed. The key issue here was not about the agreement as that was never accepted; it was more about the removal of the facilitator. 'We think the facilitation is over, it led to [a] power-sharing agreement that is flawed,' she said.

The visit of Fraser followed the removal of Mbeki from office and this was seen as an opportune moment to get South Africa and the SADC leadership to change their policy positions on Zimbabwe, including ditching the GPA and removing Mbeki as the facilitator. This objective of removing Mbeki was achieved nine months later at the August 2009 SADC Summit in Kinshasa, but the GPA remained and is the basis on which the Inclusive Government (ZANU-PF and the two MDC formations) was constituted.

In November 2008 the Elders (a group of eminent global leaders who included former UN secretary-general Kofi Annan, former US President Jimmy Carter and Graça Machel, children's rights activist and wife of Nelson Mandela) attempted, without success, to visit Zimbabwe. The government of Zimbabwe had asked them to delay their visit until the Inclusive Government had been constituted, so they could interact with the new government to determine how Zimbabwe could be assisted to recover from its crisis.

The Elders believed they should proceed to Zimbabwe irrespective of the government's wishes, as they felt the country needed help sooner rather than later. When the Zimbabwe government informed them that they would not be officially received if they came without an invitation, the Elders camped in South Africa, using it as a base for meetings with representatives of Zimbabwean civil society, business and political parties, as well as donors and UN agencies. According to the Elders' website, the visit 'shifted world and media attention from the protracted political negotiations between Zimbabwe's political leaders to the humanitarian crises in Zimbabwe'.

Some of the major powers made great efforts both overtly and covertly to influence SADC and AU leaders to turn against Mbeki and his approach. Some countries were persuaded, but the majority stuck with their choice of Mbeki as facilitator, believing that Africans should be allowed to choose their own strategies to resolve the problems affecting the African continent. The message was clear: let Africans deal with African problems in the way they see fit. This notwithstanding, the pressures continued. Some unsuccessful attempts were also made to create parallel processes to take over the facilitation process. In some instances plans were put in place to bring in more facilitators in order to negate or neutralise Mbeki's approach. These, too, failed.

Some of the countries on the African continent shared with us the extreme forms of pressures to which they were subjected, including threats to withdraw financial or budget support. Countries which depend on external funding for budget support have to take such threats seriously. I see threats of this nature as terrorism of the highest order. If there were no consequences, many presidents would testify to this form of terrorism, perpetrated by those who have the leverage of international power and resources.

Among the pressures that were applied were promises of grants in one form or another, a method used, too, when key posts are filled within the international governance system or when crucial decisions have to be made in international fora. Interestingly, no one has been bold enough to call this international cancer what it is: corruption of the highest order in the global governance system.

Punching above its weight: An irritation!

Some would say that South Africa punched way above its weight when it came to international politics. Its influence had been felt in relation to global policy issues such as the Proliferation of Weapons of Mass Destruction, matters dealt with within the World Trade Organization (WTO) and issues related to human rights.

The most critical of these has arisen in relation to decisions of the UN Security Council. Even when South Africa was not represented on the Security Council, its views were sought and, in many instances, carried the day. Thus, with the help of other allies South Africa was able to block a vote on Côte d'Ivoire (sought by France) and two votes on Zimbabwe (sought by the US), which might have further complicated the conflict situations in those countries. These successes made Mbeki's position more vulnerable. How could a small country like South Africa thwart the wishes of the permanent members of the UN Security Council? This was unimaginable to them and was not taken kindly.

Mbeki left for Sudan immediately after Zimbabwe's GPA was signed to assist with the resolution of the conflict there. In a joint statement with Sudanese President Omar al-Bashir on 16 September, Mbeki warned that charges of genocide against al-Bashir would undermine the peace efforts in Darfur and 'the promotion of long-lasting peace and reconciliation in the Sudan as a whole and, as a result, may lead to further suffering of the people of the Sudan and greater destabilisation with far-reaching consequences for the country and region'. As would be expected, the statement Mbeki made was in line with the position taken by the AU, which called on the International Criminal Court (ICC) 'to suspend its decision to seek al-Bashir's arrest for a moment until we sort out the primary problems in Darfur and Southern Sudan'.

Once again, Mbeki's position did not meet with the approval of powerful international forces, especially major countries within the European Union and civil society groups. This crucial matter, which had serious implications not only for Sudan but also for the African continent and the international community, received little publicity at home, where the media were focused on the noisy debate that followed the Nicholson judgment.

The momentum builds up

By the time Mbeki returned from Sudan, the momentum was building up to remove him from office despite his successes in the international arena. The most dramatic of these attempts came from ANCYL leader Julius Malema, in defiance of the stance taken by ANC President Jacob Zuma. Zuma believed (at least in terms of his public posture) that, despite Judge Nicholson's observations, there was no need to remove Mbeki a mere seven months before the end of his term. He is quoted as having said that Mbeki's administration was coming to an end and if you remove him now 'you are like someone who beats a dead snake. It died long ago, but you are still beating it ... wasting your energy.' The use of the imagery of a snake was unfortunate because of its negative connotations. The media played on this but the message Zuma wanted to convey was clear. In contrast Malema, who represented a particular view within the ANC, was unequivocal about the removal of Mbeki. He is reported as having said that people should wait 'until Sunday' and the ANC president would be saying what he (Malema) was saying. Those who watched the press conference will recall that this matter was treated like a joke – a laughing matter that in my view denigrated the president of the ANC.

Behind the scenes, at some point before the NEC met on Friday, Mbeki and Zuma held a meeting at which Zuma assured the president that notwithstanding Malema's statements, which represented an angry grouping within the ANC, Mbeki would be allowed to serve his full term. There is a debate about whether or not Zuma meant what he said both in public and in private about the removal of Mbeki. Unfortunately, this has to be left in the realm of speculation. Whatever the case, Mbeki had, in turn, said that if his organisation made a decision that he should leave, as a disciplined member of the organisation he would comply.

Anticipating the removal of Mbeki

As alert civil servants responsible for managing government and state, the management in the presidency could not observe these developments and debate without examining the implications of whatever decision the ruling party might take. I asked our legal unit and the president's legal adviser to look at the Constitution and advise on the legal implications of such decisions. Various scenarios were mapped out, together with a variety of options.

Interestingly, our constitution-makers did not anticipate a case in which a sitting president might be recalled by his own party. In terms of the Constitution the president is elected by parliament and not by the ruling party (s 86 and schedule 3). Parties in parliament (including the ruling party or a coalition of parties) may nominate a president, but parliament decides, by a simple majority, which of the nominees to select. So, only parliament can remove a sitting president.

Sections 89 and 102 of the Constitution are the only sections which could be used to remove a president from office. Section 89, with the heading 'Removal of President', reads as follows:

> (1) The National Assembly, by a resolution adopted with a supporting vote of at least two thirds of its members, may re- move the President from office *only* on the grounds of
>> (a) a serious violation of the Constitution or the law;
>> (b) serious misconduct; or
>> (c) inability to perform the functions of office.
> (2) Anyone who has been removed from the office of President in terms of subsection (1) (a) or (b) may not receive any ben- efits of that office, and may not serve in any public office. [My emphasis.]

This section was found not to be applicable to the case we were dealing with as the operative words were 'serious violation of the Constitution' and 'serious misconduct'. There were no grounds on which President Mbeki could be accused of such misdemeanours. The president was very particular about his responsibility to 'uphold, defend and respect the Constitution as the supreme law of the Republic' (s 83[b]). Secondly, there was no question of misconduct. The reality was that the drive to remove the president was motivated by intra-party issues, not by poor government or governance. Accordingly, this section of the Constitution could not be used to remove the president from office. The question of 'inability to perform the functions of office' did not arise at all as Mbeki was effectively managing government.

In s 102, which concerns 'Motions of no confidence', subsection (2) reads as follows:

> If the National Assembly, by a vote supported by a majority of its members, passes a motion of no confidence in the President, the President and the other members of the Cabinet and any Deputy Ministers must *resign* [my emphasis].

Again, this section refers to 'a motion of no confidence in the President' as president of the country rather than as a member of his political party. Such a motion of no confidence required a vote of more than 50 per cent of the members of parliament, a most unlikely situation, given the divisions within the ruling party at the time. If the 60/40 per cent division at Polokwane in favour of Zuma was anything to go by, a 50 per cent vote in parliament would have been a risky affair.

Based on this analysis it was clear that there was no way in which the president could be removed from office constitutionally. The Constitution did not even provide for the option of voluntary resignation.

Although the exercise was useful, enabling us to prepare ourselves for any eventuality, it was also both theoretical and speculative. We had to wait for the NEC to make its decision before we could determine the implications.

The need for stability

Uppermost in our minds was the commitment to maintain stability in the country, whatever the outcome of the NEC meeting. President Mbeki had made this very clear. His attitude was based on two hallmarks of ANC policy and Mbeki's presidency.

The first was that comrades, past and present, had made such sacrifices for this new democratic order that we could not allow it to be destabilised, whatever the circumstances. A Samsonian going down with the Philistines was not an option as far as Mbeki was concerned. Nothing would be done at the expense of the people of South Africa.

Solomon's wise suggestion – that the baby be cut in two, thereby determining its real parentage – has application in this case. Like the mother of the baby, Mbeki chose to let the baby live rather than see it cut into two pieces.

Both these solutions have wrought havoc in the world, with many living in a state of permanent war because of a leader's desire to cling to power at any cost. Mbeki would not allow this to happen even if it cost him his position; he would rather leave office than cause pain to his people. He had made it clear to us that everything had to be done to ensure that stability was maintained, whatever decision the party might make.

There was another reason for Mbeki's determination to maintain stability. He had spent much of his time in office (both as deputy president and as president) working for stability and peace on the African continent in the interests of development. Because of this legacy, built up over years, he could not, as a matter of principle, afford to be associated with instability and chaos. His legacy of peacemaking on the continent, including the vision of the African Renaissance and related programmes such as the New Partnership for Africa's Development (NEPAD) and the African Peer Review Mechanism (APRM), could not be allowed to be compromised because of differences within his party.

His advisers in the presidency, particularly those who had worked with him for years to develop the vision of the African Renaissance, totally agreed with him and were committed to ensuring that his legacy was not compromised.

There was a third reason, though, which could not be spoken about: it was the knowledge of how far some comrades were foolishly prepared to go to remove Mbeki and take over the reins of government. Some of this was just careless talk of comrades who believed that they were in power already. Nevertheless, the state security establishment was always ready to execute its constitutional responsibilities against illegal or unconstitutional activity, especially the removal of a duly elected president. This, too, Mbeki would have wanted to avoid.

People who are privileged tend to take their privilege for granted. South Africans are no exception in this regard. We take for granted the extraordinary struggle our people waged to establish the country and democracy we have today. We also forget that our struggle was waged on such high moral ground that it led to the development of a unique cadre of leaders whose concern was for the people and the country rather than for themselves, their families, factions and friends.

During that week of September 2008 it dawned on me once again that South Africans are very lucky to have the calibre of leaders they have. Without them our country would have long ago slid into a disastrous space or collapsed into chaos, as did many post-colonial states. Indeed, the events that culminated in the removal of Mbeki during that week in September brought us very close to a disaster of a magnitude that cannot even be imaged.

I have learned in life that one should never trigger events without an assurance that one can control the aftermath. In the words of one of the 'negotiating partners' at the Convention for a Democratic South Africa (CODESA), the process that negotiated the form of the new South Africa: 'Don't start a fire you cannot put out!'

I had a feeling during that fateful September that there were people who were ready to start fires without considering the consequences. There was a level of recklessness which could only be explained by a determination to have their way at any cost, even at the risk of wrecking our newly born democracy. For them it was a zero-sum game.

As head of the highest office in the land, the presidency, I felt, at the time, like the pilot of an aircraft sharing an unregulated space with other aircraft, which were unaware of what was happening in that space, lacking the sophisticated electronic sensors that might assist them to avoid danger. And when one was forced by foul weather to consider an emergency landing at the nearest airport, the control tower would announce that there were no landing lights – a severe test of one's skills. Like a pilot who has lived through near misses which were never disclosed to the passengers, I struggled through that period knowing that there was nobody with whom I could share my worries except for some of my colleagues and staff in the presidency.

I was in the presidency's cockpit with my deputies, battling a vicious, life-threatening storm, at the centre of a crisis of change in government that the Constitution never envisaged. We must all learn from the events of that week, to ensure that we are never again pushed so close to the brink as a nation.

Running government irrespective of gathering dark clouds

Despite what was happening in the background, we had to continue with the task of governing the country and ensuring that the unfolding events did not affect any of the services provided by government. As the head of FOSAD I fielded anxious calls from fellow directors-general at both national and provincial levels. They wanted to know what was happening and what the implications were for them. My advice was simple: until further notice continue working as if nothing is happening.

I emphasised the important role they had as critical stabilising factors in a situation of political crisis. DGs were not political appointees in the American sense, where senior public servants leave office with those who appointed them. DGs in South Africa are on fixed contracts unrelated to the term of office of their political principals and are expected to continue running government whatever the nature of the political transition. They are also expected to be ready to serve whichever political principal is appointed or elected legally and constitutionally (including those of opposition parties), on the principle that there must be continuity in service delivery whatever the circumstances.

The comment of one white businessperson after the removal of President Mbeki was illuminating in this regard. He was travelling when the crisis hit the country. On his return he said to me: 'South Africa is an extraordinary country. I left a week ago with one president and I returned and found that the president had been removed and another president was in office, but the airport was still running normally and cars were still moving in the streets as if nothing had happened!' This, he said, was a miracle and gave him confidence in the country and its new democracy.

Within the presidency my task was to get everyone to continue with his or her duties as though nothing was happening. One of

the major operational matters was that the president was scheduled
to make several trips, one of which was to take place the following week. Our logistics and security teams were already deployed in
various places, including the US, to facilitate his movements. As the
noises about the possible removal of Mbeki reached its crescendo, the
commanders of these teams became restless and made calls to check
whether they should continue with their preparations. They were
ordered not to be distracted by newspaper headlines. Their responsibility was to continue until instructed otherwise. Among these trips
was one to the UN, where Mbeki was due to be the keynote speaker
at a Forum on Africa, involving many key leaders on the continent.

Overnight I was transformed from head of the presidency to
something like a commander-in-chief of the public service, managing a national crisis of enormous proportions as all the relevant
ministers were also affected by the political developments. Many of
the ministers and deputy ministers were preparing themselves to
leave office, since the removal of the president could mean the end
of their service as well.

The most challenging event was the international conference on
the African Diaspora that South Africa was due to host in a matter
of weeks. The offices of heads of state from the African continent
and the Diaspora were inquiring whether or not the conference
would proceed. The answer had to be yes, since nobody knew what
the outcome of the debate within the ANC would be. The staff involved in preparing for the conference had to continue with their
work. But this response did not help, as one head of state after another began to send signals of doubt, with others indicating without giving reasons that they were no longer able to honour their
commitment to attend.

The possible removal of the president would have implications
for the presidency staff, but here forward-planning paid dividends.
The presidency had used the first part of the year before the 2009

elections to prepare staff for the impending change of president. Over and above discussions with all staff in the presidency, consultations were held with affected staff and plans were already in place to manage the constitutionally mandated transition. If there were any change, the fast-forward button would be activated.

This assurance should have been sufficient to stabilise things but staff, quite naturally, were concerned and we realised the situation had to be managed with empathy and sensitivity. A lot of patience was required.

Friday, 19 September 2008

At Esselen Park, where the ANC NEC meeting began on the Friday, the battle to remove Mbeki was driven by a multiplicity of interests. The biggest problem among some party members, one which had been articulated for about four years, was anger at Mbeki for relieving Jacob Zuma of his duties as the country's deputy president in June 2005, following the trial of his former financial adviser, Schabir Shaik, on corruption charges. In his judgment Hilary Squires had made a connection between the illegal activities that Shaik had been convicted of and Zuma. In his statement to parliament on this matter, President Mbeki said:

> [...] as President of the Republic I have come to the conclusion that the circumstances dictate that in the interests of the Honourable Deputy President, the government, our young democratic system, and our country, it would be best to release the Honourable Jacob Zuma from his responsibilities as Deputy President of the Republic and member of the Cabinet.

Mbeki has often been asked whether, given the opportunity now, he would take a different position on Zuma's removal. His emphatic answer is always 'no'. If he were to have allowed Zuma to remain in office (as deputy president of the country) after the comments made by Squires, he would not have been able to combat corruption in government. He could not be seen to tolerate corruption in any form, as his vision of the African Renaissance and the credibility of his African renewal project were at stake. Despite what his stand had cost him, Mbeki has always maintained that he had no choice; his decision was a matter of principle rather than one of political expediency.

Some argued, though, that Zuma had not been given a chance in court to defend himself and that Mbeki's action was thus premature. Mbeki's position was that it was the prerogative of the president to appoint ministers and his decision had nothing to do with disciplinary procedures or a case of any kind. He simply exercised his prerogative to reshuffle cabinet.

This constitutional prerogative of the president became a subject of emotive debates within the party as some felt it was overriding the authority of the party or feelings of members of the party. This decision should have been made by the party and not the president, thus sparking further debate about the 'centre of power' and the constitutional powers of the nation's president.

I attended a provincial meeting in North West where I was deployed as an NEC member and listened to a heated debate about presidential 'prerogative'. Some did not even understand what the word meant, but they knew that it had led to the removal of Zuma as the country's deputy president. One speaker asked whose child this 'Prerogative' is (*Ke ngwana wa mang 'Prerogetivy' yo?*). If 'Prerogative' was in the Constitution, he had to be removed.

The campaign for Zuma to be given 'his day in court' was a risky one. My view is that some of those who demanded this did not really mean it. They were just making a point that this is what should have happened before the president made his decision. It was a rhetorical assertion. Those who did really believe that Zuma should be given his day in court, believed that he was innocent and no court could find him guilty. The challenge was that the NPA proceeded to charge Zuma for corruption, causing the campaigners to claim a conspiracy to prevent him from standing for election. One day they were demanding that Zuma be given his day in court, the next they were alleging conspiracy once Zuma was charged.

Some of those who were unhappy about the removal of Zuma from office argued that Mbeki had not consulted the ANC or its tripartite alliance partners, COSATU and the SACP, before taking his decision. Those who were in leadership positions at the time know that this is not true. Mbeki had discussed the matter with ANC officials and had also gone beyond the call of duty to convene a meeting of national and provincial leaders, the alliance partners, the South African National Civic Organisation (SANCO), the ANC Women's League and the ANCYL to brief them about the action he was contemplating. The meeting was held at Genadendal, the president's official residence in Cape Town, before the announcement was made in parliament.

For others, it was not about whether or not there had been consultation; they simply did not like the decision, feeling it was unfair to the deputy president. A few responded out of anger at the way they perceived that Mbeki had treated them in the past, in relation to positions they had coveted but not received. Still others believed the removal of Mbeki would enhance their chances of advancing in their political careers. For these people, another seven months was too long. They wanted the change *ngoko* ('now').

In some instances – the example of Kwame Nkrumah in Ghana is one – people participate in the removal of a leader for what they consider to be legitimate reasons. In many others, though, especially where the leader is a thorn in the flesh of certain global powers, external interests come to bear on the matter, plugging into the grievances of the people to advance their own national interests. In most instances this is done in an underground way, without the knowledge of most of those involved, although some may be willing or compromised collaborators, or agents.

The Nkrumah case is instructive. Declassified foreign intelligence reports show that some powers welcomed his removal, considering that their programme and strategies had succeeded. In the case of Mbeki we will have to wait until intelligence records are declassified by the various countries which were involved in this matter. The wait, unfortunately, will be a long one – 20 to 30 years, depending on the country's laws. Those of us who are older have to live with the reality that we will never know. We will have to leave this to our children, unless leaks expose the information prematurely.

Returning to the debate on the removal of Mbeki, credit must be given to some ANC leaders who worked late into Friday night to persuade the angry brigade not to recall the president. Zuma himself had indicated earlier in the week, employing an unfortunate but evocative expression, that there was no point in 'beating a dead snake', that Mbeki should be left to finish his term.

I imagine that Zuma simply used this expression to make the point that there would be no harm in letting Mbeki complete his term. The media, though, made a feast of it. The word 'snake' has a deeply negative connotation. Some would say that the English translation of the expression communicates something different from what the Zulu expression would mean idiomatically. Whatever the case, while the expression was unfortunate, what Zuma wanted to communicate was clear: leave Mbeki to complete his term as he had become harmless and there was no need to waste energy on removing him.

The ANCYL, however, led by its president, Julius Malema, publicly opposed Zuma's approach, with Malema quoted as saying:

> We have approached individual members of the ANC NEC
> to ensure that the removal of Thabo Mbeki becomes an ANC
> NEC resolution this weekend, and the majority of them are
> agreeing with us on this issue.
>
> We don't fight to lose. We will have Mbeki removed. He's
> going. It doesn't matter who says what. Mbeki won't be the
> president of this country when we go to elections. We are
> leaving no stone unturned to ensure that he leaves.

The way Malema's words ultimately became Zuma's words as
president of the ANC, raised serious concerns among many South
Africans. More worrying still is that this has become a pattern.
The first question was, who is leading the ANC: its president or
the president of the ANCYL? The second was the strength of the
faction within the ANC of which Malema was a part. There was
concern that if this faction was able to overrule the president, the
ANC itself would be at risk. Thirdly, although Zuma's position
was clearly and publicly articulated, the working committee of
the party, which had met earlier that week, took a position similar
to that of Malema rather than supporting Zuma. So it was that
Malema's word became the word of the ANC by the end of the
week, and the word of the ANC became the word of the president of the ANC by the Monday.

Some of those who responded to my articles published in the
Independent Newspapers about this matter questioned my render-
ing of this event and argued that Zuma had to take the public posture he took as a leader, but they believed that he wanted Mbeki
out. Others even went as far as to say that he was the driver of the
movement to remove Mbeki. I have chosen to work on the basis of

the public expressions of Zuma rather than just thoughts, suspicions or conjectures.

CHAPTER 8

The Puzzle about the Removal of Mbeki

It was the morning of 19 September 2008 when South Africans, Africa and the world woke up to the shocking news that the NEC of the ANC had made a decision to 'recall' Mbeki as the president of the country. Many did not believe it. Their immediate response of extreme shock was 'Hee?', 'What?', 'No!', 'It can't be true!'

Although Mbeki's loss at the Polokwane ANC national conference was dramatic, rough, very hostile and totally uncharacteristic of the ANC, many did not believe that Mbeki could or would be removed as president of the country before he completed his term of office. The vote in Polokwane was about stopping him from serving a third term as president of the ANC and not about his presidency in government.

It was known that he could not serve as president beyond the second term as that was proscribed by the South African Constitution. A 'third term' as president of the ANC was constitutionally permissible, but those who voted against him feared that he would continue influencing what would happen in government, including appointments, from the party headquarters. This vote was thus about fear of his influence from outside, rather than about completing his second term.

Serving the last fifteen to eighteen months or so as president of the country after the election of a new party leader in the ANC was not unusual and happened during Mandela's presidency. In fact, the design was deliberate and meant to allow time for the new president of the party to prepare for the national general election. Although the manner in which Mbeki was removed as president of the ANC made many fear that there could be efforts to remove him as the president of the country, this was considered a remote possibility since there was such a short time left to the end of his term.

Regarding public opinion about Mbeki's removal, one has to remember that the reasons for his removal were not about national issues or about governance. They were about internal party matters which did not affect the overwhelming majority of South Africans. In any case, the country was performing at its best and there was a huge effort in government to ensure that all the promises made in the 2004 manifesto of the ruling party would be met wherever possible. So, for the majority of South Africans the decision to recall Mbeki was a real shock.

For many the shock translated into fear of a possible violent reaction or instability. The announcement of the 'recall' threatened their feeling of security which had grown in the place of the violence and insecurity of the apartheid system. Their confidence in the country was shaken. Those who were travelling wondered whether or not their families were safe, with some wondering whether it was safe to return home.

Another question worrying South Africans was whether or not the ANC could 'recall' the nation's president without their consent as the electorate. The South African Constitution was clear. The people's representatives in parliament elect the president and not the party. In this sense the party could not 'recall' the president in the classical sense of this word as if he was the party's 'ambassador' in government. The popular concept of 'redeployment' could not be used either as it would be unconstitutional in this regard. Given the context, 'recall' could only mean 'withdrawing the party's support' for him as the president of the country and 'asking him to voluntarily resign'.

The force of the resolution of the party to 'recall' him depended entirely on his willingness to comply with his party's wishes and had no legal force. If enforced by the party it would be equivalent to a *coup d'état*. It is important to understand that Mbeki had the right to say, 'No, I am not resigning. I am going to complete my term of office as provided for in the Constitution.' If he did, the country would have been thrown into a serious crisis, and the only legal or constitutional way to deal with the crisis would have been the parliamentary route. There was no guarantee as well that the parliamentary route would produce the desired effect as this was the pre-Polokwane parliament and not the post-2009 election parliament.

There are some who still believe that Mbeki should not have agreed to resign. From my recollection of the time, in our interaction with Mbeki this option was clearly not in his mind. He was clear that he would not want to stay any day extra beyond the wishes of his party. Mbeki was a child of the ANC, a disciplined cadre of the movement, and was not about to defy it. Defiance would have been like defying his being, his life and history. His consideration on this matter was not about government but about his party.

The question which still puzzles many – both inside and outside the country – is why Mbeki was removed from office just seven months before the end of his two terms as president of the country. He had served the post-apartheid government for almost fifteen years, first as deputy president and then as president for almost two terms. In terms of our Constitution the second term was the last he could serve as president and the question is, why was he removed so dramatically and unceremoniously so close to the end of his term? There are many reasons given for his removal but they do not explain the sudden haste with which it had to be done.

Although I worked with Mbeki in government, I cannot claim that I know everything he did or was doing, especially at a party political level where he was first the deputy president (1991–97) and then president (1997–07). But what I do know is that after the December 2007 ANC Polokwane conference, Mbeki was aware that the upheaval, particularly the manner in which it occurred and the attitudes expressed, meant that from then on it could not be business as usual even in his role as president of the country. He knew that the best he could do for the last eighteen months or so in office was to complete the programme of government which had been agreed upon and was within the policy framework of the ANC election manifesto. On this programme there could be no differences to occasion any conflict with the party.

After Polokwane he relinquished party political business and left it to the new leadership in Luthuli House. Although as former president of the ANC he had a right to attend their meetings he chose not to, unless specifically invited for a particular purpose. This was well meant but it left a gaping hole in the communication between Luthuli House and the Union Buildings. Efforts were made to setup regular meetings between Mbeki and Zuma, the new ANC president, but this was not successful as the meetings were irregular and infrequent. With the appointment of Kgalema Motlanthe as a minister in the presidency, leadership communication with Luthuli House was improved, but Mbeki still kept his distance from the party and its activities to avoid further conflict.

Mbeki's extra-cautious approach was strategically pragmatic. He understood that the new circumstances required high levels of sensitivity. He was also determined to complete his term of office with dignity and honour, notwithstanding the changes at the party level. As far as I can remember he was careful not to do anything that would threaten the interests of those who had taken over the leadership of the ANC. In fact, he concentrated on ensuring that the government's POA was implemented to the best of his abilities and those of government, with the next election date as its target for completion.

This was done not only in the interest of the people, especially the poor and disadvantaged, but also in the interest of the ANC given the impending elections. Someone else might have viewed this differently as an effort to destroy the chances of the new leadership winning an election. But not Mbeki, who took seriously his party, the ANC, whatever the events of Polokwane.

The only challenge was in the area of Mbeki's responsibilities as the head of state and the head of the national executive (government) in terms of section 84 of the Constitution. He took an oath of office and could not violate it. Some demanded that the president act in a manner that would have violated his constitutional mandate. These people either had no respect for the Constitution or were oblivious to its prescripts. This happened mainly in the area of appointments, the processing of Bills and assenting to and signing of Bills. The processing of the Amendment of the Police Act to replace the Scorpions with the Hawks and the appointment of the SABC board were further cases in point.

On the SABC board the problem was within the party rather than with the president but it was portrayed as if Mbeki was defying the post-Polokwane leadership. The media were not interested in the reality but were more interested in seeing a gulf building between Mbeki and his party. This was more interesting than the technical details on how the party handled the recommendations for the SABC board.

Although there was consensus about the problematic way in which the Scorpions operated and carried out their functions, and about the need to change this without the Scorpions losing their capacity to fight corruption and organised crime, the final Bill had amendments that were unlikely to pass the constitutional test. Mbeki left it to the party to shape the Bill in the way they saw fit. For me this was the first time I saw Mbeki letting go something he did not believe was correct or in the national interest. But because of the bad blood, the resolution from Polokwane, and the fact that he was about to leave office, he let it go. Some would say that he did so for the sake of democracy as this was a decision of the ANC conference.

Even after all this there was nothing to suggest that there would now be a radical decision to remove him from office. In any case, if he had not contested the Polokwane election he would have been in the same situation of there being a new ANC President whilst he was president of the country.

At an international level, especially on the African continent, many still ask the question of how the removal of Mbeki could happen in post-apartheid South Africa with its glorious history of peacemaking and reconciliation (with the worst enemies) and a democratic system with one of the most progressive constitutions in the world. Many could not understand how the ANC could do this, whatever the challenges, as one of the oldest political parties on the continent that many looked to as a shining example of what parties should be like in Africa. They could not believe that this could happen in the land of Nelson Mandela, Walter Sisulu, Govan Mbeki, Oliver Tambo, Albert Luthuli, Helen Joseph, Lillian Ngoyi, Beyers Naudé, and the many others they held in high esteem.

Those who watched the performance of the government Mbeki led were also bewildered by the fact that his removal happened at the time when government was performing at its best. The anniversary of fifteen years of freedom was approaching and all of government was working towards its goals in preparation for the fourth democratic elections in 2009. The POA with its timeframes for implementation was for the first time posted on the government website so that the public could monitor it. As part of the achievements of government one could talk about the 12 million vulnerable South Africans – the aged, people with disabilities and children – who were now on social grants; a national budget that had started releasing more money on basic needs, contrary to what had been expected by critics of the austerity measures the government had taken in the 1990s; and the 2010 FIFA World Cup preparations which were well ahead of schedule.

At an international level, the African Renaissance programme was at full speed notwithstanding the slow pace at which most African countries and some of the regional economic communities were responding. NEPAD and the APRM were in place. The G8 and the G20 were beginning to take African developmental issues seriously by listening more to African leaders rather than prescribing solutions for them. The Africa Partnership Forum (APF) was well established and managed the donor-recipient relationship in a more progressive way, as equal partners in the quest to develop the continent.

South Africa had just demonstrated its capacity to serve in the UN Security Council in a way that made a difference for developing and vulnerable countries, holding the line against the dictates of the powerful permanent members and making an effort to level the playing field in international relations.

Given all these developments, the sudden removal of Mbeki – at a crucial moment – was a shock to most African leaders. It took away one of their own brothers and impacted negatively on programmes which involved him or on which they were working with him. Many knew that the removal of Mbeki would weaken the advanced programme of building a solid African solidarity that would allow African countries the space to determine their own destiny instead of being dictated to by their former colonisers or those who wish to turn them into their proxy government. In fact, many Africans, especially the thought leaders on the continent, believe that if Mbeki were still there the crisis of Libya would not have been handled the way it was handled, which caused enormous pain to ordinary citizens of Libya. The reality, though, is that his term of office would have ended and he would have had to deal with the matter as a former president, as he tried to do without much success. But others argue that if he was not removed the way he was, his influence would have averted the disaster.

Those who followed political developments within the ANC were not surprised by the noises of those who wanted him to be removed earlier. There were dark, gathering clouds of resentment and disaffection by some within the party. Anything seemed possible after Polokwane if one took seriously these noises. But even then many of them did not expect this sudden and dramatic removal of Mbeki.

Many would agree that the clouds began gathering in June 2005, following Mbeki's use of his constitutional prerogative to release Zuma from his position as deputy president of the country. This became the rallying point for all those who were unhappy with Mbeki for whatever reason and saw his removal from the positions of president of the ANC and of the country as a solution. Polokwane was a culmination of this campaign against Mbeki, which had gathered momentum as many rallied against the charges of corruption levelled against Zuma.

Others go further back, to the allegations of a plot by Cyril Ramaphosa, Tokyo Sexwale and Mathews Phosa against Mbeki. For some reason this affected deputy president Zuma in a way that did not make sense to me, but nevertheless Zuma made a public statement denying that he had any presidential ambitions. Given that Mbeki and Zuma historically had a long close relationship, this was the first indication that something had gone wrong.

Some think that Mbeki's removal was associated with the HIV and AIDS matter. But the HIV and AIDS matter was resolved in 2003, and by 2008 South Africa had one of the best HIV and AIDS programmes, as I have referred to earlier.

The actual trigger for the removal of Mbeki was the flawed Nicholson judgment, which gave an opportunity for the removal of Mbeki at a moment when even the average member of the ANC least expected it. The Nicholson judgment linked Mbeki with the charges against Zuma, as well as said that Mbeki had interfered with the NPA processes to ensure that Zuma was charged. Nicholson also implicated cabinet members and even dragged me, the secretary of cabinet, into it.

It is now history that this judgment was later set aside by the SCA in Mangaung (Bloemfontein) as baseless. The SCA said that Nicholson failed to confine his judgment 'to the issues before the court; by deciding matters that were not germane or relevant; by creating new factual issues; by making gratuitous findings against persons who were not called upon to defend themselves; by failing to distinguish between allegation, fact and suspicion; and by transgressing the proper boundaries between judicial, executive and legislative functions'. The SCA went on to say that Nicholson let his personal opinions on matters cloud his judgment. Judges, the SCA said, are not 'entitled to inject their personal views into judgements or express their political preferences'.

But the damage was done and Mbeki had been removed from office. In this regard Judge Nicholson is reported to have said that he did not foresee that his judgment would lead to the removal of a president, but it did. His statement is also surprising because he should have known that the 'personal views' he was expressing in the form of a judgment that coincided with the accusations of those opposed to Mbeki would have dire consequences, especially when given the authority of a court of law.

After the meeting of the NEC of the ANC that decided on the recall of Mbeki, senior officials of the ANC made public statements to either explain or justify the basis of the decision, relying mainly on the faulty Nicholson judgment. I do not recall Mbeki, as a member of the ANC, being called to answer to the allegations levelled against him. Nicholson's judgment was considered sufficient basis for their action. Interestingly, one of the key aspects of the SCA's rebuttal of Nicholson was that he judged people who had not been given an opportunity to defend themselves. Using the Nicholson judgment to act against Mbeki violated the *audi alteram partem* rule, which is considered key to the justice system the ANC believed in. Interestingly, the legal minds within and outside the ANC were never heard to address this matter.

The more I think about and listen to those who campaigned for Mbeki's removal, the more I become convinced that his sudden and dramatic removal was not mainly about the fact and the way in which he had removed Zuma from cabinet, but about the fact that Zuma was charged and that they believed Mbeki was responsible. This is also what Nicholson declared, without evidence. Mainly they feared that as long as Mbeki was president the case would be reinstituted once the procedural flaws Nicholson had referred to were corrected.

The Nicholson judgment simply fuelled the fires which consumed the ANC with Mbeki as their main target. Their perspective was emotional and this emotion was the best tool for mobilisation. The solidarity presence at court appearances, the protest actions outside the court, the ugly songs about Mbeki and the burning of T-shirts and posters with his image all testify to this.

An indication of the extent to which the charges against Zuma were the driving factor was the setting up of a special operation to make sure that the case 'goes away'. The unseating of Mbeki became part of this project, as there was a feeling that as long as he was in office it would not be possible to execute the special operation successfully. A risk assessment found him to be the greatest risk to a project whose objectives had to be achieved within the seven months that he would still be president. For this reason he could not be allowed to remain in office.

Notwithstanding all the emotions, the anger and the bitterness against Mbeki before and after Polokwane, nothing could justify his immediate removal. The way he conducted himself, as indicated earlier, made it even more difficult to find a good reason to remove him from office.

There was also the challenge that the problems the party had with Mbeki were internal party matters and had nothing to do with the public. As his popularity was waning among some within the party, with the public, Africa and the world it was growing exponentially, especially within the continent and the developing world. The saying that 'a prophet has no honour in his house, his hometown or country' was proven to be true.

Even those matters which were considered by some as negative about Mbeki were behind him at that stage. But as fate would have it, a flawed judgment with the authority of a judge provided the emotional fuel for that fleeting moment that justified the action to get Mbeki out of the way immediately. Francis Thompson is credited for the expression 'the fairest things have fleetest end', but this was the ugliest thing that had the 'fleetest end', an end without a possibility of correction. Whatever other gripes people may have, Mbeki deserved a better fate.

CHAPTER 9

Conflating State and Party

A National Security Threat

One of the challenges we had to deal with in the new democratic government, which played itself fully during the crisis related to the removal of Mbeki, was the relationship between the state and the ruling party. The apparently natural tendency to want to conflate the two presented us with various challenges, including the risk of compromising the integrity of our democracy and the threat to the security of the state and its people.

The nature of the apartheid state, on the one hand, and the liberation movement's historical relationship with the state, on the other, were at the root of this challenge.

The apartheid state was a racially defined, white racist state designed to serve the interests of the white minority against those of the black majority and concerned itself with the security of the minority against that of the majority, who were excluded from the state. It was about a part of society and not about all the people of the country.

During the 46 years of National Party rule, the apartheid state became an embodiment of a racist ideology that constitutionally excluded the black majority from the central government. The police, the defence force, the public service, the prosecution authority, the courts, parliament – everything constituting what is understood as the state – were designed to guarantee the interests of the white minority against those of the black majority. At the time of the first non-racial democratic elections in 1994 the apartheid state was synonymous with the National Party and the party was in control of the state.

The apartheid state was similar to colonial states, which were designed to serve the interests of the colonialists or colonial power against those of the colonised. The only difference was that the apartheid state was a 'neo-colonial state of a special type', as it became known in the course of our struggle for liberation.

In a colonial state the colonial rulers are the state and the state is the colonial rulers. In a sense colonial rule was like a one-party state which allowed no democracy. It is no wonder that once they gained their independence, these post-colonial states became one-party states, in line with the colonial example. So despite the fact that some of the former colonial powers adopted a 'holier-than-thou' attitude to these post-independence one-party states, in fact these new governments merely reflected what the colonial states had been about. Similarly, many of the new leaders were simply good students of the colonialists.

For this reason, democracy as practised in the former Western colonial powers did not appeal to the post-colonial leaders. It was like asking someone to remove a speck in your eye whilst he or she has a lock in his or her eye. In the apartheid state the colonial masters were the racist minority, who treated black people like colonial subjects.

The April 1994 elections ushered in a new democratic government in a state to which the values of non-racialism, non-sexism, justice and democratic practice were foreign. It was like putting new wine into old wineskins – there was a risk that the skins would burst, the wine would spill and the wineskins be ruined. Accordingly, the state had to be transformed, and radically so.

Had there been a *coup d'état* the question of transformation would not have arisen – the apartheid state would simply have been replaced by an entirely new form of state. However, ours was a negotiated settlement and this dictated the route we took – that is, the transformation of the state as part of a transitional process from an apartheid society to a non-racial, non-sexist, just and democratic society.

Naturally, we expected that there would be resistance to this transformational process. Accordingly, we had to develop strategies and tactics to effect transformation rather than use unstrategic frontal attacks that would have elicited a potentially very violent response, costly in terms of human life. Among these strategies were regular critical assessments of the balance of forces within the country and internationally, which assisted us in determining the pace at which the transformation process could be carried out and the tactics to be used. The ultimate objective was to create a constitutional state where the rights of all South Africans were protected and guaranteed.

We had our own challenges as we did this. Our ideological perspectives of the state were a product of the nature of the struggle we had waged and of our historical experience. For almost half a century the white racist regime had ruled out any form of negotiations with the oppressed and exploited black majority. Peaceful protests and peaceful resistance were met with unbridled violence by the apartheid security forces. This forced the liberation movement to resort to the armed struggle as the only way to liberate the people from a brutal neo-colonial power.

The armed struggle meant establishing an army in exile with all that goes with it – that is, military intelligence, civilian intelligence, and so forth. It required a change in the nature and character of the liberation movement which now had to set itself up as a government in exile with a president who was the commander-in-chief of the armed forces.

This did not mean that all the other strategies used by the liberation movement were abandoned. It simply meant that these strategies without the armed struggle would not succeed.

The December 1994 *Strategy and Tactics* policy document of the ANC considered the 'armed struggle' or the 'underground armed resistance' to have been one of the four pillars of struggle during the period from 1961 to 1990. The other pillars were 'mass mobilisation' of the people not only to resist the system but to replace 'apartheid structures with structures of mass resistance and popular governance'; the building of underground structures of the movement inside and outside the country when the movement was prohibited, banned or operated under conditions of illegality; and the mobilisation of the international community not only to isolate the apartheid regime, whose policy was declared a 'crime against humanity', but also to mobilise resources for the liberation movement and have official representatives (ambassadors) of the movement where it was recognised. The international work included a campaign for comprehensive sanctions against the regime. These four pillars were utilised in 'an integrated manner' to ensure 'mutual reinforcement of one another'.

The paradigm shift in the life of the liberation movement to include armed struggle conceptually moved the movement from struggling to force the regime to negotiate with the legitimate leaders of the people to actually forcing it out of power. This is where the concept or slogan of 'seizure of power' came from. The *Strategy and Tactics* document explicitly says that 'the formation of

Umkhonto we Sizwe in 1961 ... placed on the agenda the *seizure of power* by the people from the white minority regime' (my emphasis). This concept envisaged, in a sense, the collapse of the apartheid state and its replacement by a non-racial, non-sexist, democratic state. Accordingly, as we entered the politics of negotiations, 'seizure of power' lingered in our subconscious minds.

There was also the challenge of the popular view that the ANC was the 'parliament of the people'. Indeed, when the ANC was formed in 1912 it was considered to be the 'parliament of the people' as blacks were excluded from the Union government and its apartheid parliament, which had been constituted in 1910 after what was called the Anglo-Boer War.

There is an interesting legend about the Union Buildings – the seat of government in Pretoria, Tshwane. Unfortunately, I left government before I could establish its factual basis. The story is told that a third wing was designed but was never built. It is said that the architect of the Union Buildings, Herbert Baker, felt that it wasn't appropriate to build the third wing since it represented the missing African majority.

The painful aspect of this Union between the English and the Afrikaners, which excluded the black majority, was that it came after what was then called the Anglo-Boer War. This was not just a war between the English and the Afrikaners; it included blacks, many of whom died in combat or in supporting roles. Many more suffered and some died in the concentration camps established by the British army. This is why the new democratic government re-named it the South Africa War.

The representations by the African leadership to the British about their exclusion from the Union government fell on deaf ears, as might be expected of a colonial power. As a result the ANC became the only organisation that represented black interests. The movement included all Africans, irrespective of their areas of origin within the country, their language, traditions or culture. It is out of this reality that the concept of the 'parliament of the people' arose, especially because there were no rival groups at the time. This is where the demon of tribalism was buried in South Africa.

Following the overwhelming victory of the ANC in the 1994 elections, the concept of the 'parliament of the people' became a reality as all other contesting parties (apart from the National Party) were reduced to insignificant minorities. In the next ten years the ANC's support in elections grew from just less than two-thirds (62.65 per cent) of the vote to 70 per cent in 2004.

Although the Interim Constitution, which provided for a Government of National Unity, constrained the new government in terms of the possibility of radically transforming the apartheid state, it did not challenge the view of the ANC as a 'parliament of the people', especially among the party's older members.

The need to transform the state raised the question of what a state is about. In normal democratic countries an election might change the government but it would not change the state. As Matthew Arnold wrote, 'the State is properly ... the nation in its collective and corporate capacity'. Using this definition one might say the state is about the totality of the nation or country. In fact, the word 'state' is used interchangeably with the word 'country'.

The state is about its people and their welfare. And its people means all its people and not just a particular group or sector. The welfare of an entire people also includes that of foreigners within its borders. It is about the government and the services it offers its people. It is about parliament or the elected representatives of the people. It is about the judiciary and the justice system. A state is a sovereign, self-governing political entity that is the totality of all these elements and represents the people internationally. The capitalised form of State emphasises the authority, sovereignty, or official character of a nation, according to the *World Book Dictionary*.

In a constitutional state like South Africa the Constitution defines how the state is constituted and how it functions. The 'founding provisions' of the Constitution of South Africa describe 'The Republic of South Africa' as 'one, sovereign, democratic state founded' on 'values' outlined in Section 1(a)–(d) of the Constitution. It provides for a 'Head of State' and a 'Head of the National Executive' in the form of the president of the country who is responsible for promoting 'the unity of the nation and that which will advance the Republic' (s 83[c]). As head of the state the president is expected constitutionally to be an expression of the unity of the nation, rather than an expression of narrow political interests.

The president is also expected to 'advance' the interests of 'the Republic' rather than just those of the party or, worse, more a faction of a party. That is why our Constitution was designed in a way that anyone elected president cannot remain a member of parliament. Once elected as president, one has to resign from parliament.

During the thirteen and a half years that I was in government we grappled with the subtle difference between the role of the president as head of state and that of head of government. There were times when the president acted as head of state and there were times when he acted as head of government. There were also times when he acted as the president of his political party, the ANC. In this regard the presidents I served under – Mandela, Mbeki and Motlanthe – had great respect for the Constitution and also respected the subtle differences between party and government activity and between the state and the (ruling) party.

I also had the opportunity to serve under Zuma between 1999 and 2005, when he was deputy president of the country, and he, too, worked within this framework or construct. Mbeki, whom I served under all the time I was in government, was always ahead of us in differentiating between the different roles the president had to play. He had an extraordinary mind and the sensitivity to ensure that the different roles were never confused or conflated. There was a clear understanding that the party was not the state, just as the state was not the party. In fact it would be unconstitutional to conflate the two.

Another way of dealing with this complex concept is to say what the state is not. It is not about a particular government, although the government of a sovereign state is a part of the state and represents the state internationally. The state is also not the ruling party, although the ruling party is part of it through the government of the day. Not only does the Constitution differentiate clearly between the party and the state, it also draws a clear distinction between parliament, the executive and the judiciary. It was designed to avoid exactly what the National Party was in relation to the apartheid state and it was in this context that the apartheid state had to be transformed. The historical 1994 *Strategy and Tactics* document of the ANC considers the transformation and restructuring of the organs of 'state power' as constituting 'one of the most important tasks in the process of broadening and consolidating the national democratic settlement'.

The qualitative changes in this respect had to reflect the 'national character and social content' of our country; the affirmation of deprived social classes; the affirmation and promotion of gender equality; and the 'democratisation' of all 'organs of state power'. This involved restructuring and transforming the machinery of state at all levels, covering areas of the public service, the judiciary, the armed forces, the police and correctional services and the intelligence services in order to 'guarantee the defence of the constitution, protection of citizens of the country, protection of public and private property and the preservation of the *integrity of the state*' (my emphasis).

While many of these objectives were achieved within the first term of democratic governance, changes within the judiciary have taken longer to achieve. The qualitative changes referred to above are also still a subject of the national discourse.

Given the high level of understanding of the nature of the state and its transformation and the concern about its integrity, one would have thought it would be easier to preserve the constitutional design. In practice, or what I call 'in real life', this was not always the case. Firstly, the history of the liberation movement in exile is that of a government in exile, with its own army and intelligence services, which fought a war against the apartheid regime. The president of the liberation movement was the commander-in-chief of the armed forces, and the intelligence services reported to him via the relevant heads of intelligence and the head of the army (Umkhonto we Sizwe) or its intelligence chief.

We who worked underground in the country also considered ourselves subject to the command system of the movement and ultimately reported directly or indirectly to the president of the ANC, at the time Comrade O.R. Tambo. Those of us who had assumed public leadership roles in one form or another, or in one organisation or another, also considered ourselves as being under the command of the leadership of the movement to advance the course of the struggle.

One example, which may appear to be of no consequence but had the potential to reach a crisis point and lead to loss of life, involved a courier who was caught between the internal underground and the external mission of the ANC. A courier was sent to Lusaka to collect money for a particular operation. The courier came back empty-handed as the source had said that there was no arrangement for such funds. No one believed the courier and there were suspicions that he might have embezzled the funds. The courier appealed to me to intervene, as he feared for his life. I contacted the Lusaka headquarters of the ANC via underground structures and established that the courier had indeed not received the funds, as the matter was being handled by a different arm of the ANC. This saved his life.

Another, more dramatic event was the first direct call from Tambo asking me to help resolve the matter of members of the so-called Mandela United Football Club stationed at Comrade Winnie Madikizela-Mandela's house, who were alleged to have disappeared or been killed. The case is well known and one does not need to elaborate, except to say that I had to go to the house to convey the message from the president of the ANC and, on his instructions, to remain there until I found the children or got leads to find them. This I did.

Many stories like this could be told, but these examples should suffice to make the point that during the liberation struggle cadres of the movement reported to one senior comrade or another and this chain of command continued beyond the April 1994 democratic elections. Even when new command structures were developed within government, or comrades were placed within specific command structures in government, the reporting lines to commanders within the liberation movement remained in place either because of a long-standing tradition or because there was uncertainty about whether or not the new political settlement would survive.

Operation Vula, meaning 'opening the way', was a classic example. This underground operation, initiated in the late 1980s to facilitate the process of infiltrating the leadership of the movement into the country, strengthened lines of communication between ANC in exile and the internal underground structures of the movement. It also strengthened communications between Oliver Tambo in Lusaka and Nelson Mandela, who was still in prison. After Mandela was released and the negotiations process started, Operation Vula continued.

It is history that the apartheid government chose a strategic moment at which it arrested the operatives of Operation Vula and its command structures, while we were in the middle of the negotiation process. This created tensions within the movement regarding the way in which this matter was handled and some comrades still remain aggrieved.

There was also the project to transform the state, which was moving at its own pace, causing some comrades to maintain the old command structures until they were confident about the sustainability of the process. This tendency had to be phased out as confidence built in the new democratic order and comrades were expected to report within the structures of government, if they were deployed within the government.

But some never stopped, continuing without any feeling of guilt to report to one leader or another in the liberation movement, whether or not that was outside of government structures and institutions. This was their liberation movement, which superseded the state, and their loyalty was to the party and not to the state. No oath, law or regulatory framework to protect the secrets of the state will deter such people from passing information to their former commanders and comrades.

The same was happening on the part of the apartheid security forces, whose elaborate security management systems and structures continued operating into the new South Africa as insurance in case the negotiated arrangements did not hold. Some may even have believed that it would not hold. Many of the structures, systems and individuals involved were part of the covert operations of the apartheid regime. Since much of this was decentralised and delegated to individuals, the risk of some continuing outside the official command structures was very high.

Some retired, taking with them files to ensure that they could defend themselves if they were charged in the future. I would imagine that some of those who retired at a senior level had subordinates reporting to them for a while. One example of old-order forces participating in a project which could easily have destabilised the state and the country was the Meiring Report of February 1998.

George Meiring, who was head of the SANDF, presented a report to President Nelson Mandela concerning an organisation calling itself Front African People's Liberation Army. According to the report there was a plot to assassinate the president, murder judges, occupy parliament and broadcasting stations, and cause chaos. On investigation the report proved to be fabricated.

South Africans must count themselves lucky to have gone through this period which was fraught with uncertainty and risk, without any major incidents occurring. Since the country is predominantly religious, many would attribute this to God's providence. Some would attribute it to a commitment on both sides to make things work and not to allow wayward characters to destabilise the peace process or the political settlement. Others would credit the desire of the majority of South Africans, tired of violence and conflict, for peace at any price. Whatever the case, we must count ourselves extremely fortunate.

We must also count ourselves lucky that South Africa – old or new – does not have a culture of coups; that professional members of the security forces have a respect for the law and the Constitution of the country. As a result everyone understood that no amount of agitation could move the disciplined armed forces to engage in acts of illegality. No commander of any security service could order any member of the services to obey a 'manifestly illegal order' (s 199[6]) as it would itself be 'manifestly illegal'.

Our Constitution was designed to produce this effect. That is why I had no concerns that our security forces would behave other than in terms of the Constitution during the time we were dealing with the crisis of the removal of Mbeki from office. At an appropriate time Mbeki interacted with the security forces, and at the appropriate time, when it became necessary, the acting chief of the SANDF called me for advice once the president had resigned.

This is the treasure of this country, of which no one should rob us because of their own political or personal interests. No individual within the forces and no politician should be allowed to corrupt our professional forces. Constitutionally the security services are expected 'to act ... to teach and require their members to act, in accordance with the Constitution and the law' (s 199[5]).

Although we survived this risky period, the issue of divided loyalties between the party and the state lingered on among both the members of the apartheid regime and the cadres of the movement. Is one's loyalty to the state or to the party or individuals one reported to before 1994? For me the question was easy to answer because it is meaningless. The party I am loyal to was responsible for delivering the new democratic government, a democratic state with a new Constitution which should govern every citizen's behaviour. In this regard I have no difficulty in giving my loyalty to the government and my respect to the democratic Constitution which the party that I have loyalty to put in place and is responsible for. This I do and will continue doing for as long as the government continues also to act within the parameters of the Constitution.

I also do not have difficulty being loyal to the state I participated in transforming to ensure that it properly represented the South African nation 'in its collective and corporate capacity', in the words of Matthew Arnold. We also made sure that it was accountable, responsive and open to the needs of the people (s 1[d]). This I will do and continue doing as long as the values enshrined in the Constitution are not violated or compromised.

However, the party I am loyal to cannot require me to violate or compromise the Constitution or the integrity of the state, which represents the collective interests of all the people of South Africa. For this is what we struggled and many paid a price for, even unto death. In fact this is where one should once again take a stand and be ready to die in defence of the gains of our revolution. Like members of the security services, I am also required to resist any 'manifestly illegal order' from anyone, including the president of the country or my party.

These are critical principles if we are to defend our revolution and ensure that the state and its government, parliament and the judiciary maintain their integrity and respect the values that are enshrined in our Constitution.

Between 2003 and 2010, the ANC entered the stormiest waters it had encountered since returning from exile and, like any ship battling for such a long time, it runs the risk of being wrecked. We are lucky we are still floating, and the sooner we get out of the storm the better: firstly, to be able to repair the ship; secondly, in order for the party of revolution to salvage the incomplete national democratic revolution and pursue it further; thirdly, for the sake of the people of South Africa, who desperately depend on it to ensure a better life for all; and fourthly, for the rest of the African continent, which has regarded the ANC and South Africa as beacons of hope for the future of the continent.

We all hope that the rescue strategies that have been put in place will enable the ANC to reconsolidate and repair the damage caused during these turbulent years. As I completed this book I had a serious concern that the strategies put in place by those who are in leadership were unravelling and were beginning to worry the people of this country.

During this period (2003–10) the principles referred to above were tested to the limit. Once the prosecuting authorities decided to charge Schabir Shaik with corruption, which could implicate the deputy president, albeit remotely, we knew (at least I did) that we were entering stormy waters with all their attendant risks.

I visited the president to indicate my anxiety about this development and how it would affect not only the presidency and the government but the ANC itself. I also wanted him to know that I intended to discuss the matter with the deputy president to work out strategies for handling the situation.

What followed is a long story but what was important was the way I, as director-general in the presidency and secretary of cabinet, would be expected to handle this new development. Firstly, it was agreed that the matter arising out of the Schabir Shaik case was unrelated to the presidency, as it concerned the period before the deputy president was appointed. But we also agreed that although the case was not about the presidency and did not relate to any work in the presidency, it would still affect the presidency in the public eye and thus communications strategies had to be devised.

The more challenging aspects of this development, though, were at party level and in the realm of public perceptions. To the general public it would appear that the president, as head of state and head of the national executive, might have been involved in making the decision to charge Shaik in a case that could affect his own deputy president. Some ANC cadres who understood these matters better were of the view that even if the president was not responsible for preferring the charges against Shaik, he could have used his powers to prevent or stop the prosecution or quash the case. At the extreme end, some believed the president was directly responsible.

Although Mbeki and Zuma were adamant that there was no problem between them, one could sense undeclared tension which was building up and began, gradually, to affect our work in the presidency. As the director-general I asked for two things from both principals. The first was that as they were long-term friends and comrades, they should agree on how they would deal with this situation. I also recommended that their normal weekly meetings should be kept in their diaries without fail.

My second request was that in the midst of all this my loyalty to both of them and to the state should never be questioned. As long as they were still president and deputy president I would be obliged to remain loyal to them in all circumstances, as long as it was within the law and according to the Constitution. I asked that I should not be expected to take sides, as I would not be able to execute my responsibilities if I did so and I would have to resign.

Fortunately, both of them agreed. In fact, the deputy president said I could not serve the president and be disloyal to him. He (the deputy president) expected me to continue being loyal to the president as a matter of principle.

The second challenge was that the DSO, comprising the Scorpions, and the NPA wanted original copies of the disclosure documents of the deputy president, in terms of the Executive Ethics Act in the Shaik case. I indicated to them that I was not empowered by the law to release the confidential side of the disclosure documents of any member of the executive. In any case, we did not have the original copies. Unfortunately, media reports about this short affidavit would suggest to the ordinary member of the ANC that I was involved in the case in some way. But one had to do one's job as long as one remained secretary of the cabinet.

The next challenge was a letter Zuma had sent to parliament in his capacity as leader of government business in the National Assembly (s 91[4] of the Constitution) about government's Arms Procurement Programme (which the media calls the 'arms deal'), of which I had to confirm the authenticity. For some unknown reason, the court chose to disregard the fact that the letter was from the presidency, representing government's position on the Arms Procurement Programme, instead assuming that the letter was a personal one from Zuma. Unfortunately, this has been used to suggest that the presidency had compromised the deputy president by making him sign that letter. This is far from the truth, as the presidency has always owned up to that letter; that it came from government and expressed the views of government, and that Zuma signed it on behalf of government and not on his own behalf.

Then there was the matter of payments for the defence costs in the Zuma case. We had to decide whether or not the case deserved the support of the presidency in terms of the law and, as advised by the state attorneys, decided that it did. The accounts were managed by the state attorneys and all queries were handled by them, but whenever there was a disagreement about accounting and payment it was reported as though the presidency was refusing to pay. There is a responsibility to account for taxpayers' monies and the state attorneys had to do that on our behalf with reports that met the requirements of the accounting officer in the presidency and ultimately the auditor-general.

One matter which occasioned serious differences in approach was the question of an appeal against the Nicholson judgment, which had drawn what were considered to be unfounded conclusions about people who had been given no opportunity to defend themselves. These included members of President Mbeki's cabinet and myself, secretary of cabinet. Cabinet decided to appeal despite the fact that the ANC-related committee appointed to deal with the case believed it should not do so. The logic, I imagine, was that the judgment was good for Zuma and the ANC (as they understood it) and should thus not be overturned. The problem with this position was that the judgment was bad for the president of the country and his cabinet, who were members of the ANC as well.

In any case, the more appropriate response was that every citizen, including members of the ANC, had the constitutional right to appeal against a judgment if they felt that justice had not been done, and it was on this basis that the cabinet had made its decision, which angered some within the ANC. When I was asked about this matter as secretary of the cabinet, I advised that only cabinet could rescind the decision and that as long as it stood in the cabinet minutes I was obliged to execute it. And indeed, when the attorneys acting for the government asked for an affidavit to confirm cabinet's decision I had to give it, notwithstanding the wishes of some in my party.

An emotional meeting was held to discuss this matter and again to try to persuade me to withdraw my affidavit, but there was no basis for me to do so. If a court wanted to confirm whether cabinet had made the decision, it was the secretary of cabinet who was duty-bound to depose an affidavit. This was not a question of loyalty to one or other official of the ANC or a question of a choice between the party I am loyal to and the cabinet I am legally required to serve to the best of my ability within the law and in terms of the Constitution. The only issue was about what the law and what the Constitution required me to do. Anything else would border on corruption of the law to serve the interests of some members of the party.

If this level of corruption of the system had been achieved, it would mean that the integrity of the state would have been totally compromised and a faction in a party or another entity would effectively have taken control of the state. This would be the birth of a dictatorship or a country controlled by a mafia. The Italian Mafia, which ended up corrupting or compromising the police, the prosecutors, the judges and the political leadership to have their way or avoid being brought to justice, comes into mind in this regard.

The Constitution is very clear about where our loyalty should be. One of the key values and principles governing public administration is that 'a high standard of professional ethics must be promoted and maintained' (s 195[a]) and that 'services must be provided impartially, fairly, equitably and without bias' (s 195[d]). Any party interest would have to be 'legitimate in terms of the Constitution' in order to be considered.

As I worked with comrades during these difficult times, it became clear to me that some of them really had no respect for the law, being prepared, in pursuit of their own interests, to break the law or violate the Constitution. This attitude applied, too, to sharing classified information with comrades who did not have legitimate access to such information. These comrades believe that the laws of secrecy apply only to those outside their faction or party. It felt as though they were still operating in exile against an apartheid regime and were therefore entitled to defy or violate the law.

Such an attitude threatens the security and integrity of the state. Once officials in sensitive areas such as the police, the military and the intelligence services feel that they are at liberty to violate the laws of secrecy and share information with unauthorised people, the state and its people are at great risk, especially where party factions are involved.

In an ordinary criminal case it is easier to understand the threat occasioned by such behaviour. The investigating officer cannot pass information directly or indirectly to the targets of the investigation. To do so would be 'defeating the ends of justice', which is a criminal offence. If I am placed in a position of responsibility within the security system of the state and I come across information that my own brother or sister is about to be arrested for criminal activity, I cannot, by law, tell them in order for them to remove evidence or make sure they are out of reach. If I do so I will not only have broken the law or defeated the ends of justice, I will be involved in corrupting and compromising the justice system and thereby the state.

This is even worse in the case of organised crime, which thrives by compromising targets who are likely to interfere with their criminal activities. If the perpetrators succeed in compromising senior enough people, they may put themselves in a position to determine who will investigate a particular case to make sure that it is quashed or does not succeed in court. The 1988 bombing of Khotso House, the headquarters of the SACC, was a classic example, with the security police officer who instigated the bombing acting as investigating officer for the case. The outcome was the arrest and torture of innocent comrades such as Shirley Gunn, while the actual perpetrators continued to be part of the law enforcement agencies.

At the highest levels organised crime syndicates also buy or compromise prosecutors, magistrates and judges. They have such developed intelligence systems that they infiltrate the police, the justice system and political principals to ensure that their projects succeed. In governments where the military is active in the internal affairs of the country, they, too, are compromised.

In the worst-case scenario the whole of the cabinet and its president are compromised and syndicates operate without any fear. At this point the citizens of that country have lost their government, since the government now serves the interests of a particular syndicate or mafia and not those of the people. Businesses, too, may compromise key political players to ensure that the government serves their interests at the expense of the people.

The same strategies are used by foreign countries with interests in a particular country. Where they have a long-term plan, foreign intelligence services compromise or recruit up-and-coming leaders to ensure that by the time they take the reins of power they are already at their service. In some instances they even invest money, intelligence support, and so on to ensure that their candidate wins a perfectly democratic election. The result is proxy governments that serve the interest of other forces or countries and not their own people. This is what happened in some independent countries where post-colonial powers became proxy governments to their former colonisers.

Corrupt intelligence services are the most dangerous threat to the security and integrity of the state, the country and its people. In South Africa complex factors made it particularly challenging to get a handle on corrupt systems of intelligence. After the 1994 elections some members of the old-order intelligence community retired, some to start security companies, others to establish specialised consultancy or advisory companies focusing on security advisory services, or risk analysis or assessment.

Some of these companies offered their services to the new democratic government, while others offered them to foreign governments, business entities or multinationals. Although some of these were legitimate business concerns, others operated as disguised intelligence organisations or intelligence-gathering entities, which fell outside the provisions of section 209(1) of the Constitution. In terms of this section 'any intelligence service ... may be established *only* by the President ... and *only* in terms of national legislation' (my emphasis). This means that even the president cannot have his or her own intelligence service that is not established in terms of the national legislation, which effectively prohibits personal militias.

Many of these people were still in contact with their colleagues in the official intelligence services and exchanged intelligence information with them. Some were still handlers of some of the sources used by the intelligence-collection systems, and still others had members of the intelligence community reporting to them outside the legal and constitutional framework of the country.

We also had historically compromised members of the liberation movement who were obliged to work with the old-order intelligence operatives who were their handlers. Once these cadres were strategically placed in the new government, the old handlers returned and, using blackmail and other means, caused them to serve their interests in one form or another. One former MK cadre, for instance, was given a job at a critical level of government where he used an official vehicle. His old handlers asked him to help them 'clean up' stolen vehicles by securing official documents and he obliged, using the cover of the official vehicle. In some cases the handlers became the handled and the handled became the handlers.

Some were compromised during or after the negotiated settlement which led to the 1994 democratic elections. Yet others compromised themselves by engaging in criminal activities or acts of corruption which made them susceptible to blackmail. In a strange way, after the April 1994 democratic elections we began to have corrupt old-order and corrupt new-order operatives who worked together to further mutual interests which either had criminal intent or, at worst, a political intent which became a threat to the security of the state.

The most worrying of these operations were those which also worked with foreign governments and foreign intelligence agencies. It was not surprising that false intelligence information was fed into the system to destabilise either government or the ruling party. Innocent people with integrity were framed to neutralise them and create space for further criminal activities both within and outside of government. The Browse Mole Report, a top-secret report, produced by elements within the DSO, which claimed that Jacob Zuma was involved in a conspiracy to topple President Thabo Mbeki's government, was a classic case of destabilisation of government and the ruling party and clearly involved both old-and new-order functionaries. Strangely, a copy of this document was sent to COSATU from whence it surfaced in public. Time will tell how all this happened.

A reading of this document left one with no doubt that the reasons for its production and for leaking it to the media were, firstly, to intensify the divisions within the ANC that were playing themselves out at the time and, secondly, to create an atmosphere of suspicion within government, thus destabilising its activities.

The dramatic story which purportedly implicated businessmen Cyril Ramaphosa and Tokyo Sexwale and the then premier of Mpumalanga, Mathews Phosa, in a supposed conspiracy is one of those mysteries which, for me, formed part of the disinformation projects intended to destabilise government and the ruling party. Both the ANC and government were forced to respond to the story, and there is no doubt in my mind that the first seeds of the debilitating tensions within the ANC stemmed from this time.

The most devastating of the projects run by corrupted old- and new-order intelligence operatives were the fake e-mails the details of which have been dealt with in an earlier chapter. It was a well-planned project with the clear intention of discrediting a selected set of leaders of the ANC, both within and outside government, and influencing and changing the views of targeted leaders about specific events of the time to achieve specific political objectives. They were clearly meant not only to sow distrust and the seeds of dissension among the leaders of the movement but to destabilise the remaining pillars of the movement to be able to bring it down.

I personally pursued this matter to get to the roots of it. I engaged the president of the country, who was also then president of the party, to find out where this material had come from. I interacted with the police and the intelligence services and, at a party level, I held a number of meetings with Motlanthe, then secretary-general of the ANC, to find out who was responsible for these fake e-mails. My attempts included a formal letter of protest addressed to the six officials of the ANC (that is, the president, the deputy president, the national chairperson, the secretary-general, the deputy secretary-general and the treasurer-general) and a plea to the leadership to deal with this matter. To date I have not received a response or even acknowledgement from them, except for Mbeki, who I was able to talk to directly at the Union Buildings.

It is a matter of record that both the government and the ANC investigated the matter and that the investigations led to a number of court cases. To date, however, we are no wiser about the origins of the e-mails or how they found their way into the hands of the organisation. The only thing we were told was that an 'unknown person' dropped 'a brown envelope' at Luthuli House which contained the e-mails. One would have thought that no one would act on information that was brought by faceless people, but the information was used and it had a devastating impact on the party. Unfortunately, for now we have to accept that only time will tell who was responsible.

The reality, though, is that whoever conceived this intelligence project and recruited the agents to carry it out from the early part of 2005 achieved his or her objective – broken relationships and a fragmented party. What is more worrying to me is that this was clearly a joint project between the old- and new-order intelligence services. Their intentions were different but were sufficiently compromised to allow them to collaborate. Some worked with some of the leadership or were commanded by people at a leadership level.

The risk to the security of the state occasioned by comrades who believed there was nothing illegal about reporting to outside entities was compounded by divisions within the movement, since information of that nature might be used by ANC factions to advance sectarian interests. If this tendency is not checked, it is a dangerous recipe for development of a culture of coups, which we should not allow to take root.

At a criminal level, corrupted and corrupt intelligence operatives have used strategies of diversion and decoys to ensure that the real criminals are never caught. In some cases corrupt elements from crime intelligence have run their own car-theft syndicates while successfully breaking other such syndicates. Through their successes they convinced their seniors that they were effective, thus creating a cover for their own criminal activities. An investigation of car-theft syndicates in Soweto revealed two or more levels within the syndicates, one of them run by corrupt crime intelligence operatives and police.

The Brett Kebble murder case is for me the best case study on how syndicates operate to ensure that at the end everyone who was involved goes home scot-free. At worst, it is the innocent who

ultimately go to jail. Money also creates different classes of criminals, with the poorer going to jail and the richer going scot-free.
The case of Zola Roberts Tongo in the Anni Dewani murder case
matter is an example. A plea-bargain agreement was reached and
Tongo is serving eighteen years in jail, while the Kebble killers and
their accomplices did not only do the same, but were accused of
more serious crimes and they walked!

The experiences detailed above indicate the level of vulnerability
of countries and their people where state organs are compromised
to serve the interests of individuals, interest groups or factions. An
extensive cleaning-up operation is required to protect the people
against such deviant behaviour. In addition, the international governance system is as vulnerable as its various constituent countries.
Because crime syndicates have a global reach, a global strategy is
required to deal with them.

PART THREE

Mbeki's Legacy

CHAPTER 10

Mbeki

The Kwame Nkrumah Way

In November 2009, just over a year after Mbeki, the visionary for the renewal of the African continent, was removed from office, I attended a CAFRAD forum of secretaries of cabinet and experts on Africa. CAFRAD – the Centre Africain de Formation et de Recherche Administratives pour le Développement – is an African training and research centre in administration for development, based in Tangier, Morocco.

The meeting was held at the Continental Hotel in Tangier, about 400 kilometres north of Casablanca. On a clear day one can see from here the Strait of Gibraltar, a reminder of my secondary school days when we had to remember the location of the Strait for examination purposes. If one lifted one's eyes further, one could see the coast of Europe. Indeed, the reach of the eye brought to mind the centuries-old, painful symbiotic relationship between Africa and Europe – a love-hate relationship of slavery, colonial exploitation, oppression, racism and dependency – in a startling way.

Although the theme of the CAFRAD forum was 'The Role of Governmental Institutions in Responding to the Global Economic and Financial Crisis', ultimately the discussion ended up being about the weak state institutions and governmental structures in Africa, which made it a challenge to respond effectively and in a collective way to this crisis. Poverty made Africa more vulnerable. Many of the countries did not have the resources to mitigate against the challenges of the global economic and financial crisis. Some said that South Africa was able to do what I had described in my presentation because of its economic muscle, including its independent budget management and financial resources. Many of these countries depended on budget support from the donor countries. Accordingly the scope of their independent thinking was constrained by the need for any strategies devised to meet with the consent of their donor partners, since they would have to fund them. In the worst-case scenario the donor simply dictates what decisions the country can make in the face of a crisis.

It is this symbiotic relationship between Africa and its former colonial masters that these African intellectuals and public servants reflected on, including the decolonisation struggles of Africa and the challenges that post-independence Africa faced over the past 50 years or so. But they also acknowledged that some of the woes of Africa were of its own making and they discussed the need for Africa to reverse this lamentable history.

This discussion reminded me of my pain at the Kennedy School of Government, Harvard University, about eighteen years ago, where Africa was discussed as a 'footnote' in the textbooks or case studies we used. It was a forgotten continent, of no consequence in the global political and economic discourse. I became convinced that our first task in the renewal of the African continent was to remove Africa from the footnotes of the discourse of the world community and make it the centre thereof. To achieve this we had to move beyond the experiences of the past centuries (that is, centuries of slavery, colonisation, proxy governments and client states, and just downright failures of our people and leaders) which defined the Africa of today. We needed to redefine and renew Africa through our deeds rather than just theorise about it. In the language of old, we would have called this a 'revolutionary act' aimed at a 'revolutionary change' of the continent. For us to make a real difference here we would need to be brutally honestly, surgically radical, and strategic in our approach but bold and fearless.

The African Renaissance vision leading to NEPAD was one of the key programmes aimed at achieving this objective. It is accepted that President Thabo Mbeki was the key driver of this vision within South Africa, on the continent and in the rest of the world, although he would modestly not say so. It took about five years (1996–2001) to go through the consultative processes, first within South Africa (1996–1999) and then with African leaders (1999–2001), to make this a real African vision for the new millennium. At the dawn of the 21st century, African leaders were able to boldly proclaim that the new millennium must be an African Millennium. As part of this process the OAU (Organisation of African Unity) was transformed into the AU (African Union) with better institutions and structures to carry out this new vision for the renewal of Africa.

As Africa discussed the strategies to renew the African continent, it became clear that they needed to mobilise the global community to change its view about Africa and shed its Afropessimism, as well as make sure that no one made decisions affecting Africans without Africa's participation or without considering its views. It is for this reason that the African leadership decided to engage with the G8 countries at the Okinawa Summit in Japan, in 2000. At the 2000 Togo Summit of the OAU, a decision was made that a collective of the leadership of the OAU, NAM (Non-Aligned Movement) and the G77 plus China should attend the G8 meeting and raise the concerns of Africa as well as share their vision about the African continent. The leadership of the three organisations at the time consisted of President Bouteflika of Algeria (OAU chair), President Mbeki (NAM chair) and President Obasanjo of Nigeria (chair of the Group of 77).

The conveners of the Okinawa G8 meeting found it difficult to accommodate the African delegation at their meetings, since there was no precedent to this. I personally remember the frantic, tough telephonic discussions between some of the presidents who were part of the African delegation and the leaders of the G8 countries. This resulted in a compromise arrangement for the African leaders to interact with the G8 countries without necessarily becoming part of their formal meetings. Since then, no meeting of the G8 countries has been held without the participation of the African leadership. In a sense, African leaders forced their way into the G8 meeting of the rich countries to make sure that the concerns of Africa become part of the agenda.

Although these meetings are structured like bilateral meetings between the G8 and African countries, the input made impacts effectively on the decisions of the G8. Later, representatives of all the other continents were invited to participate, resulting in the formidable forum of the G8 with countries such as China, India, Brazil, South Africa, Mexico, and others, depending on who hosted the G8 meeting. There is also now a debate on the need for a G13 structure in the place of the G8 countries. This is based on the realisation that the G8 countries can no longer make decisions about world economic issues without the participation of key developing countries such as China, India, Brazil, South Africa and Mexico. The economic and financial crises in the USA and Europe have made this reality even clearer.

The struggle to renew the African continent as well as change the relationship between the North and South, or the developed and the developing (or less-developed) countries, also resulted in the establishment of the APF in 2003 in the wake of the Evian G8 Summit, as part of the NEPAD processes. The APF is a high-powered forum of African leaders and leaders of the developed countries, including strategically placed bilateral and multilateral institutions and organisations. It consists of heads of state or government of NEPAD; the chairperson of the AU; heads of the AU regional economic communities (RECs); the head of the African Development Bank (ADB); heads of state or government of Africa's principal industrialised-country development partners; the president of the European Commission; and heads of selected international institutions, including the UN and the United Nations Development Programme (UNDP) and the Economic Commission for Africa (ECA), International Monetary Fund (IMF), the World Bank, the WTO and the Organisation for Economic Development (OECD).

Its establishment was part of a concerted effort to broaden the high-level dialogue between the G8 and African leaders and develop it into a mature partnership between Africa and the developed world. According to the APF website, the commitment of APF members is to 'work together as *equals* in the forum' (my emphasis) with the objective of turning the age-old negative traditional 'donor-recipient' relationship, a relic of the colonial and neo-colonial era, into a partnership of equals. The forum meets twice each year and is co-chaired on an alternating basis by representatives of the AU and NEPAD on the one hand, and on the other by G8 and non-G8 OECD member countries.

The point is that a titanic battle was waged to ensure that Africa is the centre of all discussions that have an impact on her or the world within which she has to live. The recent effort to deal with the global economic and financial crisis reinforces this point. The developed countries could not meet alone, as in the past, and make decisions which impact on the global community. In fact, they could not address this crisis without the participation of Africa, however limited and unsatisfactory this representation was.

All the meetings dealing with the global economic and financial crisis – whether in the form of the G20 or otherwise – included South Africa, because of the size of its economy on the African continent. This was not satisfactory, as this representation was not necessarily formally sanctioned by African countries. South Africa tried to consult other African countries through the meetings of finance ministers, but many African countries felt that they should also have been included directly, and rightfully so.

* * *

At the CAFRAD forum one could sense that we would end up reflecting on the leadership of the continent. With two Ghanaians represented in the meeting – and having just celebrated a half-century of independence a year earlier – we could not but reflect on the pioneering and heroic leadership of Kwame Nkrumah, his vision for Africa, and his daring positions that took seriously the independence of Ghana and the need for the rest of the continent to be free. Nkrumah's sin, which resulted in him being dramatically removed from government and ending up dying tragically in exile, was to toil with radical ideas and models for Africa that risked negating the Western world-view of the time, one coloured by unfortunate colonial overhangs.

During a lunch-hour discussion, one of the Ghanaian intellectuals returned to the pain related to the removal of Kwame Nkrumah and how this tragic event continues to haunt Ghana to this day. This discussion reminded me of our last state visit to Ghana with President Mbeki. The government of Ghana arranged for our delegation to visit the memorial sites for Kwame Nkrumah, which had been established only after his death in exile as part of the process of corrective measures and reparation. As the guides led us through the shrines you could feel the tension and the consciousness underlying the presentation. There was a deep feeling that a great injustice had been done to one of the greatest heroes of Ghana and a great son of the African continent. The feeling of guilt was palpable in the silence.

Our interlocutor from Ghana repeatedly said that those who distort history must remember that their lie will only last for their lifetime or while they still have power to suppress the truth. This discussion reminded me of the African idiomatic expression *maka a maoto makgutswane*, which literally translated means 'lies have short feet'. Those who suppress or distort the truth should remember that classified information gets declassified in 20 to 30 years, depending on a country's specific laws. Even if the affected country does not declassify its documents, its partners or allies will, thus exposing the lie.

We all agreed that this can be terribly embarrassing to those who were involved, as well as to their children or descendants. The stigma stays with them. They carry it like stripes on their bodies and continue to be tormented and haunted by it psychologically as long as they live.

In the case of Kwame Nkrumah, it is now known that although his removal was carried out by his own countrymen and looked legitimate and necessary to some of those who carried it out, information released later, including declassified information, shows that the hand of foreign interest was involved. Declassified intelligence and communications show that the US government, together with the British and French, was directly or indirectly involved in the overthrow, as well as ensuring that he was banished from his country because, in their view, he threatened their interests. After the Ghana coup, the then special assistant on national security to President

Johnson, Robert W. Komer, said in a congratulatory message to President Johnson: 'The coup in Ghana is another example of a fortuitous windfall. *Nkrumah was doing more to undermine our interests than any other black African*' (my emphasis). For them, Nkrumah was seen not only to be undermining their interests but as a bad example to the other 'natives' on the African continent.

A rereading of Nkrumah for a conscious African who has a heart for Africa can only be a painful experience. Nkrumah fits well within the literary theory of a tragedy. He was obviously way ahead of his time to a point of being reckless. He punched beyond his weight and responded to world events as if little Ghana, was a superpower. All this he did, not only in the interests of Ghana but for the rest of the continent of Africa. When I expressed natural disgust that he was not given a chance as he did not last long, my Ghanaian interlocutor retorted, 'Good leaders in Africa never lasted for long'. Giving them an extra day in office was seen as dangerous. Removal *ngoko* ('now') was critical.

Although the CAFRAD Forum was useful and encouraging for Africa, giving us hope that our generation has the possibility and responsibility to change the course of events, the discussion about Kwame Nkrumah remained heavy on my mind and soul. As we drove through the city of Tangier on our way to the airport, the name of King Mohammed VI, which marks major roads and landmarks, transported me again to that history of struggle. This history includes heroic leaders such as Nkrumah, Bea of Algeria, Nasser of Egypt, Nyerere of Tanzania, Lumumba of the Congo, and many others who made sacrifices for our liberation. The pain in me went deeper. It was as if salt had been rubbed into my wounds, which were renewed by the discussion about the tragedy of the Nkrumah reality. In the depths of my heart I exclaimed, 'My God, please help us!'

★ ★ ★

The forum discussion could not end without reference to the way in which President Mbeki was also removed from office. 'Whatever the issues and politics involved, we as Africans are unhappy about the way in which this matter was handled,' said my Ghanaian inter-locutor. The others who were involved in this discussion just sighed (*go kgotsa*) or simply looked at each other with bewilderment. This was like '*Ach,* this was not good for Africa ... whatever the issues'! This was clearly meant to make the point that the concern was not about the issues, which might have been legitimate or illegitimate depending on where one stood, but about the manner in which the matter was dealt with.

Those who have interacted with some of the leadership of the African continent would have experienced similar responses: 'whatever the issues'. One that comes to mind for me is the of-ficial meeting between President Sassou Nguesso of the Republic of the Congo and President Motlanthe, held at the end of October 2008, about a month after the removal of Mbeki. President Sassou Nguesso spoke like a representative of the continent's leadership and raised concerns about what was happening in South Africa, as if he were also a member of the ANC and concerned about his or-ganisation. For him the ANC was one of the lights on the continent and Africa could not afford anything going wrong with the ANC. South Africa's presidents since then and other South African leaders can testify to similar encounters.

Mbeki is one of the most well-known sons of this continent. In his own words in the 'I am an African' speech, he says that he owes his 'being to the Khoi and the San whose desolate souls haunt the great expanse of the beautiful Cape'. In his veins, he says, 'courses the blood of the Malay slaves' whose 'stripes' which 'they bore on their bodies from the lash of the slave master are a reminder em-bossed on [his] consciousness of what should not be done'. Mbeki was born at Idutywa in the Eastern Cape, the son of the Mme

Epainette Mbeki and the late Oom Govan Mbeki, outstanding and revered stalwarts of the liberation movement. Mbeki went into exile at the time that Govan Mbeki was charged with high treason with other stalwarts such as Nelson Rolihlahla Mandela, Walter Sisulu and Ahmed Kathrada in the early sixties.

Mbeki was a child of the ANC, as he was born in an ANC (and its ally, the SACP) family. He joined the ANCYL at age fourteen and went into exile as a cadre of the ANC who was sent out to go and study and prepare for the future. Besides studying, he worked for the ANC for all his exile life (about 28 years) until he returned home in the early 1990s when the ANC was unbanned. He was part of the team that started the negotiation process with groups of whites from South Africa, firstly underground and then openly. This led to the release of political leaders, including Nelson Mandela, which marked the formal commencement of negotiations at the beginning of the 1990s that led to the establishment of a non-racial, non-sexist and just democratic government in April 1994.

He became deputy president of the country during Mandela's presidency, entrusted with the transformation of the country and its day-to-day running. He was elected president of the ANC at the 1997 national conference with overwhelming support and became president of the country with an increased majority of the ANC in parliament in 1999. He was re-elected in 2002 and 2004 as president of the ANC, and as president of the country with further increased majorities, which suggested high public-approval ratings.

Unfortunately, his success in the leadership and management of government was interrupted by his forced resignation as president of the country seven months before he completed his second and last term of office. What has not been articulated clearly by analysts and commentators nationally and internationally is that his forced removal from government was purely a party matter rather than a governance issue. To date he remains a member of the ANC in good standing, notwithstanding his removal.

What made his removal so dramatic and shocking to many South Africans and most Africans is that he served the nation well as both deputy president for five years and president for two terms (minus seven months). As deputy president during Mandela's presidency, he was assigned the responsibility of driving the processes and policies of transforming the South African society from a racist apartheid society to a just, non-racial, non-sexist, democratic and prosperous society. When I was reluctantly brought to his office, first as a special adviser and later as director-general, Mandela explicitly said to me that he intended to delegate many of his responsibilities as president to Deputy President Mbeki. Together, they wanted me to create the capacity in Mbeki's office that would enable him to carry out this responsibility as effectively and efficiently as possible.

There is no gainsaying that Mbeki discharged this responsibility with distinction, notwithstanding the challenges he together with his cabinet colleagues faced. In the words of President Mandela in his address to the joint sitting of parliament to mark the tenth anniversary of democracy on Monday, 10 May 2004, no president or prime minister in South Africa's history could 'claim to have done more for the people and the country' than Mbeki. Mandela went on to say that Mbeki was 'a modest man and I know he would prefer that I do not sing his personal praises, but his achievements as president and national leader is the embodiment of what our nation is capable of'.

This task of transformation of the apartheid society and the apartheid state is what made him unpopular amongst some white South Africans. It is for this reason that a special outreach programme to the Afrikaner community was initiated after his election as president. He entered into dialogue with the Afrikaner communities and sectors to create a better understanding of the transformation agenda, which was not necessarily against whites but was for all South Africans. A transformed South Africa from an apartheid society to a non-racial, non-sexist and just democratic society would be a better place for both whites and blacks to live in.

Interestingly, the persistent voice against this transformation agenda became the liberal tradition in South Africa, which happens to be more conservative than the liberal tradition elsewhere in the world. The liberal press also became vicious – at one stage more hostile than the Afrikaans media.

Again as president Mbeki continued to execute his responsibilities with distinction, focusing on implementation of government policies and programmes during the second term of his office, given that the policy framework was now in place, with fiscal discipline over the past eight years or so and an efficient revenue collection system all combined to release more resources to meet the needs of the people, particularly the poor. As part of this effort, outreach programmes were designed to take government to the people, listen to them and act to address their concerns. This unique programme was called *Izimbizo*. There were also presidential working groups which provided opportunities for the president to interact with organised sectors of the people, such as business (big and small business; black and white business; agricultural sector; etc.), labour (represented by the three major national federations), the religious community (representative of all the religious communities and sectors in their diversity), women, and youth groups.

The main challenge was lack of capacity at the sphere of local government to efficiently carry out the programmes of government. This is where the focus was towards the end of his last term of office, before it was disrupted. The *Izimbizo* and some of the working groups (business, religious, women and youth) were roped in to assist in one way or another in this regard.

A more complex issue was that of his views about HIV and AIDS which were considered controversial, to say the least. One has to say that, like Kwame Nkrumah, Thabo Mbeki was way ahead of his time. He walked where angels fear to tread – for example, challenging the pharmaceutical industry as regards its pricing systems and monopolies that made medicines in developing countries more expensive. This dispute ended up in the international courts. He also challenged the use of certain HIV and AIDS related medicines in developing countries in a way that was different from that in developed countries. Key amongst these were Nevirapine and AZT.

Taking on the international pharmaceutical industry was like taking on a mafia. Like Nkrumah's, Mbeki's intellectual prowess simply sucked him further into dangerous territories. Their honesty was finally the downfall of both men. They just could not look at anything which they felt was going wrong and keep quiet, however risky. Again, it was a type of commitment to the truth that bordered on being reckless. I will never forget our experience of the 2002 visit to the USA, which was turned into an HIV and AIDS tour. The cumulative effect of what I heard and experienced throughout all the meetings we attended, both in private and public, was clearly that President's Mbeki's life was at great risk. To the pharmaceutical industry, every statement Mbeki made that questioned strategies and marketing of medicines to developing countries in a way that was not allowed in developed countries meant a dramatic reduction in their revenues and profits. In one meeting a figure of US$2 billion a year loss was mentioned.

I returned from the USA visit with a very heavy heart, afraid for the president and fearing for his life. I started to have a deep concern for his security, something that I never had to worry about previously. The risk for his life would clearly be from external forces rather than from his own people. Our risk assessment was that this could involve both foreign intelligence services and elements of private entities. The unpleasant memories of African leaders such as

Kwame Nkrumah and Patrice Lumumba came to mind. I recalled the three attempts on Nkrumah's life between 1961 and 1964 before the coup in 1966. I also recalled the brutal murder of Patrice Lumumba in 1961. The death of our revered friend of the liberation movements, the prime minister of Sweden Olof Palme, also came to mind.

It became clear to me that we needed to engage the president about the reality of this situation. We also assessed the nature of the forces arrayed against him which were becoming a serious threat to him and to the country. Although he believed in the correctness of the course he was following, we convinced him about the need to change strategy to avoid a head-on collision with these forces. We convinced the president that he had made his point and that he would go into history as one president who did take on the international pharmaceutical establishment to change their policies globally in favour of the poor and that he had sufficiently warned the world about the dangers of using some of the medication in a manner that was not prescribed.

Although the president was seriously concerned about the risks that some of the medication posed for our people, he accepted the advice. A strategy was developed to review the then policy on HIV and AIDS, refine it in terms of new information that was available and then present it to cabinet as the new policy for HIV and AIDS. Once approved by cabinet the president would use this policy as a reference for any engagement relating to the subject of HIV and AIDS. He then gave us the latitude and authority to develop such a policy for government. The strategy was to make this policy the centre of the discourse on this subject rather than the president. Within a year – that is in 2003 – we achieved our objective to develop a world-class policy that would stand the test of time and the scrutiny of any critique, nationally or internationally.

Ultimately, after the heated intellectual debate about HIV and

AIDS, the best policy on HIV and AIDS was adopted and rigorously implemented. Interestingly, in the midst of the negative debates and publicity both nationally and internationally, South Africa was actively implementing a policy that was considered one of the best in the world. The debate and discourse around the death of the former health minister Manto Tshabalala-Msimang reconfirmed this perspective in a way that had never been done before. The policies that were developed and implemented during the term of Manto Tshabalala-Msimang (and thus Mbeki) were ANC policies that were approved by the ANC.

Where Mbeki excelled most was on the international front. As president of the country he executed with distinction the policies of the ANC on the African Renaissance. He is credited as the driver of the African Renaissance vision on the continent for the past fourteen years or so, giving birth to NEPAD, the APF and the APRM. He participated in the development and establishment of the AU with its progressive institutions and policies to advance democracy on the continent and intensify development of the African continent. Regarding the debate within the AU on the issue of African unity, he took a cautious view on behalf of South Africa, along with many other African countries. The view here was that African unity should develop naturally from the bottom, starting with regional integration. This is where Mbeki and Nkrumah find themselves on opposite sides of this discourse, although this was at different times in history.

The one person credited with conflict resolution, mediation and peacemaking on the continent in the past fifteen years or so, is President Mbeki. It started with mediation efforts in Lesotho, followed by the Democratic Republic of Congo (DRC), Burundi, Côte d'Ivoire, Zimbabwe and Sudan. The area of his work that is not known and was never made public is his interaction with many African leaders at a quiet level about the challenging situations in their countries, as well as advising on strategies to address these problems to avoid them boiling into a crisis. Some of the leaders even asked him to talk with their own countrymen and women. In some instances he had to ask his brothers, the heads of state and government, to allow him to meet some of their citizens to assist in defusing potential conflicts. There was a preventative diplomacy that he was involved in, which could not and cannot be made public.

At a global level, South Africa always found itself punching above its weight. Under the watch of Mbeki, the G8 opened its doors to the participation of developing countries in their fora, which has led to support for the establishment of a G13 to replace the G8. South Africa also participates in the G20, a forum that has been used to deal with more practical global economic and financial issues affecting the rest of the international community. On matters of Weapons of Mass Destruction (WMD), issues related to the Non-Proliferation Treaty, the WTO, sustainable environment, and many others, South Africa has played a critical role under the leadership of President Mbeki. There is also the matter of the peace initiatives relating to the Middle East, including the Israeli-Palestinian matter, and efforts to avoid the disastrous war in Iraq which has cost many lives and continues to do so.

The independent and critical way in which South Africa dealt with these matters under the leadership of Mbeki did not endear with country to some of the major Western powers. One might ask, why the Western powers in particular? The answer is simple. As the former coloniser of a country, there is an umbilical cord which links you with the former colony in a way that is almost inextricable. The process of decolonisation was an unwelcome occurrence for the colonial powers. They reluctantly let go while building complex systems to retain the former colonies within their direct or indirect sphere of influence. In some of the former colonies they ensured that client states or proxy governments were established to secure their interest. And this was not based on any sense of morality or interests of the people in that former colony. It was downright, cold national interest in the crudest form. The pretence of defending democracy and human rights is negated by history. Most of the regimes supported by the Western powers were undemocratic and outright dictatorships in some instances. Zaire, the former Belgian colony, was a classical example.

Where there were hostile leaders – in the view of the former colonial masters – they changed them by any means at their disposal, including coups against democratically elected leaders. The Robert Komer quote we referred to earlier clearly suggests direct interest of the USA in the coup in Ghana which he called 'a fortuitous windfall' and continues to say that the new military regime (in Accra) is almost *pathetically pro-Western*' (my emphasis).

Earlier, Komer had reported that they 'may have a pro-Western coup in Ghana soon', that the 'plotters are keeping us briefed' and that 'all in all, [it] looks good'.

In the case of Patrice Lumumba of the Congo, he was not given a chance. He was murdered within the first year of becoming the prime minister, during the watch of the major Western countries and the UN forces that had been deployed in the Congo. In modern political parlance this would be called regime change.

An independent and critical state anywhere in the world does not sit well with the world powers, who want to exert their influence. They feel more comfortable with pliable governments rather than independent-thinking states. The most dramatic expression of this discomfort of the major powers with small independent-thinking states like South Africa was during one critical discussion with a major power about an issue that had the potential of disastrous global consequences.

One of the delegates exclaimed: 'The problem with you [South

Africans] is that you are correct most of the time, but and unfortunately the positions you take are not in line with our national interests and geo-political plans.' The correctness of the issue here did not matter; what mattered was the narrow national interests of the power affected. In this regard, the critical positions held by South Africa – which in general are informed by a concept of the indivisibility of justice that has no respect for the position, power and status of a country – makes South Africa an uncomfortable ally of the major powers of the world. In the words of the delegate referred to earlier, 'This position of South Africa makes you look like our enemy. We do not want to treat you like our enemy, but the problem is that you [your policies and positions] are always in our way!' The problem with being in the way of a huge elephant is that you could be trampled on and you will be lucky to come out alive.

The discomfort also affects the smaller, more vulnerable states, since it is worst for those who depend on the developed world for their budget support. An agreement could be reached today between African countries on a critical global matter and tomorrow they would act differently. Initially I was shocked by this behaviour but learned later about the terrorism of the powerful against the weaker states. One country did something contrary to what was agreed a few days earlier, and in a president-to-president discussion the president said to his counterpart, 'My brother, I got a call at midnight and was told that if I did not change the position we had taken I could rest assured that my budget support would be pulled instantly, so I had to comply. Please understand.'

This is the case where you just *kgotsa* ('sigh') and say, 'God help us!' As I have said before I call this the highest form of terrorism, which this modern world, petrified by terrorism, is not ready to confront. This is like the highest levels of corruption when the international community fills a critical international post. They buy states or countries by promising them one form of assistance or another, and they even buy leaders directly to ensure that they vote in the way that serves the interest of their own countries or regions. This act by the privileged and powerful is not named for what it is, corruption or fraud. Instead it is termed influence or lobbying. Nobody thinks to set up a commission of enquiry to investigate and expose this high-level form of corruption and fraud in the international governance system.

As we indicated earlier, the engagement of South Africa globally, resulting in her punching above her weight, caused feelings of discomfort in many ways and areas. Our involvement in processes to make peace in the DRC, Burundi, Côte d'Ivoire, Zimbabwe, Sudan, the Middle East, Iraq, and other places has invited the wrath of powers that have interests in those countries. This is like a love-hate relationship. You are loved for doing good but hated for doing it in a way that does not serve their narrow nationalistic interests. The most dramatic event for me was related to the DRC negotiations. Before the negotiation teams arrived at Sun City in the North West province, the various intelligence services of interested parties checked into the local hotels to monitor and influence the negotiation processes.

The most critical engagement related to the facilitation of the peace processes in Côte d'Ivoire and Zimbabwe. There was a time when France took a contrary view to that of the facilitator during the negotiation processes on Côte d'Ivoire. This ended up at the UN Security Council, where France lost the matter. The same happened with Zimbabwe, where both Britain and the USA felt the facilitation was not serving their own interests. They tried twice to scupper this process at the Security Council and failed. In both cases South Africa found itself opposing positions taken by the major superpowers who are members of the Security Council. As one would expect, this was not taken kindly by the affected countries that lost, causing us to worry about the security of the president and the country, as well as the security of the information he was dealing with to find solutions to these challenges.

Mbeki and Kwame Nkrumah

I started this chapter with a discussion of the African intellectuals who were at the CAFRAD conference in Tangier, leading us to observations about African leaders and their failures and successes. In terms of the efforts to radically challenge the lot of the people of the African continent, the names of Kwame Nkrumah and Thabo Mbeki were singled out. In the discussion, one could not miss the remarkable similarities of the lives of Nkrumah and Mbeki. This discussion inspired me to look critically at these two figures in a comparative way. The histories of the two figures are striking and enlightening.

Similarities

Firstly, the two leaders were both outstanding intellectuals who were fortunate to receive the quality education that made them what they are.

Secondly, they engaged in student and youth struggles, and these experiences shaped their perspectives on life.

Thirdly, they were totally committed to the freedom of the African continent and its people, and focused on changing the quality of the lives of their people and the people of the rest of the continent.

Fourthly, both failed to give sufficient attention to their own parties, which were the vehicles of their mission, and believed that their parties and their people were so revolutionary that they did not need nurturing.

Fifthly, for both, the freedom and liberation of the African continent included the right to make decisions without being manipulated or dictated to by other foreign countries or governments, especially the former colonial powers.

Sixthly, both believed that the unity of the African people and the rest of the developing world was critical to ensuring that they had a stronger voice in international fora to advance the interests of Africa and the rest of the developing world. (Note Nkrumah's OAU, Ghana-Guinea federation and the Ghana-Guinea-Mali federation on the one hand, and on the other Mbeki's AU, India-Brazil-South Africa (IBSA), Brazil-Russia-India-China-South Africa (BRICSA) and the G8 plus G5.)

And seventhly, both were independent thinkers and resisted any attempt to manipulate Africans to achieve the interests of others rather than those of Africans. They were uncompromising when it came to the right of Africans to make their own decisions and find their own solutions to the challenges they faced. This they did irrespective of the consequences and they paid a price.

Differences

The fundamental differences between the two leaders are mostly defined by the period at which they exercised their leadership.

Firstly, Nkrumah was the first African in sub-Saharan Africa to lead an independent country after a long period of colonisation. Mbeki on the other hand, exercised his leadership at a time when all the African countries, except for the Sahrawi Republic, were free.

Secondly, Nkrumah's was a liberation task, while Mbeki's was a renewal task.

Thirdly, Nkrumah moved more into alliances with the East because the West consisted mostly of former colonial powers that were still colonising other African countries and saw his views on the decolonisation of Africa as hostile. Mbeki, on the other hand, had the task of a balancing act between the East and the West, with a clear bias towards justice for all irrespective of their power.

Fourthly, Nkrumah's time allowed for one-party states as a way of consolidating the new states against hostile former colonisers. Human rights were sacrificed in defence of their freedoms within the context of an East-West cold war. Mbeki's time was about democratisation of all of government and society, including respect for human rights.

The CAFRAD conference and the extensive discussions we had with the African intellectuals were very enlightening for me and got me to think about the legacy of Mbeki in a way I had not considered before. Like Kwame Nkrumah, Mbeki's legacy will be appreciated and celebrated later, once the dust of the battles within the ANC has settled. When generations to come look back his contribution will loom high above many.

CHAPTER 11

Mbeki

The Person and His Legacy

From the moment I thought of writing this book, I wrestled over the inclusion of a chapter or chapters dealing with Mbeki as a person. On the one hand, I knew that I could not do justice to him and his legacy in just one or a few chapters. His is a story that can fill volumes. On the other hand, I had to keep in mind that this book is not about Mbeki per se but about my experiences in government.

In fact, I need to state clearly that this book is also not about the ANC, government or any other person or institution as some have surmised from articles published in Independent Newspapers. The book is about some of the things I could not say, which were part of my experiences over the thirteen and a half years I was in government. The things I could not say involved other players and organisations, but the book is not about these players or organisation. As I worked through the book I also found out that this limited scope was an impossible task, since one cannot accommodate all the things one could not say, let alone all one's experiences.

Nevertheless, my experience in government would not be complete without my experience of Mbeki, whom I worked with for almost all the time I was in government. Indeed, there are things I could not say about him while I was in government. Now that I am out of government, I have some freedom to reflect on my experiences with him, although, unfortunately, some things remain classified.

Initially I had planned chapters with titles like 'Understanding the Real Mbeki!', 'Mbeki: What is Enigmatic about Him?', 'Mbeki and the Media', 'The Legacy of Mbeki' and 'The Blind Spots of Mbeki'. Ultimately I settled for 'Mbeki: The Person and His Legacy' as it allows me freedom to deal with all the matters in the other themes that were part of my experience. The only risk here is that this might suggest that I will be dealing with everything regarding Mbeki. I need to state clearly again that this book is not a biography of Mbeki, but my reflections on him as I experienced him.

When Mbeki left the country and went into exile in the early 1960s I was too young to have known him. My memories of that time about the struggle against the apartheid system are about 'Free Mandela' and 'Stay Away' posters and writings on walls. I also remember the huge, strange vehicles that occupied Soweto for a while. The banning of the liberation movements had an enormous impact, as it sent people underground and silenced them to an extent that they could not even talk about their experiences in the struggle, nor talk about the leaders and organisations which were involved, and as a result it deprived the younger generation of knowledge about the history of the struggle. Our parents were afraid to discuss anything that had to do with the banned organisations in the 1960s because of the risk of being victimised or imprisoned. By the late 1960s I began to learn more about the liberation movement and its leadership, as the older generation got up the courage to talk about it.

The first underground literature I saw was about the Rivonia Trial and Mandela's gallant speech from the dock. We knew it was underground literature because it was packaged in a way to disguise it, in order to avoid detection by the apartheid security forces, which could have resulted in harassment or imprisonment. Through this literature I came to know more about the ANC and the Rivonia trialists, including Govan Mbeki and, to a certain extent, his family.

My recollection is that I only learned more about Thabo Mbeki as part of the leadership of the ANC in the early 1970s, through underground structures and literature or through the media. I do not remember meeting Mbeki in person in my errands to neigh-bouring countries (Botswana, Lesotho and Swaziland) to speak or preach at church and student Christian movement conferences and at universities, and later as part of the underground operations of the ANC. During the latter part of the 1970s the apartheid regime withdrew the travel documents of some of us, to cut our direct contact with the liberation movement in exile. This meant that all communication with the liberation movement was conducted through underground structures and couriers were used on a needs basis to avoid detection, detention and even imprisonment. As a result I had no opportunity to meet Mbeki in person during this time.

When our passports were reissued towards the end of 1984 and leaders such as Albertina Sisulu and others were unbanned, I got an opportunity to travel outside the country. My recollection is that it was during this time that I met Mbeki. I was in transit at Heathrow Airport en route to Sweden when comrades whisked me away, drove around London with me, including going through basements of buildings and changing cars, to end up in a house where Mbeki was. The meeting involved briefings and debriefings about the situation in the country and what was being done, including plans ahead of us. Another interaction would have happened during the first quarter of 1986, following the 1985 Treason Trial of the UDF leaders where I was one of the accused, and before the declaration of the State of Emergency in June 1986, which forced some of us to go underground, while many others were detained for long periods.

There were memorable interactions with him during this difficult period, after I left the country while underground in September 1986, and spent about five and a half months outside the country before returning underground again. At one stage we had to discuss my return back home, which was a difficult decision because of its attendant risks. Ultimately we agreed that I had to come back, as this was where I was needed most. At that time the strategic tasks for the liberation movement were more inside the country than outside. Exile was the last resort and only when conditions were such that one could not continue executing tasks internally.

It was only after my appointment as the general secretary of the South African Council of Churches (SACC), in July 1987, that I found more opportunities to meet him and other exiled ANC leaders, while travelling internationally on SACC business and during the campaign for comprehensive sanctions against the apartheid system. I also had opportunities in my capacity as general secretary to attend funerals of ANC leaders in exile (such as that of Johnny Makhathini) as well as visit places such as Morogoro, in Tanzania. These were defiantly considered pastoral visits and assignments which a general secretary of the SACC had to undertake as part of its ministry to exiled South Africans, especially because the regime had arrangements for its soldiers to be ministered to by military chaplains. We also held formal meetings from time to time between the ANC and the SACC leadership on critical matters affecting the people of South Africa.

After the unbanning of the liberation movements Mbeki, to-gether with other ANC leaders, paid me a courtesy call at home in Diepkloof, Phase Two, Soweto. But most of the interactions were more at an official level between the ANC and the SACC, rather than personal. These included meetings regarding the return of exiles and their care; getting the church to understand the ANC better; and dealing with the various crises in the country during the negotiation period, the violence which was unleashed by the apartheid regime and interventions we had to make. Once a set-tlement was reached at the negotiations table, I was appointed to the Independent Electoral Commission (IEC) at the end of 1993, which created platforms for interacting with leaders of all the par-ties, including Mbeki as a representative of the ANC.

When I was called towards the end of 1995 and asked to join Mbeki as head of his office, I was surprised as I had not expected it nor thought about it at all. In any case, I had no intention of join-ing the public service, as I did not think of myself as a civil servant.

Before I responded I engaged in a number of consultations to find out more about Mbeki in terms of his background, personal-ity, character, political perspectives and the way others viewed him within the movement. Naturally, those I consulted were in exile with him, where he spent about 30 years of his life. All of them painted a positive picture of him, especially his intellectual prowess and his knowledge and experience regarding the ANC, as well as the fact that he was among the few who learnt at the feet of O.R. Tambo, with whom he worked closely for many years. They also talked about his extensive knowledge of international affairs be-cause of his work as a representative of the ANC in various coun-tries and his deployment to the ANC's department of information and international relations.

Some of the comrades I consulted also referred to the fact that he was a complex and difficult character to fathom. He was considered an intellectual powerhouse, which at times intimidated his peers, and this made him seem aloof and distant. He was intellectually ahead of most of his comrades, especially in his understanding of the world, the complexities of the struggle, and where the movement should be heading, especially during the 1980s and the 1990s. They referred to his foresight in starting the negotiations with the apartheid regime, the interactions with delegations from South Africa and his charm towards white South Africans who met the ANC outside the country. In particular, he charmed business into accepting the ANC as something they did not need to fear.

Although he was known for his flexibility and readiness to make strategic compromises where solutions could be found to complex political and economic issues, he was uncompromising on matters of racism and those affecting the rights of Africans, including their human dignity after many years of slavery and colonial oppression and exploitation. He held uncompromising Africanist positions on matters which involved relations between South Africa and Africa with the rest of the world.

Having worked with him closely for more than thirteen years, I came to understand that his perspectives on the world all hinged on the issue of the right of Africans to determine their own destiny in the way they saw fit. This is clearly demonstrated in his handling of the conflict resolution processes in the DRC, Burundi, Zimbabwe, Côte d'Ivoire and Sudan. In this regard, he is a classical cadre of the ANC as these positions form part of the DNA of the party. It is for this reason that the ANC has never contradicted his handling of these situations, even at the height of his sharp differences with his comrades. The right of Africans to determine their destiny is a matter on which Africans and African leaders do not differ, even under enormous pressure. These positions did not endear Mbeki to some Western countries and in civil society circles that were issue-based in their orientation.

Another aspect of Mbeki's character is his commitment to the right of Africans to be treated equally with others, whatever their race, nationality or class. This is demonstrated in his stance towards the use of drugs such as Nevirapine and AZT in developing countries in a manner that was different from the way in which such drugs were used in Europe and the USA. The permissible risk and benefit ratio was lowered in poorer countries when compared to rich countries, thus putting the lives of poorer people at higher levels of risk. Although this position made perfect sense in rational terms, it was considered to be seriously flawed, especially by those who were infected and affected by HIV and AIDS, who felt that his position deprived them of medication which could save their lives. Mbeki's position on this matter proved to be the most controversial in his career and generated the most vicious campaign against him and his ministers of health. To some, especially those who were affected by HIV and AIDS, it made Mbeki look cold and uncaring.

The complex issues relating to the concept of equality also reared their head where human rights issues were concerned. Mbeki, in a classic ANC manner, resisted selective enforcement of human rights by powerful Western countries, since these countries did so to pursue their narrow national interests and not because of human rights per se. In fact, human rights issues were used strategically as tools to achieve their objectives, rather than as a principle. This is demonstrated by the way in which they would close their eyes to gross violations of human rights by countries which advanced their interests. There was also the tendency to use the UN Security Council selectively against smaller countries on human rights issues, instead of referring them to the UN Commission on Human Rights (UNCHR). This approach by Mbeki and the ANC was always misunderstood, as it looked like a rights-based country in terms of its Constitution and history was now supporting or tolerating violations of human rights in other countries. The challenge here is not about closing one's eyes to human rights violations. It is about the equality principle.

As the one African leader who pursued these principles of equality with uncompromising zeal, Mbeki was identified as a hindrance to the interests of dominant countries in the global governance system, which is based on the relics of colonial traditions and practices. At times he appeared to them as a puzzle, an enigma as some have called him. On these matters I had no difficulties with Mbeki as I was brought up under the same school of thought.

Another concern I had about joining Mbeki's office was the fear that I could just be caught up in the internal politics of the ANC, which could impact negatively on my ministry. Up to 1994 I worked within the church at the highest level of the ecumenical movement and I could not imagine allowing myself to be caught up in cleavages within the movement or becoming part of any divisions. I engaged my interlocutors regarding all the personalities within the leadership of the movement and the risk of association with one leader being construed as being against another.

What I heard was not different from what we experienced inside the country: there were at times different signals from Lusaka at the height of the struggle in the 1980s. One example was the extremely angry position advocating military attacks on strategic targets even if it meant exploding bombs in Wimpy Bars and other public places where innocent lives could be lost. This I understood later when we dealt with the Iraqi invasion, as the loss of innocent lives was coldly called 'collateral damage'. It felt so cold and callous to us. The other was a more moderate approach, which expected operatives to be cautious when selecting targets to make sure that the loss of innocent life was avoided as much as possible, which was in line with the 1961 MK manifesto.

The attacks on Wimpy Bars led to a special meeting between the heads of churches of the SACC and the top leadership of the

ANC, which I facilitated as SACC general secretary, to discuss our serious concerns over this new development. In that meeting the leadership of the ANC assured the SACC leaders that attacks on soft targets such as Wimpy Bars was not part of its policy and that everything would be done to ensure that it did not happen again. They warned, though, that there could also be agents of the apartheid regime or provocateurs that were involved.

The differences in handling these difficult situations were manageable, since once they were reduced to the policy of the ANC, there could be no differences. In this regard I was satisfied that I would be able to manage these internal cleavages of the ANC, as the policy positions were clear. In any case, this was about government and not the party.

Although I was unhappy at being made a public servant, which I believed would rob me of my public advocacy role for justice, peace and righteousness, I accepted the challenge purely because of the respect I had for the leadership of the movement, particularly Nelson Mandela, who then was president of the ANC and the country.

Once in the office, first as a special adviser and then as director-general, I was immersed in the life of the man who was described as a 'complex', 'aloof', 'distant' intellectual and an 'enigma'. As is always the case, when one got closer to him the first thing one found was that Mbeki was just a human being like all of us, with weaknesses and strengths. But his superior intellect made up in large measure for his weaknesses.

As in Western societies where politicians are expected to walk around holding hands with their wives, Mbeki was expected to do the same with Zanele Mbeki. Coming from exile and having worked in different and distant capitals, some of which was underground work, walking around and holding hands was the last thing on their minds. Like many families that were in exile, they lived a life which was similar to that of two married soldiers who were deployed in different places or posts and at times had to play down the relationship for security reasons. But Zanele Mbeki was also a professional in her own right, who was involved with the Women's Development Bank (WDB) and assisting poor rural women with microfinance facilities to run small businesses.

Neither of them is a showy person and they hated playing to the gallery. They resisted attempts to make them do what they were expected to do and in this regard they were just outright rebels.

Unlike many politicians, Mbeki did not believe in premeditated media exposure or branding. At the beginning, a number of companies offered to assist him with branding and building his image and his response was a categorical no. Like a traditional ANC cadre, he did not believe that the individual mattered. What mattered was the image of the organisation, its policies and what it was able to do for the people, especially for those who had been victims of the racist apartheid system. He believed that what he was doing would speak for itself and did not need to be marketed. Posing for photos and making sure the angles were right was totally reprehensible to him, while media appearances were limited to the minimum and only when it was absolutely necessary. Electronic media sound bites were also a no. Time had to be made for engagement and analytical work. It was substance that mattered, not sound bites, which is why he was said to be media-shy.

When one came to know his extended family, particularly his parents and their history, one began to appreciate that he did not grow up in a normal family, as the struggle kept them apart most of the time, with his father spending 25 years in jail. A reading of Mbeki's upbringing, a subject of many other publications, does not describe him as the typical family man, as he and his siblings never had a normal family life. It is said that their parents prepared them for a life without the parents being around. In this regard he is atypical. That is why at the beginning of his term of office in the presidency he was subjected to unfortunate criticisms of 'being aloof' or 'feeling awkward' in picking up babies or relating to them. He was too hardened for soft issues like picking up babies and playing with them. As time went by he adjusted – walked an extra mile – and began to relate to ordinary people and children in a normal way. The picture of him sitting on the floor surrounded by elderly women and men at Khayamnandi, outside Port Elizabeth, remade his image in a way that no branding company could do.

One of Mbeki's greatest weaknesses was directly related to his greatest strength – his intellect. Because of his high intellect, many people misunderstood him or found it difficult to understand him. He always took a discussion beyond the ordinary to a level that stretched the imaginations of his listeners to a point where many simply failed to comprehend. Further, he did not have much time for people who could not think strategically, especially those who were placed in positions of responsibility. Here again his intellect was his greatest enemy, as he expected his colleagues and staff to operate at the same level. He understood that ordinary people on the ground would not be able to operate at that level, but he expected something different from high-level staff, political appointees and office bearers.

He was also a prolific reader with an extraordinary memory. He possessed great abilities to do his own research about any subject, even specialised matters. Having done this over years, he accumulated a huge bank of information which put him ahead of his colleagues, including officials in their own areas of speciality. Half-baked material never survived his critique and he picked holes in what others would have thought was perfectly done. Although this was normally done in a cool and collected manner without any emotion being displayed, many felt they had been sent packing and feared any further engagement. This extended even to his intelligence officers at times leaving him to his own devices.

His prodigious memory made note-takers irrelevant, since he remembered better what happened in meetings than the minute-takers. In any case, having worked underground most of his life in exile, he had a natural aversion to note-takers and insisted on fewer participants in meetings than would normally be the case for heads of state.

The unintended consequence of this was that many drifted away from him or, if they remained, avoided any serious intellectual engagement with him on difficult issues. At best, they were reduced to admirers of his intellect. As a result, his advisers were few and far between. To advise Mbeki, one had to be bold and ready to accept when one had not done enough homework or did not have all the information, should one be found to have missed the point. As one of those who spent enormous amounts of time with him, I always took the opportunity to raise areas of concern I felt needed to be addressed or those that were raised by others who could not approach him directly.

One thing about Mbeki that many have missed is that he never lived for himself. The victory of the ANC in 1994 was the victory of the people, and the ANC government had to be the government of the people and for the people. For the thirteen years I worked with him he was concerned about two things: the defence of the revolution and changing the conditions of lives of the people by meeting their basic needs. Defence of the revolution involved defending the rights of the historically oppressed and exploited to determine their own destiny. This put him at loggerheads with those who wanted to keep elements of racist practices or economic dominance.

He also led the ANC at a time when unpopular decisions had to be made to restructure the economy strategically to ensure that it served the interests of the people. That is where the Growth, Employment and Redistribution (GEAR) programme was developed to grow the economy, create employment, redistribute the country's resources equitably, and compensate for the damage caused by the apartheid system. The restructuring had to be done without reducing social expenditure, which gradually grew over the years.

The 'Ten Year Review' published at the end of ten years of democracy showed that all the objectives which were a sole responsibility of the government were achieved to a greater extent than those which required the involvement of the private sector. Failure to create as many jobs as projected in the GEAR strategy is attributed to this challenge. It is for this reason that those who critiqued GEAR argue that it had resulted in jobless growth. Interestingly, no one has critiqued the redistribution strategy, as this was achieved to a greater extent, although the gap between the poor and the rich kept on growing.

One thing that the GEAR strategy achieved, which has been underplayed, was the reduction of the budget deficit, which has since released resources to improve the quality of our national infrastructure, a key to economic growth, as well as meet the basic needs of the people through the provision of clean water, sanitary services, access to electricity, housing, health services and education, amongst others.

There are two elements in the person of Mbeki that, together, sum up what he is all about. One is the African Renaissance and the other is his belief in the cadre of the ANC.

The African Renaissance vision and subsequent programmes are part of the legacy of Mbeki that cannot be taken away from him. Even his worst enemies cannot but acknowledge that the African Renaissance became synonymous with Mbeki over the entire period when he was in government.

From a historical perspective his signature speech on the African Renaissance was the 'I am an African' speech delivered in parliament in May 1996 on the occasion of the adoption of the new Constitution for democratic South Africa. In a sense the adoption of the Constitution in 1996 signalled the consummation of the struggle for self-determination and the right of 'Africans' to determine their own destiny. It was a moment one could only be proud of. As Mbeki said, 'As an African, this is an achievement of which I am proud, proud without reservation and proud without any feeling of conceit.'

The historical moment brought out in Mbeki his deeper feelings about his identity which went beyond just being an Mbeki (of which he was robbed), his identity as a South African (of which he was also robbed) and his identity as an African (which was reduced to slavery and service to others while being exploited and robbed) and his broader definition of being African (which went beyond the narrow traditional concept). He submits that he owes his being 'to the Khoi and the San'; he was formed of the 'migrants who left Europe to find a new home on our land'; that in his 'veins courses the blood of the Malay slaves' who came from the East; that he comes of those who were 'transported from India and China'. He then concludes that 'being part of all these people, and in the knowledge that none dare contest that assertion, I shall claim that – I am an African'.

Over the years that I worked with him to develop and popularise the vision of the African Renaissance, he never claimed it as his own, nor did he claim to be the pioneer thereof. As a revolutionary he knew that making such claims would alienate those whom he wanted to be partners in this project. Whatever we did had to ensure that the leadership of the continent felt that this was their project and vision and made it their own. He recognised the historical visionaries of the African Renaissance, such as Kwame Nkrumah and others who came before him. He built his new vision on the foundations laid by the African leaders before him. In

fact, he derived his legitimacy and authority from them as he mobilised South Africans, his fellow African leaders and the people of
the African continent, including the African Diaspora.

Furthermore, he understood that the vision of the African
Renaissance was a core policy of his party, the ANC. One could
say that the vision of the African Renaissance is part of the DNA
of the ANC as it was formed precisely for this purpose. Its objective was to unite all Africans irrespective of their geographic origins, language or culture, to enable them to fight effectively against
colonial and oppressive systems and develop Africa to its fullest
potential. From its beginnings the ANC had a continental and
global Africanist perspective and reach, which is demonstrated by
its choice of the anthem '*Nkosi sikelel' iAfrika*', which is about the
continent rather than South Africa alone. The 1906 speech of the
founder and former president of the ANC, Pixley Ka Seme, which
also starts with the words 'I am an African', indicates the state of
mind of the leaders of the ANC even before the party was formed
in 1912. The ANC was conceptualised as a party for all Africans
beyond the borders of South Africa.

In preparation for taking over government in 1994, the ANC
worked on policy positions on international relations which
made the African Renaissance the centrepiece of its foreign policy. The first speech of President Nelson Mandela at the Tunisia
OAU Summit focused on the renewal of Africa and its people.
He announced that the new democratic South Africa was now
ready to make its contribution in the rebuilding of the African
continent.

After the 'I am an African' speech, I, together with Mbeki's advisers of the time – namely, Vusi Mavimbela, Mojanku Gumbi and
Moss Ngoasheng – developed strategies to make the vision articulated in the speech a truly African vision. Essop Pahad initially
participated as the parliamentary counsellor to Mbeki and later as

a deputy minister in the office of the deputy president. A national conference, bringing together key thinkers in the country, was organised to reflect on this vision, as well as develop a South African programme to promote the vision.

Mbeki's first step was to engage with his key political and economic ministers and their directors-general to reflect on this matter and advise accordingly. This happened over a period of many weeks before a document, which was used to consult and mobilise other heads of state and government to buy into the project, could emerge, entitled the Millennium African Recovery Plan (MAP). The second step was to engage with key African leaders who were responsible for certain continental and international organisations at the time to get them to work together to promote this vision. The countries were Algeria (then chair of the OAU) and Nigeria (then chair of the Group of 77 plus China). South Africa at the time was the chair of NAM. The third step was to get a decision of the OAU to endorse this vision and then develop it further together with them and translate it into a programme which became known as NEPAD followed by APRM.

The fourth step was to break into the exclusive courts of the powerful countries such as the G8, to force them to make the African continent's development part of their agenda. The principle again was that the powerful G8 countries could not make decisions about the world without the participation of Africa and the rest of the developing world. The poor had the right to determine their own destiny. Initially the G8 countries resisted this determined approach by African countries, but ultimately they relented and since then they have not had meetings without Africa's participation. Today there is an African Partnership Forum (APF) with developed countries where the priorities of Africa are addressed. Interestingly, this success of the African leaders in penetrating the forums of the powerful G8 countries opened the way for the rest of the developing countries, which is why there is now talk of a G13 forum which will include other major developing countries such as China, Brazil, and India over and above any key African countries.

Throughout all this Mbeki proved to be an extraordinary visionary, a strategist per excellence, with exceptional patience to see the project through against the odds. He treated his fellow African leaders with respect as he mobilised them to support the vision. He led the process of breaking into the forums of the G8 countries and still kept excellent diplomatic relationships with them. In the concluding words of his 'I am an African' speech he said:

> This thing that we have done today [the adoption of the new Constitution in South Africa in 1996] ... says that Africa reaffirms that she is continuing her rise from the ashes.
>
> Whatever the setbacks of the moment, nothing can stop us now!
>
> Whatever the difficulties, Africa shall be at peace!
>
> However improbable it may sound to the sceptics, Africa will prosper!
>
> Whoever, may be, whatever our immediate interest, however much we carry baggage from our past, however much we have been caught by the fashion of cynicism and loss of faith in the capacity of the people, let us err today and say – nothing can stop us now!

For Mbeki, the renewal of the African continent and the freedom of Africans to determine their own destiny defined everything he was about. Even when he was asked to talk about South Africa as its president, he talked about Africa. The 'I am an African' speech is a classical example where a speech on a major South African event became a speech about the continent. He was at it when he was removed from office, having just facilitated an agreement amongst

Zimbabwean parties and then returning from Sudan on a peace mission. He lost his position as president of the country as a soldier of the African Renaissance project. He continued as a facilitator of the Zimbabwean settlement well beyond his removal as president, until the Inclusive Government was formed. Six months after he was removed from office, the leadership of the African continent showed their confidence in him by appointing him the chair of the AU high-level panel on Sudan, and his achievements there speak for themselves.

His removal from office felt like the removal of the African Renaissance vision from the agenda of the African continent and a dampening of the spirit of enthusiasm. But his later speech at the launch of the Thabo Mbeki Leadership Institute and the announcement of its programme raised new hopes that the vision of the African Renaissance may not be lost after all.

Where Mbeki got it radically wrong was about the cadre of the ANC, which in my opinion was one of the reasons for his downfall. The nature and length of time of our liberation struggle in South Africa produced unique cadres such as Albert Luthuli, O.R. Tambo, Nelson Mandela, Govan Mbeki and Walter Sisulu, among others. Our struggle was not about ethnic or narrow nationalistic interests. It was a struggle against one of the most blatantly racist and obnoxious systems, which was declared by the international community a crime against humanity. It denied millions of South Africans their human rights and used the worst forms of violence to suppress any form of resistance to the system. Many people died over years either because of the policies of the regime or while resisting it. Many were detained, tortured and sent to prison for long periods, some for life, while many others were hanged. Many others left their families and went into exile either to seek refuge or to fight the system.

The uniqueness of this struggle is that it was against a

blatantly immoral system and it produced a great moral commitment. Resistance to apartheid became a highly moral issue, which went beyond a revolutionary morality to a religious morality, with a commitment to die for the cause. Many activists began to talk about dying for the cause, rather than just because of apartheid. They differentiated between what they called a useless death and a meaningful death. For them, a useless death was merely being a victim of apartheid and a useful death was dying in the course of resisting or fighting to remove the apartheid system.

The struggle stripped activists of their self-interest and put the interests of the people and the course for liberation at the centre of their lives. Once one was forced to go underground, or was detained, imprisoned, banned, banished or exiled, the immediate interests of the self, family or friends faded away and the higher calling to the removal of the system loomed larger than anything else. The reward for getting involved in the struggle for liberation was police harassment, detention without trial, solitary confinement, torture, imprisonment, bannings, banishment, exile or death. In exile most of the cadres of the movement lived on allowances to cover their basic needs. It is these experiences and this reality that shaped the quality of the cadre of the movement, a cadre who was not easily corrupted.

When the ANC returned from exile at the beginning of the 1990s, an allowance of about R2 500 was made available to those who worked for the movement, and others got grants from the National Coordinating Committee for the Return of Exiles (NCCR). But our victory radically changed our terrain of struggle as it opened us to new opportunities both negative and positive, which were bound to change the character of the cadre of the movement. Following our first democratic elections in April 1994, our praxis of struggle changed radically. In the past, becoming a leader in any structure of the movement either made one a sitting duck or one qualified to be arrested or forced into exile; now it was a status symbol to be in leadership and came with lucrative benefits, which included a large salary, cars, houses, and so forth. Whereas in the past money was scarce and only used for basic needs, now the national budget made money accessible not only to change the conditions of life for the people; people also began to devise corrupt means of accessing the money for personal gain, at the expense of the people.

The natural consequence of this changed praxis was that it was bound to make elections within the movement from branch levels to the national level a highly contested terrain, with violent and corrupt means becoming part of the new culture of the cadre. Lest I be misunderstood, this is not a unique challenge of the ANC, as it happens in all parties to different degrees. What is glaringly apparent in the ANC is that with its cadre starting from a higher level of revolutionary morality and descending to the level of the other political parties, this could not happen without being noticed. The *ngena-phuma* ('come in and go out') language which demands that those who are in government should give way for others to get a chance is taking root and in the process the interests of the people are trampled upon or ignored completely.

The ANC NGC in 2000 spent its time analysing this phenomenon of a new cadre and took resolutions to combat it, but without much success. The problem with corruption is that it corrodes the system and spreads like cancer unless a radical intervention is devised to combat it. Moreover, once one is corrupt, the only way to protect one's self is by corrupting others or allowing others to be corrupted. If this fails, violence and the misuse of state power becomes the only way.

Although Mbeki was aware of this development and tried his best to combat it, he did not believe that the ANC cadre – what he calls the 'real cadre of the movement' – could behave in this manner. For instance, he believed in his action against his deputy president and expected the cadre of the movement to understand why he had relieved Zuma of his duties. The July 2005 meeting of the NGC shocked him, although he still believed that it was a few leaders and individuals who misled the cadre as he understood it to be – revolutionary, pure and perfect.

At the May 2007 policy conference he stoically maintained his position, which he believed was what the ANC was about, even if this alienated some of the ANC's alliance partners. On ANC policy issues one could not find fault with him. He also had a sophisticated understanding of Marxist theories and related ideological perspectives, which enabled him to differentiate between what the roles of the alliance partners, COSATU and the SACP, should be in relation to each other and the ANC. Mbeki had a further advantage: personal knowledge of the relationships between the ANC and its alliance partners over a period of more than 40 years.

He came out of the policy conference a victor conceptually and ideologically, but the ground was busy shifting under his feet because of considerations other than purity of policies, ideas and the high-level cadre of the movement. People were aggrieved for one reason or another, rightly or wrongly, and found the action against the deputy president the best rallying point to remove Mbeki as their leader. The coalition against him was diverse, with some who genuinely had grievances – whatever their merit – while others were strategically using the tragic matter affecting the deputy president to further their own personal interests.

The ultimate test would be the 2007 Polokwane national conference, where Mbeki went believing that the 'real cadre' of the movement would prevail. He got the shock of his life, especially at the behaviour of the majority of those cadres at the conference. Until the last minute he still believed that in a secret ballot the real cadre would show up. This was not to be, as only about 40 per cent did. He lost the election to continue as the president of the ANC and was later unceremoniously removed from the presidency of the country.

Despite this, he remains convinced that the electoral college at the conference was not representative of the real cadre of the movement, but as a democrat he had to accept the outcome of the election. He remains an ANC member in good standing and believes that the ANC has natural mechanisms to correct itself, which it has to do for its own sake and for that of the country and its people.

For now, he has given his life to help Africa to resolve its intractable problems, and to create conditions conducive to achieving the vision of the African Renaissance.

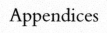

Appendices

Statement by the NEC of the ANC on the 'Recall' of Mbeki

20 September 2008

Over the past two days, the National Executive Committee of the ANC has deliberated on the Pietermaritzburg C!ember [*sic*] by Judge Chris Nicholson.

In particular, we have focused on the implications of the judgement for our movement, and for our people as a whole.

The judgement has had a profound impact on many aspects of our legal system. It has obviously also had an impact on the affairs of the ANC.

We wish to assert to you that our most important task as a revolutionary movement is the stability of our country and the unity and cohesion of the ANC. Our movement has been through a trying period and we are determined to heal the rifts that may exist.

In the light of this, and after a long and difficult discussion, the ANC has decided to recall the President of the Republic before his term of office expires.

Our decision has been communicated to him.

The formalities are now [the] subject of a Parliamentary process and, we can assure you, will take place in a way which ensures smooth running of government.

We acknowledge with deep admiration all the great strides our country has made under the stewardship of President Mbeki. He remains a loyal cadre of our movement and we will continue to work closely with him on matters relating to our desire to achieve a developmental state.

We will follow with precision all the constitutional requirements to ensure that interim arrangements are in place to ensure the smooth running of the government.

In the coming days, the President of the ANC will meet with ANC deployees in Government to assure them that the NEC would wish for them to remain in Government.

To the citizens of South Africa, we make the commitment that we share their desire for stability and for a peaceful and prosperous South Africa. We believe that our decision is in the interests of making that a secure reality.

Issued:
African National Congress

For more information contact national spokesperson:
Jessie Duarte on 079 506 6756

Mbeki's Address to the Nation on His Resignation

21 September 2008

Fellow South Africans,

I have no doubt that you are aware of the announcement made yesterday by the National Executive Committee of the ANC with regard to the position of the President of the Republic.

Accordingly, I would like to take this opportunity to inform the nation that today I handed a letter to the Speaker of the National Assembly, the Honourable Baleka Mbete, to tender my resignation from the high position of President of the Republic of South Africa, effective from the day that will be determined by the National Assembly.

I have been a loyal member of the African National Congress for 52 years. I remain a member of the ANC and therefore respect its decisions. It is for this reason that I have taken the decision to resign as President of the Republic, following the decision of the National Executive Committee of the ANC.

I would like sincerely to thank the nation and the ANC for having given me the opportunity to serve in public office during the last 14 years as the Deputy President and President of South Africa.

This service has at all times been based on the vision, the principles and values that have guided the ANC as it prosecuted a difficult and dangerous struggle in the decades before the attainment of our freedom in 1994.

Among other things, the vision, principles and values of the ANC teach the cadres of this movement life-long lessons that inform us that wherever we are and whatever we do we should ensure that our actions contribute to the attainment of a free and just society, the upliftment of all our people, and the development of a South Africa that belongs to all who live in it.

This is the vision of a South Africa that is democratic, non-racial, non-sexist and prosperous; a country in which all the people enjoy a better life.

Indeed, the work we have done in pursuit of the vision and principles of our liberation movement has at all times been based on the age-old values of Ubuntu, of selflessness, sacrifice and service in a manner that ensures that the interests of the people take precedence over our desires as individuals.

I truly believe that the governments in which I have been privileged to serve have acted and worked in the true spirit of these important values.

Based on the values of Ubuntu, the significance of which we learnt at the feet of such giants of our struggle as Chief Albert Luthuli, OR Tambo, Nelson Mandela and others, we as government, embarked, from 1994, on policies and programmes directed at pulling the people of South Africa out of the morass of poverty and ensuring that we build a stable, developed and prosperous country.

Accordingly, among many things we did, we transformed our economy, resulting in the longest sustained period of economic growth in the history of our country; we introduced an indigent policy that reaches large numbers of those in need; we made the necessary advances so as to bring about a developmental state, the better to respond to the many and varied challenges of the transformation of our country.

This is, of course, not the occasion to record the achievements of government. An additional critical few are however worth mentioning. They include our achievements with regard to many of the Millennium Development Goals, the empowerment of women, the decision to allow us to host the 2010 FIFA Soccer World Cup and our election as a non-permanent member of the UN Security Council two years ago.

Despite the economic advances we have made, I would be the first to say that even as we ensured consistent economic growth, the fruits of these positive results are still to be fully and equitably shared among our people, hence the abject poverty we still find coexisting side by side with extraordinary opulence.

Importantly, we had an obligation to ensure that democracy becomes the permanent feature of our lives and that all our citizens respect the rule of law and human rights. This is one of the cornerstones of our democracy, which we have consistently striven to protect and never to compromise.

We have also worked continuously to combat the twin challenges of crime and corruption, to ensure that all our people live in conditions of safety and security. We must admit that we are still faced with many challenges in this regard.

Work will therefore have to continue to strengthen and improve the functioning of our criminal justice system, to provide the necessary resources for this purpose, to activate the masses of our people to join the fight against crime and corruption, and to achieve new victories in the struggle for moral regeneration.

With regard to the latter, our successive governments from 1994 to date have worked consistently to encourage the entrenchment in our country of a value system whose observance would make all of us Proudly South African, a value system informed by the precept of Ubuntu – umuntu ngumuntu ngabanye. Among other things this means that we must all act in a manner that respects the dignity of every human being.

We have sought to advance this vision precisely because we understood that we would fail in the struggle to achieve the national and social cohesion that our country needs, as well as the national unity we require to enable us to act together to address the major challenges we face.

Fellow South Africans, since the attainment of our freedom in 1994, we have acted consistently to respect and defend the independence of the judiciary. For this reason our successive governments have honoured all judicial decisions, including those that went against the Executive.

This did not mean that the Executive did not at times have strong views which we would have publicly pronounced upon. The central approach we adopted has always been to defend the judiciary rather than act in a manner that would have had a negative impact on its work.

Indeed, on the infrequent instances when we have publicly expressed views contrary to those of the judiciary, we have done so mindful of the need to protect its integrity. Consistent with this practice, I would like to restate the position of Cabinet on the inferences made by the Honourable Judge Chris Nicholson that the President and Cabinet have interfered in the work of the National Prosecuting Authority (NPA).

Again I would like to state this categorically that we have never done this, and therefore never compromised the right of the National Prosecuting Authority to decide whom it wished to prosecute or not to prosecute.

This applies equally to the painful matter relating to the court proceedings against the President of the ANC, Comrade Jacob Zuma. More generally, I would like to assure the nation that our successive governments since 1994 have never acted in any manner intended wilfully to violate the Constitution and the law.

We have always sought to respect the solemn Oath of Office each one of us made in front of the Chief Justice and other judges, and have always been conscious of the fact that the legal order that governs our country was achieved through the sacrifices made by countless numbers of our people, which included death. In this context it is most unfortunate that gratuitous suggestions have been made seeking to impugn the integrity of those of us who have been privileged to serve in our country's National Executive.

Compatriots, again, as you know, we have often pointed to the fact that our liberation movement has always been pan-African in its outlook and therefore that we have an obligation to contribute to the renaissance of the African continent. All of us are aware of the huge and daunting challenges that face our continent.

In the short years since our freedom, as South Africans we have done what we could to make our humble contribution to the regeneration of our continent. We have devoted time and resources to the task of achieving the Renaissance of Africa because this is what has informed generations of our liberators, even before the ANC was formed in 1912. We have done this fully understanding that our country shares a common destiny with the rest of our continent.

I therefore thank the many dedicated compatriots – men and women – who have made it possible for us to contribute to the resolution of conflicts and the strengthening of democracy in a number of countries including the Kingdom of Lesotho, the Democratic Republic of Congo, Burundi, Côte d'Ivoire, Comoros, Zimbabwe, Sudan and elsewhere. We have also done this work conscious of our responsibilities as a State Member of both SADC and the African Union.

I would like to thank my colleagues, the many Heads of State and Government on the African continent whose abiding vision is that Africa must be free; that all our countries, individually and collectively, should become democratic, developed and prosperous, and that Africa must unite. These African patriots know as I do that Africa and Africans will not and must not be the wretched of the earth in perpetuity. Similarly we have worked to contribute to the achievement of the aspirations of the countries and peoples of the South, conscious of the need for us to act in solidarity and in unity with the billions with whom we share the common challenge to defeat poverty and underdevelopment.

Accordingly, I depart the Office of President of South Africa knowing that this country has many men and women who have dedicated their lives to ensure that South Africa, Africa and the countries of the South will, in time, manage to ensure a better world for all of humanity. I depart this Office conscious that the sterling work done by the Presidency, the Ministries and departments, the provinces and local government structures will continue, driven by the determination to achieve the goal of a better life for all.

I am convinced that the incoming administration will better the work done during the past 14-and-a-half years so that poverty, underdevelopment, unemployment, illiteracy, challenges of health, crime and corruption will cease to define the lives of many of our people. I have received many messages from South Africans, from all walks of life, through e-mails, telephonically and through cell phone text messages as well as those conveyed through my colleagues.

I thank all of you, fellow South Africans, for these messages. To everyone, and responding to these messages, I would like to say that gloom and despondency have never defeated adversity. Trying times need courage and resilience. Our strength as a people is not tested during the best of times. As we said before, we should never become despondent because the weather is bad nor should we turn triumphalist because the sun shines. For South Africa to succeed there is more work to be done and I trust that we will continue to strive to act in unity to accelerate the advance towards the achievement of our shared national goals.

In this regard, it may be worth repeating what I said during the inauguration of the President of the Republic in 1999. Using the metaphor of the Comrades Marathon, I said then that: 'Those who complete the course will do so only because they do not, as fatigue sets in, convince themselves that the road ahead is still too long, the inclines too steep, the loneliness impossible to bear and the prize itself of doubtful value.'

Once more, I thank you most sincerely for affording me the opportunity to serve you and to serve the people of Africa.

Thank you,
Ngiyathokoza,
Ke ya Lebogang,
Ndo livhuwa,
Ndiyabulela,
Ndza khensa,
Baie dankie,
Ngiyabonga.

Statement of the President of the ANC, Jacob Zuma (on Behalf of the ANC), on the 'Recall' of Mbeki

22 September 2008

The National Executive Committee of the ANC met over the weekend of the 19th to 21st September 2008, to deliberate on various pertinent issues.

After careful debate and discussion the NEC decided to recall Comrade Thabo Mbeki. This was one of the most difficult decisions the NEC has ever had to take in the history of the ANC.

We fully understand that the decision comes with a degree of pain to Comrade Mbeki, his family, friends, members of the ANC, ordinary South Africans and members of the international community with whom we interact.

Comrade Mbeki has devoted decades of his life to the ANC and our country. The decision to recall him was not taken lightly, but it had to be taken in the interests of making the country move forward.

The country needs a strong and united ruling party at the helm of government, capable of galvanising support for the government's development agenda.

As the ruling party we need to sustain the confidence of our people in the ANC and its government. Once this level of confidence is weakened, the ANC has no alternative but to take action.

We appreciate the cooperation of Comrade Mbeki and the dignified manner with which he has conducted himself during this difficult situation.

When he met with the President of the ANC on Friday morning, ahead of the NEC discussion, he said that as a disciplined cadre of the movement he would readily accept and abide by any decision of the organisation and subject himself to its wishes. The ANC prides itself on having leaders who rise to the occasion, who put the organisation and the country first, no matter how challenging the circumstances may be.

Comrade Mbeki will continue to be given tasks as a cadre and one of the senior leaders of the movement.

We are united in our appreciation of the important role that Comrade Mbeki has played in the organisation and broader liberation movement.

The achievements of government during Comrade Mbeki's Presidency are impressive. The ANC government has created conditions for a sustained expansion of the South African economy since the Second World War with the rate of growth averaging over 4.5% a year since 2004.

Government also scored several gains in the social arena such as increasing access to housing, water, education, electricity and other basic services.

Comrade Mbeki also succeeded in placing Africa in the forefront of international debates. He made his mark in promoting an African renewal as well as South-South cooperation, between our country and the developing world. In addition, our country made history as we joined the UN Security Council as a non-permanent member.

The Mbeki administration, building on the legacy of our icon President Nelson Mandela, has definitely created a strong foundation for the ANC to successfully contest next year's elections.

In light of this weekend's developments, we will do all in our power to ensure that stability is maintained in governance and service delivery.

The Speaker of the National Assembly has informed us that she has received the letter of resignation from President Mbeki.

Working together with Parliament, we will ensure that the election of a new President takes place as speedily as possible.

There is no reason for South Africans to be apprehensive. The transition will be managed with care and precision.

We will announce the name of our Candidate in Parliament at an appropriate moment. We have in Cabinet many experienced Ministers including the Deputy President of the ANC, Comrade Kgalema Motlanthe. I am convinced that if given that responsibility he would be equal to the task.

It should be borne in mind that Comrade Mbeki led an ANC government.

We therefore expect a smooth transition, as this is not a change of party but only leadership in government.

We call upon all ANC Ministers and Deputy Ministers, to continue their work and serve the people of our country, supported by the Public Service, which is not affected at all by these changes.

We also appeal to all South Africans to support the government and its new leadership, and work with them to promote access to a better life for all.

Within the ANC we will continue the work for organisational renewal and unity. We will be sending NEC deployees to all provinces and regions to brief our structures on the new developments.

We will also brief civil society formations and other key stakeholders to ensure their understanding of the decision.

Most importantly, we will be hosting the 2010 FIFA World Cup. We will support our government to make the World Cup a huge success for the African continent and the world.

The ANC led by its President and the NEC will now focus energies on preparing for the 2009 elections and the new administration next year.

After the elections, the ANC will take further the fight against crime to build safer communities, as stated in our Polokwane resolutions.

We will focus more on improving the quality of health service delivery and the reduction of diseases such as HIV and AIDS, tuberculosis and others.

We will prioritise education and skills development, as well as land and agrarian reform, as key tools in the fight against poverty.

We have decided to make the creation of decent work opportunities the primary focus of our economic policies. This means we have to achieve sound economic growth and development, in spite of the global economic crisis.

Our economic policies will remain stable, progressive and unchanged, as decided upon in previous ANC national conferences including Polokwane.

We will take forward the transformation of our criminal justice system, to promote access to justice for all, poor and rich, rural and urban, men and women.

The rule of law and the independence of the judiciary are amongst the most fundamental principles in our country's Constitution, which the ANC will always protect and defend.

We would like to underline that we acknowledge and accept the ruling of Justice Chris Nicholson and reiterate that we will, as always, abide by the decisions of this and all courts in our country.

We appreciate the prevailing atmosphere of calmness and maturity that has accompanied the recall.

We have clearly matured as a democracy and we should all be proud.

We have made a painful and difficult decision, and we are convinced that it will bring about much needed stability in government and public life and enable us to focus on the challenges facing our country.

Thank you.

Mbeki's Farewell Letter to Cabinet

24 September 2008

Dear Colleagues,

To all Members of the National Executive.

As you know, tomorrow, September 25, the National Assembly will elect the next President of the Republic of South Africa, who will also swear his or her Oath of Office on the same day.

By law, I will therefore cease to be President of the Republic with effect from midnight today.

I thought I should send you this letter as one of my last communications to you as Head of our country's National Executive.

First of all I would like to thank you for having agreed to serve in the National Executive when you were requested to do so.

This demonstrated your selfless commitment to serve the people of South Africa, which told me that I was indeed very privileged to have the possibility to work as part of such a collective of South African patriots.

All of us, together, have always understood that as members of the National Executive, we carry the heavy responsibility to stand in the front ranks of the national forces charged with the historic task to achieve the goals of the national democratic revolution.

All of us know that, by definition, all revolutions are not, to quote Nelson Mandela, an 'easy walk to freedom'. Accordingly, our own continuing revolution has also not been, is not, and will not be an easy walk to freedom.

It will constantly test and pose a challenge to everybody, including ourselves, to prove through our deeds, rather than our words, that we are true revolutionaries.

This will demand that we demonstrate that we are able and willing to walk the long and hard road to freedom, always conscious of our obligation to serve the people, rather than promote our personal interests.

As tried and tested combatants for the victory and consolidation of our democratic revolution, you have had no need for an instructor to educate you about the challenges we would face, and face, to achieve the objectives of the revolution.

Your decision to serve in the National Executive has therefore meant that you are willing to walk a hard road that would necessarily demand personal sacrifices.

It is for this reason that I have thanked you for your conscious and voluntary agreement to join the National Executive.

In this regard I must emphasise the fact that the charge given to the National Executive during the years of our freedom, since 1994, mandated by the people through democratic elections, has been to pursue the goal of the revolutionary transformation of our country.

I make this observation in part to pay tribute to you for the loyal and principled manner in which you have consistently and consciously approached your responsibilities as revolutionary democrats.

I also make it to thank you for the contribution you have made towards the achievement of the revolutionary goals of the democratic revolution.

Fifteen years ago now, on the eve of the victory of the democratic revolution, the movement to which I belong took various decisions about the immediate tasks of this revolution. These were encapsulated in two important documents, these being:

- 'Ready to Govern'; and the
- 'Reconstruction and Development Programme'.

Repeatedly, over the years, we have summarised the strategic focus of these documents, and therefore the democratic revolution, as:

- the creation of a non-racial society;
- the creation of a non-sexist society;
- the entrenchment and defence of the democratic order, as reflected in our National Constitution;
- the restructuring, modernisation and development of our economy to create a prosperous society, characterised by the eradication of poverty and underdevelopment, and a shared prosperity;
- the implementation of social policies consistent with the preceding goals;
- the transformation of the state machinery to ensure that we build a developmental state; and,
- the Renaissance of Africa and the building of a better world, focused on the challenge to defeat global poverty, underdevelopment and inequality.

Over the years, since 1994, the objectives of the movement to which most of us belong have served as the centrepiece of the Election Manifestoes on whose basis the people of our country mandated the ANC to assume the honoured position of the ruling party of South Africa.

With immense pride, I would like to convey to you my firm conviction, empirically demonstrated by life itself, that you have indeed honoured your responsibilities to our country and nation, as mandated by the people in the 1994, 1999 and 2004 General Elections.

If need be, it would not be difficult to detail the factual accuracy of this statement. Neither would it be difficult to demonstrate the appreciation of the overwhelming majority of the masses of our people for what has been done to improve the quality of their lives.

Apart from the ever-increasing levels of approval stated by the people in all the General and Municipal Elections after 1994, I have experienced this popular sentiment personally in the many Community Izimbizo we have convened in all parts of our country, both urban and rural.

The fundamental message I would like to communicate to you in this regard is that you have indeed discharged your revolutionary obligation further to advance the goals of the national democratic revolution.

At the same time, I am certain that during the years we have served as members of the National Executive we have made mistakes. I am equally convinced that the only way we could have avoided these mistakes would have been if we had done nothing to strive to achieve the fundamental social transformation of our country.

In this context, as revolutionaries, we must at all times remain open to criticism and self-criticism, precisely to ensure that we identify whatever mistakes might have occurred and correct these.

At the same time, I am aware of the reality that there are some in our country who are convinced that such mistakes as we might have made, as well as the reality that in fifteen years we have not eradicated a 350-year legacy of colonialism, as we could not, derive from our strategic commitment to a reactionary, neo-liberal perspective and programme.

In addition, it is also clear that there are different views in our country with regard to the assessment of the objective national and international circumstances within which we have sought to achieve the goals of the democratic revolution.

Some claim that we have deliberately overestimated the constraints posed by this objective reality, precisely to justify our failure to undertake what they consider to be an imperative obligation to implement what they regard as a more revolutionary and appropriate programme for the fundamental social transformation of our country.

Further to complicate the challenges with which we have had to contend, the matters that have been raised by some of our opponents have required that we engage a discourse that relates to intellectual paradigms relating to philosophy, ideology and politics.

All this, including the practical politics to which we necessarily had to respond, has imposed on the National Executive the obligation to consider and respond correctly to the dialectical relationship between the two phenomena of human existence, the objective and the subjective.

Confronted by the reality that as Government we must govern, and therefore take decisions that have a national, structural and long-term impact, we have consequently had the task to relate the subjective to the objective, to find the necessary relationship between theory and practice.

During our years as members of the National Executive we have discussed all these matters, which relate to the fundamental and critically important issue of the strategy and tactics of the democratic revolution.

I remain convinced that on all occasions we have addressed these matters in an open, honest and objective manner, always informed by our fundamental understanding of the nature and goals of our national democratic revolution.

Among other things, in the end, this has found expression in various documents we have adopted, which have, without let or hindrance, sought honestly to review the performance of the Government in which all of us have been honoured to serve, centred on the impact its policies and programmes have had on our society.

By decision of the ruling party, the ANC, acting within its rights, the current government I have been privileged to lead has been obliged to end its tenure a few months ahead of its popularly mandated term.

In the interest of the masses of our people and country, personally I accepted this eventuality without resistance or rancour, and acted upon it accordingly. I trust that all of us, members of the National Executive, will respond in similar fashion.

At the same time, as we bid farewell to one another as members of the elected 2004–2009 National Executive, we must do so with our heads held high.

We must adopt this posture not out of any sense of arrogance or self-satisfaction.

We must do so, as I suggest, because we can honestly say that we did the utmost, to the best of our ability, as a united collective:

- to advance the goals of the democratic revolution;
- to accelerate the advance towards the achievement of the goal of a better life for our people;
- to pursue the objective of the fundamental reconstruction and development of our country;

- to honour the mandate, and respect the expectations of the masses of our people; and,
- to meet our obligations to the peoples of Africa and the rest of the world.

I am proud without reservation of what you have done to achieve these historic achievements. I am proud of the manner in which you have functioned, in the context of the intricacies of our democratic and constitutional governance system, to do the detailed work which constitutes the daily fare of our Ministries and Departments.

As you lead your lives in the aftermath of the early termination of the term of the life of the 2004–2009 National Executive, and with all due humility, I plead that in addition to what I have already said in this letter, you should do everything you can, constantly to:

- affirm your personal integrity, refusing to succumb to the expedient;
- assert your commitment to principle, rejecting opportunism and cowardice;
- reaffirm your commitment selflessly to serve the people, determined to spurn all temptations to self-enrichment, self-promotion and protection of material personal benefit, at the expense of the people;
- remain loyal to the values of truthfulness and honesty; and,
- respect the views and esteem of the masses of our people.

I make these comments, at this particular moment, to reemphasise the value system that has informed all of us as we served in the National Executive, concerning our quality as individuals charged with the responsibility to play a leading role as revolutionary activists of the democratic revolution.

In this regard and in the end, the ultimate motive power that would inform and has informed our behaviour as individuals are our conscience and self-respect, individually.

I am absolutely certain that at this particular moment in the history of our country, the masses of our people need the unequivocal assurance, demonstrated practically, that they continue to be blessed with the kind of ethical leadership they have seen serving in our country's National Executive during the last fourteen-and-a-half years.

Surely, as we sought to achieve what Nelson Mandela described as 'the RDP of the soul', as well as implement the Moral Regeneration Programme, we have known that we must lead by example, serving as role models in terms of the morality and value system we have urged our people to respect!

I thank you most sincerely for the comradely manner in which we have worked together in the National Executive, the openness of our debates, the friendship among ourselves we have enjoyed, and your firm commitment to the realisation of the goals which our history and reality have dictated.

I wish you success in all your future endeavours, convinced that you constitute a corps of patriots on whom the masses of our people can continue to count as their reliable and selfless leaders, regardless of whether you occupy positions in organs of state or you do not.

You, an outstanding and immensely talented collective of patriots, have, during the years we have worked together, placed and demonstrated confidence in me as the leader of the National Executive.

Please accept my humble thanks to you for this, as well as my apology that it is only now, as I leave Government, that I convey this sentiment to you. However, in this context, I would like to assure you that I am fully conscious of my responsibility to you, at all times to honour your confidence and respect.

This has told me that I owe an obligation to you and the masses of our people at all times to remain loyal to the morality of our revolution.

It has told me that I must always strive to serve the people.

It has told me never to betray those who are my comrades-in-arms, committed to achieve agreed common objectives.

It has told me never to dishonour the revolutionary democratic cause, by allowing my personal desires to assume precedence over the interests of the masses of the people.

As we part, I would like to assure you that I am determined to respect and act in accordance with the value system I have just described.

Today is Heritage Day. It may therefore be appropriate that today this outstanding collective of South Africans, the National Executive, should make a commitment to hand to our people, as part of their heritage, a tradition of honest government which is firmly opposed to corruption, duplicity and disrespect for principle.

I trust that, in time, history will hand down the judgement that when we, as our country's National Executive, were given the opportunity, we lived up to the expectations of the masses of our long-suffering people to serve them as honest and selfless leaders – men and women of conscience.

Please convey my humble thanks to your families that they released you to enable you to perform the outstanding public service for which I sincerely thank you.

I bid you a fond farewell as a member of the National Executive.

Because we are, or have become comrades, friends and partners in the pursuit of a common cause, I trust that it will be possible for us informally to continue talking to each other and one another, concerned, still, together to serve the peoples of South Africa, Africa and the rest of the world.

Yours sincerely,
Thabo Mbeki.

President Motlanthe's Acceptance Speech in Parliament after His Election as President

25 September 2008

Madame Speaker of the National Assembly,

Acting President

Our esteemed Chief Justice

Honourable leaders of our political parties

Members of Parliament

Ministers and Deputy Ministers

Mr Jacob Zuma, former Deputy President of the Republic and President of the ANC

Ahmed Kathrada, Isithwalandwe Seaparankoe

Chairperson of the National House of Traditional Leaders and honoured Traditional Leaders

Heads of State Organs supporting our constitutional democracy

Directors-General and leaders of the Public Service

Your Excellencies, Ambassadors and High Commissioners

Distinguished guests, friends and Comrades

People of South Africa

Today, I make a solemn pledge that I will do all to live up to these expectations and to undertake this task to the best of my ability.

I wish to record my sincere thanks and appreciation to outgoing President Thabo Mbeki, in whose Cabinet I have had the honour to serve these last few months.

I know that I speak on behalf of all the people of this country when I say that we have been privileged to have you as our President these last nine years. There is no value that we can place on the service you have rendered to your country, nor any tribute that can adequately capture your contribution to building this nation.

For all that you have done for South Africa, for our continent and for the advancement of the global community, we remain forever indebted.

Madame Speaker,

I wish also to express my gratitude to my cabinet colleagues, most of whom were appointed in 2004 in my presence while I was Secretary General of the ANC, and with whom I have been part of a team in government.

I am grateful to the African National Congress for the tasks and responsibilities it has given me over several decades, for providing the political and analytical grounding that is so essential for effective public service.

The African National Congress is a movement with a rich political tradition. While conditions have changed, and tactics have had to be adapted, the policy orientation of the ANC has remained consistent for over 50 years.

The vision espoused in the Freedom Charter remains at the core of the work of this movement, reflected in the mandate of this government.

Since the attainment of democracy in 1994, as the leading party in government the ANC has kept a steady hand on the tiller.

Even when faced with difficulty, and confronted by unanticipated challenges, the ANC has remained unwavering in its commitment to advance the interests of all the people of South Africa.

This has been reflected in the policies of three successive ANC governments, as it will continue to be reflected in the final months of this, the country's third democratic national government.

In 2004, the people of this country gave a clear and unequivocal mandate to this government to forge a people's contract to create work and fight poverty. It placed on this government the responsibility to use all means at its disposal to ensure that by 2014 we would be able to reduce poverty and unemployment by half.

When its term ends next year, this government will be able to report to the people that indeed it has done as it was mandated.

It will be able to report on an economy that has sustained a pace of growth unprecedented in recent South African history, that has created jobs at an accelerated pace, and that has enabled government to dedicate greater resources to meeting the basic needs of our people.

It will be able to report on significant progress in pushing back the frontiers of poverty. This government will be able to report on tangible advances in the provision of housing, electricity, water, sanitation and other basic services to millions of our people. And it will be able to report on major improvements in the access of poor South Africans to health care, education and social security.

South Africans across the length and breadth of the country will attest to these and many other achievements.

But they know too that much work still lies ahead. They know the challenges our country faces, and the hardships that many of our people continue to endure.

To them, and to the world at large, we say that we shall not falter in leading the national effort to build a society in which all South Africans, regardless of their background, race or gender, have equal access to an expanding array of opportunity.

To them, and to the world at large, we say that this government will continue, as it has done under the leadership of President Thabo Mbeki, to dedicate every day that it remains in office towards the achievement of this goal.

The resolve of this government will not slacken. The pace of implementation will only quicken, and the fulfilment of its mandate will only ever draw closer.

Madame Speaker,

We are able to make such pronouncements with neither hesitation nor doubt, precisely because the policies we are charged to implement are the policies of the African National Congress.

These policies, which government will continue to implement unchanged, are the product of an extensive consultation and decision-making process.

These policies are the property of a collective. They do not belong to any one individual. And it is not for any one individual to change them.

The policies of this government are clear.

They are based on the 2004 Manifesto of the African National Congress, enhanced by the decisions of both the ANC's Policy Conference as well as its 52nd National Conference held in Polokwane in December 2007.

Mine is not the desire to deviate from what is working. It is not for me to reinvent policy. Nor do I intend to reshape either Cabinet or the public service.

We will not allow that the work of government be interrupted.

We will not allow the stability of our democratic order to be compromised.

And we will not allow the confidence that our people have in the ability of the state to respond to their needs to be undermined.

At this moment in our history, as we stand poised to make still further advances towards the achievement of a better life, it is as important as ever that we stand united as a nation.

It is as important as ever that we retain our faith in the resilience of our constitutional order and the vibrancy of our democracy.

Though we may at times experience difficulty, though we may suffer moments of doubt and uncertainty, we have both the will and the means to rise above the challenges of the present, and to forge ahead with our historic mission to liberate all our people from discrimination, oppression and want.

Therefore, we stand here to send out a message that government remains on course to deliver on its commitments to the poor, who rely on us daily for the fulfilment of their basic needs and for the provision of important services like health, education, and social security.

We remain on course to halve unemployment and poverty by 2014.

We remain determined to stamp out crime, violence and abuse, whomever it affects and wherever it manifests itself. We remain committed to building safer communities and protecting the vulnerable in our society from abuse. But in doing so, we need all our people to work with, and within, the criminal justice system so that together we stamp out crime.

We are here to assure all those on our continent and in the world that we will continue to meet our international obligations. We will continue to play a positive role within international institutions and forums. We will continue to provide whatever assistance we can in the pursuit of peace, security, democracy and development in Africa.

We remain on course to host in 2010 the best FIFA World Cup ever – An African World Cup. We fully expect to meet every commitment our nation has made to the football world.

In a turbulent global economy, we will remain true to the policies that have kept South Africa steady, and that have ensured sustained growth.

We will intensify the all-round effort to accelerate the rate of growth and job creation, and ensure that the benefits of growth are equally shared by all our people.

In the spirit of building a united democratic, non-racial, non-sexist and prosperous South Africa, I look forward to a constructive relationship with all parties within this assembly, even as we begin preparations for next year's elections. I hope to benefit from the critical eye that a vibrant and alert opposition brings to politics.

We will continue the regular engagements between government and the various working groups representing vital sectors within our society. These, together with initiatives like the nationwide Izimbizo programme, provide a crucial opportunity for enhancing popular engagement with the highest levels of government.

Madame Speaker, in the interest of establishing immediate stability and certainty, I have thought it important not to delay in filling whatever vacancies may have occurred in government and confirming the Cabinet. I am therefore intending appointing the following into the Cabinet of the Republic of South Africa. (List to be distributed in due course)

We live in challenging times. We see before us many mountains that are yet to be climbed, and numerous rivers that still need to be crossed.

Yet, for all the challenges that lie ahead, the incontrovertible truth is that never before has South Africa been closer than it is today towards the achievement of a better life for all its people.

We therefore have a shared responsibility to build on these results and to strive together – sparing neither courage nor strength – towards the achievement of a better South Africa, a better Africa and a better world.

I thank you.

The Oath of Office of the President

Schedule 2 – Oaths and solemn affirmations

The text below includes all amendments, up to and including the 16th Amendment, to the Constitution (disclaimer).

Sections
1. Oath or solemn affirmation of President and Acting President
2. Oath or solemn affirmation of Deputy President
3. Oath or solemn affirmation of Ministers and Deputy Ministers
4. Oath or solemn affirmation of members of the National Assembly, permanent delegates to the National Council of Provinces and members of the provincial legislatures
5. Oath or solemn affirmation of Premiers, Acting Premiers and members of provincial Executive Councils
6. Oath or solemn affirmation of Judicial Officers

[Schedule 2 amended by s.2 of Act No. 35 of 1997 (Eng text only) and substituted by s.18 of Act No. 34 of 2001.]

Oath or solemn affirmation of President and Acting President

1. The President or Acting President, before the Chief Justice or another judge designated by the Chief Justice, must swear/affirm as follows:

In the presence of everyone assembled here, and in full realisation of the high calling I assume as President/Acting President of the Republic of South Africa, I, A.B., swear/solemnly affirm that I will be faithful to the Republic of South Africa, and will obey, observe, uphold and maintain the Constitution and all other law of the Republic; and I solemnly and sincerely promise that I will always

- promote all that will advance the Republic, and oppose all that may harm it;
- protect and promote the rights of all South Africans;
- discharge my duties with all my strength and talents to the best of my knowledge and ability and true to the dictates of my conscience;
- do justice to all; and
- devote myself to the well-being of the Republic and all of its people.

(In the case of an oath: So help me God.)

Oath or solemn affirmation of Deputy President

2. The Deputy President, before the Chief Justice or another judge designated by the Chief Justice, must swear/affirm as follows:

In the presence of everyone assembled here, and in full realisation of the high calling I assume as Deputy President of the Republic of South Africa, I, A.B., swear/solemnly affirm that I will be faithful to the Republic of South Africa and will obey, observe, uphold and maintain the Constitution and all other law of the Republic; and I solemnly and sincerely promise that I will always

- promote all that will advance the Republic, and oppose all that may harm it;
- be a true and faithful counsellor;
- discharge my duties with all my strength and talents to the best of my

knowledge and ability and true to the dictates of my conscience;
- do justice to all; and
- devote myself to the well-being of the Republic and all of its people.

(In the case of an oath: So help me God.)

Oath or solemn affirmation of Ministers and Deputy Ministers

3. Each Minister and Deputy Minister, before the Chief Justice or another judge designated by the Chief Justice, must swear/affirm as follows:

I, A.B., swear/solemnly affirm that I will be faithful to the Republic of South Africa and will obey, respect and uphold the Constitution and all other law of the Republic; and I undertake to hold my office as Minister/Deputy Minister with honour and dignity; to be a true and faithful counsellor; not to divulge directly or indirectly any secret matter entrusted to me; and to perform the functions of my office conscientiously and to the best of my ability.

(In the case of an oath: So help me God.)

Oath or solemn affirmation of members of the National Assembly, permanent delegates to the National Council of Provinces and members of the provincial legislatures

4. (1) Members of the National Assembly, permanent delegates to the National Council of Provinces and members of provincial legislatures, before the Chief Justice or a judge designated by the Chief Justice, must swear or affirm as follows:

I, A.B., swear/solemnly affirm that I will be faithful to the Republic of South Africa and will obey, respect and uphold the Constitution and all other law of the Republic, and I solemnly promise to perform my functions as a member of the National Assembly/permanent delegate to the National Council of Provinces/member of the legislature of the province of C.D. to the best of my ability.

(In the case of an oath: So help me God.)

(2) Persons filling a vacancy in the National Assembly, a permanent delegation to the National Council of Provinces or a provincial legislature may swear or affirm in terms of sub-item (1) before the presiding officer of the Assembly, Council or legislature, as the case may be.

Oath or solemn affirmation of Premiers, Acting Premiers and members of provincial Executive Councils

5. The Premier or Acting Premier of a province, and each member of the Executive Council of a province, before the Chief Justice or a judge designated by the Chief Justice, must swear/affirm as follows:

I, A.B., swear/solemnly affirm that I will be faithful to the Republic of South Africa and will obey, respect and uphold the Constitution and all other law of the Republic; and I undertake to hold my office as Premier/Acting Premier/member of the Executive Council of the province of C.D. with honour and dignity; to be a true and faithful counsellor; not to divulge directly or indirectly any secret matter entrusted to me; and to perform the functions of my office conscientiously and to the best of my ability.

(In the case of an oath: So help me God.)

Oath or solemn affirmation of Judicial Officers

6. (1) Each judge or acting judge, before the Chief Justice or another judge designated by the Chief Justice, must swear or affirm as follows:

I, A.B., swear/solemnly affirm that, as a Judge of the Constitutional Court/
Supreme Court of Appeal/High Court/ E.F. Court, I will be faithful to the
Republic of South Africa, will uphold and protect the Constitution and the
human rights entrenched in it, and will administer justice to all persons
alike without fear, favour or prejudice, in accordance with the Constitution
and the law.

(In the case of an oath: So help me God.)

(2) A person appointed to the office of Chief Justice who is not already a
judge at the time of that appointment must swear or affirm before the
Deputy Chief Justice, or failing that judge, the next most senior available
judge of the Constitutional Court.

(3) Judicial officers, and acting judicial officers, other than judges, must
swear/affirm in terms of national legislation.

Extracts from the Constitution on the 'Removal' of and a 'Vote of No Confidence' in the President

Chapter 5 – The President and National Executive

The text below includes all amendments, up to and including the 16th Amendment, to the Constitution (disclaimer).

89. Removal of President

1. The National Assembly, by a resolution adopted with a supporting vote of at least two thirds of its members, may remove the President from office only on the grounds of
   a. a serious violation of the Constitution or the law;
   b. serious misconduct; or
   c. inability to perform the functions of office.
2. Anyone who has been removed from the office of President in terms of subsection (1) (a) or (b) may not receive any benefits of that office, and may not serve in any public office.
3. [2]

90. Acting President

1. When the President is absent from the Republic or otherwise unable to fulfil the duties of President, or during a vacancy in the office of President, an office-bearer in the order below acts as President:
   a. [3] The Deputy President.

b. A Minister designated by the President.

c. A Minister designated by the other members of the Cabinet.

d. The Speaker, until the National Assembly designates one of its other members.

2. An Acting President has the responsibilities, powers and functions of the President.

3. Before assuming the responsibilities, powers and functions of the President, the Acting President must swear or affirm faithfulness to the Republic and obedience to the Constitution, in accordance with Schedule 2.

4. A person who as Acting President has sworn or affirmed faithfulness to the Republic need not repeat the swearing or affirming procedure for any subsequent term as Acting President during the period ending when the person next elected President assumes office.

[Sub-s. (4) added by s.1 of Act No. 35 of 1997]

102. Motions of no confidence

1. If the National Assembly, by a vote supported by a majority of its members, passes a motion of no confidence in the Cabinet excluding the President, the President must reconstitute the Cabinet.

2. If the National Assembly, by a vote supported by a majority of its members, passes a motion of no confidence in the President, the President and the other members of the Cabinet and any Deputy Ministers must resign.

---

1. Until 30 April 1999, s. 84 is deemed to contain sub-s. (3) as set out in Annex B to Sch 6. See Sch 6 item 9 (2).

2. Until 30 April 1999, s. 89 is deemed to contain sub-s. (3) as set out in Annex B to Sch 6. See Sch 6 item 9 (2).

3. Until 30 April 1999, s. 90 (1) *(a)* is deemed to read as set out in Annex B to Sch 6. See Sch 6 item 9 (2).

4. Until 30 April 1999, s. 91 is deemed to read as set out in Annex B to Sch 6. See Sch 6 item 9 (2).

5. Until 30 April 1999, s. 93 is deemed to read as set out in Annex B to Sch 6. See Sch 6 item 9 (2).

6. Until 30 April 1999, s. 96 is deemed to contain sub-ss. (3) – (6) as set out in Annex B to Sch 6. See Sch 6 item 9 (2).